PATENTS, COPYRIGHTS, & TRADEMARKS

PATENTS, COPYRIGHTS, & TRADEMARKS

SECOND EDITION

Frank H. Foster
Robert L. Shook

JOHN WILEY & SONS, INC.
New York • Chichester • Brisbane • Toronto • Singapore

This publication is designed to provide accurate and
authoritative information in regard to the subject
matter covered. It is sold with the understanding that
the publisher is not engaged in rendering legal, accounting,
or other professional service. If legal advice or other
expert assistance is required, the services of a competent
professional person should be sought. From a *Declaration
of Principles jointly adopted by a Committee of the
American Bar Association and a Committee of Publishers.*

Library of Congress Cataloging-in-Publication Data
Foster, Frank H.
    Patents, copyrights, & trademarks / by Frank H. Foster and Robert
L. Shook. —2nd ed.
        p.   cm.
    Includes index.
    ISBN 0-471-58123-2 (cloth : alk. paper)
    ISBN 0-471-58124-0 (pbk. : alk. paper)
    1. Intellectual property—United States—Popular works.
I. Shook, Robert L., 1938–   .   II. Title.   III. Title: Patents,
copyrights, and trademarks.
KF2980.F67   1993
346.7304'8–dc20
[347.30648]   92-33071

I dedicate this book to my wife, Sandy, who taught school while I went to law school; Jerome R. Cox, who first employed and taught me intellectual property law practice; Frank T. Kremblas, who became my first partner as I ventured out on my own; and Debra Bright, my secretary, who has long made me look better than I am. For the second edition I am proud to add my son Jason, currently in law school and soon to join me in the practice of intellectual property law. Perhaps he is the professional second edition of me.

F. H. F.

To my dear friend Linda, with love.

R. L. S.

PREFACE

As a layperson, you are likely to find most reading material about patents, copyrights, and trademarks far too legal-oriented, complicated, and dull. That is a shame, because it does not have to be that way. Unfortunately, however, the majority of books on these subjects have been written in textbook form, generally by patent attorneys directing their messages toward other attorneys.

For this reason, we believe a definite need exists to provide an interesting, easy-to-comprehend book about what we feel is a fascinating topic. We want you to enjoy the second edition of *Patents, Copyrights, & Trademarks*, and most importantly, we want you to gain adequate knowledge so you can make the right decisions about your creative work. The Patent Act, the Trademark Act, and the Copyright Act represent the best protection of our intellectual effort in America, and with this in mind, it is in your best interest to have a clear understanding of these regulations. While this book does not guarantee to make you an expert, it will provide enough information to enable you to communicate effectively with experts in the field, and it will give you a better insight about the technical end of patent, copyright, and trademark law. This new edition includes five new chapters that cover patent licensing, foreign patents, protecting computer technology, selecting a new trademark, and trade secrets.

As you read this book, you will realize that the law involving patents, copyrights, and trademarks is not an exact science. You will discover that even the experts are likely to disagree in certain areas. Some of the law is subject to individual judgment, and it is possible that any specific ruling in a court of law can go either way. Yet, in other situations, the law is quite clear and unlikely to be disputed. We recommend that you work closely with an attorney who specializes in this field of law. Keep in mind, however, that while your attorney is hired to render legal decisions, it is up to you, the patent owner, the copyright owner, or the trademark owner, to make the business decisions on your work. It is our sincere hope that this book will guide you to make the *right* decisions.

FRANK H. FOSTER
ROBERT L. SHOOK

Columbus, Ohio
September 1993

CONTENTS

CONTENTS

CONTENTS

CONTENTS

A BRIEF HISTORY OF PATENTS, OF PATENTS, COPYRIGHTS, AND TRADEMARKS

THE HISTORY OF PATENTS

The history of patents is both interesting and informative. A knowledge of the historical background will enable you to understand the world of patents more easily. This information will also provide you with the basic principles behind the laws that govern patents today.

GREECE, ROME, AND VENICE

One of the earliest references to patents is a message by the third-century Greek historian Phylarchus in the *Banquet of the Learned*. Phylarchus writes about Sybaris, a Greek colony that was famous in 500 B.C. for luxurious living and self-indulgence. The historian states that if a confectioner or cook invented an unusual and outstanding dish, no other artist was allowed to prepare it for a period of one year. The granting of a monopoly thereby served as an inducement for others "to labour at excelling in such pursuits."

Although the Romans scorned monopolies, they recognized the value of rewarding creative citizens. In A.D. 337, the Roman Emperor Constantine decreed that artisans of certain trades who resided in cities would be exempt from all civil duties. Particularly noted were those craftsmen whose leisure hours were spent in perfecting themselves and instructing their sons. These privileged individuals included chariot makers, engineers, and locksmiths—undoubtedly the majority of Rome's inventors at the time. The Romans, however, refused to grant monopolies and, in fact, in A.D. 483, the Emperor Zeno decreed that there was to be no monopoly of any kind pertaining to clothing or food, even if the monopoly was re-

3

quired by order of an emperor. This principle still exists in the patent law of many countries and has been extended to medicine. However, it was not carried into U.S. law.

For centuries, the early Republic of Venice controlled the majority of trade between Europe and the rest of the world. Its influence on world trade continued until the discovery of the sea route to the East around the Cape of Good Hope. In 1297, a Venetian decree was passed stating that if a physician made a medicine based on his own secret, it had to be kept within the guild and all guild members were required to swear an oath not to pry into it. The first actual patent of invention on record anywhere in the world is said to have been granted in 1443 to Antonius Marini, who offered to build 24 flour mills for each of Venice's boroughs. Although his devices were not new, he requested the right to build them and asked the Senate not to permit anybody else to construct a mill that operated without water for a period of 20 years. The Senate granted his petition on the condition that a test be made on one of the borough's mills; if it worked, Marini would receive his monopoly. The mills worked and Marini received the exclusive rights on his waterless flour mills.

Of course, the most famous inventor to receive a patent from Venice was Galileo, a professor of mathematics at Padua. On September 15, 1594, he received a patent for a device that raised water and irrigated land. Galileo claimed that his invention was capable of discharging water through 20 spouts with the motive power of a single horse! His rights extended for 20 years, and the decree provided that infringers would lose their machines and be fined 300 ducats.

The history of patents is an inseparable part of the history of monopolies that were popular in the Middle Ages. While the practice of monopolies is by no means limited to the British, our U.S. patent laws stem, for the most part, from England. For this reason, the remainder of this chapter will focus on English and American history.

ENGLAND

Queen Elizabeth I's sovereignty in the sixteenth century is often referred to as the birth years of the English patent system because of her unprecedented and frequent exercise of her prerogative to grant monopolies and privileges to inventors. It is true, however, that for centuries before, the English sovereigns were endowed with the power to bestow various freehold interests, franchises, and other liberties to favored subjects. These grants were often referred to as the Letters Patent, because they described and enabled all to see the favor bestowed (the words "letters patent" are linguistically derived from words meaning "public letters"). In addition to granting favors to friends and family members, English kings and queens handed out monopolies as a means of raising money. Most often the grants were given when the monarchs were short of cash to operate their kingdoms. While the cost to purchase one was quite expensive, a good monopoly provided many privileges, often producing considerable wealth for its holder. Records indicate that these grants date back as far as the Conquest.

During the Middle Ages, the nature of these monopolies varied considerably. For example, a town might purchase the exclusive right to hold a fair or market. Or, in other cases, a municipality might buy the right to collect a toll for merchandise passing through the town. Other times, both merchants and manufacturers in a community would organize a guild for their mutual protection. The purpose of a typical merchant guild was to acquire such rights from the Crown so it could monopolize all of the local trade. Craft guilds also sought monopolies and were quite popular during this period.

Letters of protection can be traced as far back as 1324, when Edward II gave his protection to skilled German miners to induce them to come to England. Both Edward II and Edward III made strong efforts to attract skilled artisans to reside in England and engage in their trades. In particular, the English were eager to establish a cloth industry and, perhaps more than to any other trade, the sovereigns granted special privileges to dyers, fullers, weavers, and other clothing workers. In 1327, Edward III went so far as to prohibit his subjects from wearing foreign cloth. In 1331, John Kempe of Flanders received the first royal grant for the purpose of building the clothing industry in England, and under the protection of the king, he induced weavers, dyers, and fullers of woolen cloth to cross the Channel to reside and practice their trade somewhere in England. Later Edward III extended this policy to other trades. While these letters of protection did not grant monopolies, they served as passports and therefore enabled individuals to overcome the strict guild regulations against competition. In part, as the number of these letters of protection increased, the power of the guilds diminished.

These early letters of protection encouraged foreign artisans to migrate to England so that they could establish their trades, but keep in mind that more often than not these immigrants were not inventors. It is not clear when the first actual British patent was issued, but historians have several different interpretations. Some consider the first British patent to be the letter of protection granted to John of Shiedame in 1440 for a newly invented method of making salt on a scale never previously attempted in England. Another early "patent" was granted by Henry VI in 1449 to John of Utynam, upon his return to England from Flanders; this granted him exclusive rights to practice his art of making colored glass for 20 years, and nobody else had the right to do so without John's consent. It is not known whether John was the actual inventor of the process, but until 1977, unlike U.S. patents, British patents were issued to the first person to introduce and actually do something commercially with an unpublished invention. In return for his patent, John was obligated to instruct others in his art so that they too might practice it when his exclusivity of 20 years had expired. Because his monopoly privilege extended beyond trade and crafts to an actual process, the rights granted to him have a particular significance in patent history.

A milestone in patent history occurred in 1559 when Giacopo Acontio, an Italian, petitioned Queen Elizabeth I for protection on certain furnaces and "wheel machines" that he invented. Acontio feared that others would copy his work, so he appealed to the queen's sense of fairness, citing, "Nothing is more honest than that those who by searching have found out things useful to the public should have some fruits of their rights and labors, as meanwhile they abandon all other modes of gain, are at much expense in experiments, and often sustain much loss." Queen Elizabeth found his contention to be reasonable, and by granting Acontio the protection he sought, she inaugurated the British policy of rewarding inventors by granting them patents for their discoveries.

Although Acontio was granted a patent by the queen for his ingenuity, there were still many abuses during the Elizabethan rule. For instance, Sir Walter Raleigh was given rights to license tavernkeepers and to take possession of foreign real estate even though he originated neither. And in 1575, the queen granted a patent for the transmutation of iron into copper and of lead and antimony into mercury, which proved to be scientifically impossible. The queen also denied a patent to John Harington for his invention of the water closet, which delayed the introduction of its use for an estimated 150 years. Other noteworthy inventions that were refused patents during her reign include Stanley's armor plate, Gainibelli's method of land reclamation, and the stocking frame of Lee, which was subsequently accepted in France.

Nevertheless, as a result of Queen Elizabeth's involvement, the use of the patent privilege in England was off and running. In spite of her abuses of monopolies, she created a basis of the present patent law. It was only when the Crown's treasuries were low that she granted monopolies strictly for mercenary reasons; these called for either an out-and-out cash payment or a part of the profit in exchange for the Crown's favors. During the first 10 years of Queen Elizabeth's patent grants, 23 original grants were made, and during the next 20-year period there was a total of 25; from 1591 to 1600 only 6 were granted. Then, from 1600 until her death in 1603, none was issued. While these numbers of patents are low, her reign marked the first time in English history that inventors received patents regularly and is therefore considered historically significant in the development of patent law. Because Elizabeth's abuses of granting monopolies were not well received by her subjects, the first public denunciation of monopolies in Parliament occurred in 1571. While the denunciation didn't by itself change the law, it did mark the beginning of other criticisms, court cases, and finally actual bills that were introduced and passed in Parliament.

Following Queen Elizabeth's reign, under James I, the Statute of Monopolies was passed in 1624. But even then an inventor was not assured of the right to a patent, and he remained in the position of a humble petitioner of the king's grace. The new statute did put a stop to the granting of monopolies for anything other than new inventions. This 1624 legislation, considered the grandfather of all patent laws, remained the only English act governing patents until well into the nineteenth century. Although many changes have since been made, the English Statute of Monopolies remains the basis of both the British and U.S. patent systems to this day. Interestingly, the original term for a patent was established at 14 years. At the time, in 1624, an English apprentice's service was seven years, so two generations of apprentices were given an opportunity to learn an invention. The American patent term was originally 14 years with a renewal option of 7 additional years; however, it is presently 17 years (which was a compromise between 14 and 21 years).

THE UNITED STATES

Our American patent system was strongly influenced by British common law. It started, perhaps, when bounties, premiums, and subsidies were used to induce skilled craftsmen and industrialists to settle in the New World. Familiar with the monopoly system in England, these individuals asked the colonies for monopoly patents. Due to the strong need for industry, these patents were granted from time to time. The "Body of Liberties" legislated by the General Court of Massachusetts in 1641 expressly prohibited the granting of monopolies, except when a new invention was profitable to the country. Even then the patent was issued for a short time. The Colony of Massachusetts granted the first patent in the Western Hemisphere in 1641. Its recipient was Samuel Winslow for his invention of a process for manufacturing salt. It was granted on the condition that Winslow set up his production within one year; if he did, his monopoly stated that all others were prohibited "from making this article except in a manner different from his." The first American patent for machinery was issued five years later by the Massachusetts Colony to Joseph Jenkes for his invention of "engines of mills to go by water." Massachusetts was the colony to grant the most patents, followed by Connecticut.

After the revolution, the states continued to grant monopolies to inventors, copying the practice from the British. There was a strong need for acts of the legislature to be enacted so that the rights of an inventor did not depend on a special favor being granted by a person in a high-ranking position. It wasn't until 1784 that the state of South Carolina even attempted to pass general patent legislation. Its 1784 Act provided for the copyright of books and included a short section that extended monopoly rights to inventors of useful machines to 14 years. Although two patents were granted in South Carolina in 1786, in actual practice it still took a special act of the legislature for one to be obtained. Following the Revolutionary War, Pennsylvania led the other states in the number of patents granted. Even after the federal Constitution, Pennsylvania continued to grant its own patents. For a while, other states did the same, but gradually stopped.

In May 1787, the Constitutional Convention began to meet daily, and it recognized the abuses in the granting of monopolies practiced by the British. A lot of discussion centered on formulating a system to protect authors and inventors so they would have the exclusive rights to their work. By August 18, 1787, Charles Pinckney and James Madison both submitted proposals for additional powers to be granted to the federal government to secure such rights, and by September 5th, Article I, Section 8, Clause 8 of the Constitution was drafted. It states that Congress shall have the power "to promote the Progress of Science and useful Arts, by securing for limited Times to Authors and Inventors the exclusive Right to their respective Writings and Discoveries."

For the first time in the history of the world, a constitutional instrument had recognized that individuals have property rights in the products of their intellect and that it is in the interest of progress to protect those rights for a limited time. Interestingly, the words "patent" and "copyright" were not used in the original clause of the Constitution. Not only was the word "trademark" not mentioned, but it was not until many years later that the federal government exercised the power to regulate trademarks under the interstate commerce clause of the Constitution (see Chapter 3). On September 17, 1787, the delegates signed the Constitution, to become effective later upon ratification. It is important to note that the constitutional provision was the first of many steps taken to protect the rights of authors and inventors. During the Second Session of the First Congress in 1790, in his first annual speech to Congress, President Washington urged the "expediency of giving effectual encouragement" to the introduction of new and useful inventions from abroad, and "to the exertions of skill and genius in producing them at home." A patent bill was later passed by both houses of Congress, and on April 10, 1790, President Washington signed the first patent act. A separate copyright act was enacted on May 31st.

Once the patent act was passed, a patent board consisting of the secretary of state, the secretary of war, and the attorney general had the responsibility to review and issue patents. George Washington and Thomas Jefferson actually signed the first U.S. patent. Obviously, the members of the board were unable to spend their time productively administering patents. It is no wonder there were only 3 patents issued in 1790, 33 in 1791, 11 in 1792, and 10 in 1793. A new act was introduced and passed in 1793, and the number of issued patents began to increase substantially. By the time the Patent Act of 1836 became the law of the land, 752 patents had been issued during the year 1835. The more comprehensive act established the U.S. Patent Office as a separate bureau with a commissioner of patents. It also kept the duration of a patent to 14 years but contained an option to appeal for a seven year extension. It also provided for the construction of a new patent office building. On December 15, 1836, the U.S. Patent Office was completely destroyed by fire. The loss included 7,000 models, 9,000 drawings, and 230 books. The following year, Congress appropriated $100,000 to replace the records as well as the most valuable and interesting of the destroyed models. In 1837, probably as a result of the previous year's fire, Congress provided for the submission of a duplicate set of drawings so that one could be attached to the grant itself. Until 1951, when the present patent law was legislated, the 1836 Patent Act was only slightly modified from time to time. Some of the changes made prior to 1951 include the following:

- In 1839, Congress authorized the employment of two assistant examiners to handle the increased work load.
- In 1842, an amendment made designs patentable for seven years and also required that a patented product have a patented mark.
- In 1848, the commissioner of patents was given the sole power to extend a patent.
- In 1849, the U.S. Patent Office was placed under the newly created Department of the Interior.
- In 1861, Congress created a Board of Appeals consisting of three examiners-in-chief.

Because there were so many amendments added to the 1836 Act, the Act of 1870 was passed, in part, to consolidate all of the laws into a single entity. This act also conferred power on the commissioner to establish regulations consistent with law for the administration of the office. The patent term was also increased to a maximum of 17 years. From this time on, until a general modernization in 1951, the patent laws remained basically unchanged. One significant change did occur in 1930, when plants became patentable. Previously, no protection was given to the breeder or discoverer of a new variety of plant. The law was passed shortly after the death of renowned horticulturist Luther Burbank, who had said, "A man can patent a mouse trap or copyright a nasty song, but if he gives to the world a new fruit, he will be fortunate if he is rewarded by so much as having his name connected with the result."

The number of patents issued in the United States has increased dramatically in the twentieth century. In 1935, patent number 2,000,000 was issued; in 1961, patent number 3,000,000 was issued. Today, over 4.7 million have been issued.

In 1940, the National Committee for the U.S. Patent Law Sesquicentennial Celebration chose the following 15 "outstanding great inventions" through the nineteenth century:

Date of Patent	Inventor	Invention
1794	Eli Whitney	Cotton gin
1811	Robert Fulton	Steamboat
1834	Cyrus H. McCormick	Reaper
1840	Samuel F. B. Morse	Telegraph
1844	Charles Goodyear	Vulcanization
1846	Elias Howe, Jr.	Sewing machine
1868	C. Latham Sholes	Typewriter
1869	George Westinghouse	Air brake
1876	Alexander Graham Bell	Telephone
1878	Thomas A. Edison	Phonograph
1880	Thomas A. Edison	Incandescent lamp
1888	Nikola Tesla	Induction motor
1889	Charles M. Hall	Aluminum (production of)
1890	Ottmar Mergenthaler	Linotype
1893	Thomas A. Edison	Motion picture projector

A National Inventors' Hall of Fame was created more recently; each year it inducts new inventors at its new permanent home in Akron, Ohio.

The above list does not suggest that a majority of the wonderful inventions had already been invented before the beginning of the twentieth century. Based on past history, and with the incredible amount of technological advancements made in our modern day space age, we can assume that an increasing number of patents will continue to be issued in future years.

THE HISTORY
OF COPYRIGHTS

2

ENGLAND AND OTHER EUROPEAN COUNTRIES

Like the U.S. patent law, copyrights in this country can be traced back to Anglo-American common law that developed over the course of centuries in the courts. While there are some early references to the rights of writers and artists, from a practical point of view the need for copyright protection did not become widespread in England until 1476. This was the year William Caxton became England's first printer, opening his shop in Westminster. The Crown became concerned that the new and growing trades of printing and bookselling would wrongly influence the public with dangerous political and religious ideas. With this thought in mind, the government recognized the need to regulate the printing industry in order to maintain a strong grip (censorship) on what was written.

To accomplish this, the sovereign established royal restrictions on the right to print, including (1) the issuance of royal grants and patents that provided the exclusive right to print certain books, (2) the demand that the author's and printer's name appear in each copy, and (3) the requirement that a printed copy of each work be submitted to the sovereign's private collection. In 1557, Queen Mary I established the Stationers' Company of London, a trade association of printers and booksellers. The Stationers' Company held one of the royal patents that permitted it to print books for resale in England, and without its approval, no one could print books for sale. The company also maintained a register in which each printer and bookseller entered the title of each book that was purchased from an author or from another member. Although the organization established a court to govern claims of priority and piracy, it also had the responsibility to keep track of heretical authors and to make sure they were properly punished (put in the stocks, or worse) for their misdeeds.

Another important function was destroying works unworthy of publication. It seems that book burning has deep roots—even today the censorship of certain books exists in many countries around the world. Unfortunately, due to the intangible nature of the intellectual contents of a manuscript, the history of the rights of authors, artists, and composers has been a sad one. Rarely were the creative works of such individuals commended like products made on the workbench. Because of their potential influence, unauthorized books were considered dangerous. Although the beginning of copyrights did not have the best interests of the writer in mind, it did mark the start of some form of regulation that later evolved into benefits for everyone, including the writer.

Throughout the seventeenth century, the English Crown continued to control the licensing of authors, booksellers, printers, and publishers. If censorship did not plague authors, literary piracy did. By the beginning of the eighteenth century, the mistreatment of authors had become a national outrage. Influential men such as Swift, Addison, and Steele and respected publishers told their friends in Parliament that reform in the publishing industry was vital—traditional common law was not sufficient. Under Queen Anne's reign, in 1709, legal protection of an author's rights was granted for the first time in history. The Statute of Anne is recognized as the first statute of modern copyright. The act's opening words read as follows:

> *Whereas printers, booksellers, and other persons have of lately frequently taken the liberty of printing, reprinting, and publishing books without the consent of the authors or proprietors . . . to their very great detriment, and too often to the ruin of them and their families: for preventing therefore such practices for the future, and for the encouragement of learned men to compose and write useful books, be it enacted . . . .*

The law gave protection to the author by granting a 14-year period to own the sole rights of a work, and a second 14-year renewal period was permissible on registering the title at the Stationers' Hall and furnishing nine copies for deposit at various university and other official libraries. The act also stated:

> And . . . if any bookseller, printer, or other person whatsoever, shall print, reprint, or import any such book or books, without the consent of the proprietor . . . then such offender shall forfeit such book or books to the proprietor of the copy thereof, who shall forthwith damage and make wastepaper of them; and farther, that every such offender shall forfeit one penny for every sheet which shall be found in his custody.

Other European countries followed England's example. In 1741, Denmark enacted its first copyright law, which stated that books could be reprinted only with the consent of the author or the first publisher. Among the exceptions to the Danish law: hymnals, Luther's catechism, and "abc books."

In 1793, France enacted its first copyright laws, and under the influence of Napoleon, the laws were passed on to Belgium, Holland, Italy, and Switzerland. The French laws protected all authors, artists, and composers, regardless of citizenship, with the exclusive lifetime right to sell, distribute, or assign their works throughout the republic. During Isabella II's turbulent reign, in 1847, Spain passed its original copyright law. It protected the works of Spanish authors, whether they were published in Spain or in one of the Hispanic colonies. However, the Spanish-written works of colonial writers could only be imported into Spain with the consent of the government.

Because Germany lacked a strong central government, and was composed of many autonomous states, the country was slow to enact copyright laws. In 1838 Germany passed its first copyright law to protect the citizens of its many states. The laws, however, were ineffective, and literary pirating was commonplace. It was not until Germany's first national copyright law was passed in 1870, when a stable government existed, that German authors had real protection.

THE UNITED STATES

For the most part, the American colonies based their copyright laws on the English system. By 1786, 12 of the original 13 states (with the exception of Delaware) had passed copyright acts before the federal Constitution was adopted. Their purpose was clearly to protect the authors' rights, as witnessed from the actual titles of their acts. Connecticut's new act was called "An Act for the Encouragement of Literature and Genius," and New York's was titled "An Act to Promote Literature."

In 1790, the first U.S. federal Copyright Act that protected books, maps, and charts was passed and, like English law, it had a 14-year period and a 14-year renewal period. The act's provisions stated that a copy of the title page of a forthcoming copyright book should be deposited before publication, and required that the copyright owner run a newspaper advertisement of the facts of publication during the first two months after publication. A copy of the book also had to be deposited within six months after publication with the U.S. secretary of state. Once the copyright was established, if a publisher should infringe on the work by issuing a piratical edition, it would forfeit all copies on hand. In addition, the publisher would be liable for a fine in the amount of 50 cents for every sheet found; half of the fine would be paid to the author and the remainder to the U.S. government.

While the first U.S. federal copyright laws protected our citizens and residents, they did not provide the same protection for foreigners. In fact, it has been said that the government gave its blessing to the pirating of foreign books in this country. With no provisions to protect the rights of foreigners, U.S. printers and publishers were able to pirate and reprint foreign publications of all books they desired. At the time, American books were only a small number of the total that were published, and the demand for imported books far outnumbered the domestic supply. With no restrictions, U.S. citizens were able to buy the pirated books at considerably lower prices than if copyright laws had been in place to prohibit this practice. For good reason, other countries bitterly protested—Britain in particular. From our point of view, American literary piracy was believed to be in the best interests of the country. The United States was by no means the only nation to have such laws, and even in England, which had the best copyright laws in the world, piracy of foreign publications existed. Later, when fine American books were produced by some of our great writers, pirated editions of these works began to find their way to the shores of England.

Throughout the nineteenth century, amendments were added to the original copyright laws. For example, in 1802, books were first required to carry a notice of copyright. The law was also extended to cover designs, engravings, and etchings. In 1819, the U.S. circuit courts were declared to be the courts of original jurisdiction in all copyright cases. In 1831, music was added, and the first term of protection was extended to 28 years. In 1846, a permanent index of all copyright material was initiated when the law made it necessary to send one deposit copy to the Library of Congress, and a second copy to the newly founded Smithsonian Institute. In 1856, performance rights were granted to dramatists. In 1859, copyright matters were transferred from the State Department to the Department of Interior. In 1861, copyright cases could now be appealed in the Supreme Court, regardless of the amount. Previously, only cases in excess of $5,000 were eligible. In 1865, photography was covered by copyright law. In 1870, the U.S. Copyright Office was placed under the Librarian of Congress. At this time, paintings, drawings, statues, chromos, models, and designs were also brought under the umbrella of copyright law.

The Chace Act, passed in 1891, finally extended copyright protection to foreigners in this country—but only to those books manufactured here with a U.S. copyright. The passing of this act was begun in part by the strenuous petitioning over the years of such great American writers as Longfellow, Holmes, Emerson, Whittier, and Twain. Because the leading English writers, such as Charles Dickens and Robert Louis Stevenson, had been freely pirated by U.S. publishers, many good American books were being ignored in favor of royalty-free British works. It was as if the British works had become "public domain" in this country and, consequently, placed in unfair competition with our writers. In 1905, foreigners were further protected by being given one year following the publication of a foreign language book to make a decision to reprint in the United States. The Copyright Act of 1909 enacted the last changes made in this country until the Copyright Revision Act of 1976 was enacted. The 1909 Act allowed a book of foreign origin in a foreign language to secure a copyright in this country without having to be reprinted here. The copyright term also was changed to start from the date of publication instead of the date of registration and deposit, and the renewal term was extended to 28 years.

To many copyright experts, the present 1976 Act has been viewed as an entirely new body of law rather than an amended version of the Copyright Act of 1909. However, it includes most of the "old" copyright law that is still applicable. Perhaps the most significant change in the present law is that it strengthens the rights of authors and deemphasizes the rights of publishers. The following are nine major changes enacted by the new law:

1. In the past, prepublication protection was referred to as *common law copyright*. For this protection, no legal formalities had to be observed so long as the work remained unpublished. Previously, a copyright was obtained in two ways: one, by publication of the work with a proper notice of copyright, and two, by registration of certain works (such as lectures, dramatic and musical compositions, motion pictures, works of art) before publication. On such publication or registration, the common law copyright terminated. For this reason, U.S. copyright law had been referred to as "a right of first publication," and the question of whether a particular work had been published was often a major consideration. Now, this cumbersome and confusing dual system of protection is replaced by a single federal system of statutory protection for all copyrightable works, both published and unpublished.

2. A work is now automatically protected on "creation"—that is, once the work has been fixed in a tangible medium. The work need not be published or registered to be entitled to copyright protection. The copyright registration does, however, provide important rights and remedies.

3. Any one of the group of rights comprising the copyright in a work can be separated and treated independently from the remaining rights.

4. Unless specified otherwise, it is presumed that the author retains all of the rights in a work except what is expressly transferred. However, an employer may be the author of a work actually made by an employee.

5. With the exception of nonexclusive licenses and transfers by operation of law, all transfers of ownership of a copyright must be in writing to be enforceable.

6. The length of period of a copyright has been extended with the base being the life of the author plus 50 years. And for certain other works, particularly works "for hire," the term is 75 years from publication or 100 years from creation, whichever is less. The term of copyrights that existed when the 1976 law was enacted has also been extended. Furthermore, any copyrights under the old law that must be renewed now have a longer renewal term.

7. Pantomimes and choreography reduced to a tangible form, such as by notation, are now covered under the law. Computer programs and data bases are also protectable.

8. Certain provisions explaining what constitutes noninfringing fair use of a copyrighted work were added.

9. An administrative tribunal was created to handle the distribution of royalties under newly enacted compulsory licensing provisions.

Some of the other important changes in the Copyright Act of 1976 pertain to cable television, library photocopying, and educational, religious, and nonprofit use of copyrighted works. Other changes include a large reduction in the number of classes of works for registration, new copyright forms, increases in U.S. Copyright Office fees, and changes in the deposit requirements. Based on past history of copyright law, we can anticipate little change in the foreseeable future.

THE HISTORY OF TRADEMARKS

3

ANCIENT CIVILIZATION
TO NINETEENTH-CENTURY ENGLAND

The history of trademarks goes back much further than patents and copyrights. Archaeologists have found markings on pottery of the Stone Age period, around 5000 B.C. Animals were also marked, as witnessed by cave drawings found in southwestern Europe of bison with symbols on their flanks. These ancient marks presumably were used to identify ownership rather than to serve some business function.

Potter marks from around 3200 B.C. identifying the source of fired clay pots, including jars buried in tombs of the First Dynasty Egyptian kings, have also been dug up. It is believed that these marks were used to identify the maker so that he or she could be held responsible for defective merchandise and be appropriately punished. Often the blame for inferior workmanship was passed on to an unfortunate slave. Building stones during this period were marked with symbols to identify either their quarry or the masons who prepared them, and roof tiles and bricks were stamped with their makers' names. Among the Sumerian cities of Mesopotamia (3500 B.C.), cylindrical seals were used to identify the person who supplied commodities taken to the temple exchange.

Many stone seals found at Cnossus on Crete have inscriptions cut in reverse so that they can be impressed into clay. These seals date back to 3500 B.C. Near Corinth, clay bowls and saucers bearing potters' marks from around 2000 B.C. have been unearthed. It was the Roman civilization that existed between 500 B.C. and 500 A.D., however, that provides us with the earliest documented records of an economy that used trademarks on an everyday basis. Latin literature contains actual references to the use of makers' marks on cheese, wine, lamps, medicine, ointment, metallic ornaments, and glass vessels. Other available evidence includes seals used for marking cloth, masons' marks chiseled on building stones, and tiles and bricks with impressions that identify their makers. Most prominent, however, has been pottery, the most commonly uncovered relic from ancient civilizations. An estimated 6,000 different Roman potters' marks have been identified. These marks were often in the form of a picture such as a bee, a heart, an animal, a Christian symbol, initials, and a lion's head. Interestingly, some of these marks were quite clever and surprisingly up-to-par with today's trademarks. For example, Marcus Rutilus Lupus, a maker of oil lamps, used the design of a wolf's head as his trademark. *Lupus* in Latin means wolf.

During the Dark Ages, which covered the period of the fifth century A.D. through the eleventh century A.D. (the fall of the Roman Empire), there is not much available information on trademarks. In the Middle Ages, from the twelfth century on, however, the use of many kinds of trademarks on a variety of goods was commonplace. Throughout Europe, under the control of the guilds, merchants were not permitted to advertise. Consequently, as a quality standard that the guilds guaranteed to customers, trademarks were used as evidence of a product's manufacturer. For a similar reason, merchants used a "merchant's mark," and between the fourteenth and seventeenth centuries, they actually had more commercial importance than a maker's mark. This is true because a merchant dealt in goods acquired from many different sources, and one's reputation depended on the quality of handled goods. These merchant's marks can be traced through English literature as far back as the fourteenth century. Because the marks were often compulsory, they were also called "police marks." Merchant's marks appeared on either goods or their wrappings, as well as on the bills of lading or entries of ships' registers when shipped by sea. An English statute enacted in 1353 provided that a foreign merchant could obtain restitution for lost goods if his mark proved ownership.

Typically, guild regulation required every article produced by one of its members to bear both the guild symbol and the mark of the individual artisan. The guild's mark let the public know that the goods were not contraband. But it also held the artisan responsible for poor craftsmanship, and if guild standards failed to be met, disciplinary action was in order.

What is believed to be the earliest recorded reference to a trademark in English law is contained in a 1266 statute during the reign of Henry III. The statute required every baker to have a mark for each sort of prepared bread. Also dating back to the thirteenth century are bell-founders' marks, and the use of watermarks on paper in the fourteenth century. In 1373, an ordinance was passed that required London bottlemakers to place their individual marks on all "vessels made of leather."

In the fifteenth and sixteenth centuries, armorers, metalworkers, papermakers, printers, tapestry weavers, smiths, and tanners commonly used trademarks. At the time, there were strict laws that punished anyone who copied someone else's trademarks. In the Palatinate in the fourteenth century, an innkeeper was hanged for passing off cheap wine as Rudesheimer. Still, many products did not have marks because, unlike today, most sellers were personally known by the customers who bought their products. In France and Italy, the goldsmiths and silversmiths stamped their marks on their wares; in England, the woolen and linen weavers; in Austria, the hammersmiths.

Cyphers were often used by well-to-do merchants as a kind of bourgeois heraldry. When these traders were later accepted as gentlemen, their marks evolved into coats of arms. Some of these symbols of trade are still evident in the brasses and stained glass windows of ancient colleges, abbeys, and cathedrals of England and the rest of Europe.

An identifying mark also served another purpose in the British insurance industry. When fire insurance was first introduced, the insurance companies would use metal stakes and other marks to identify the properties that they insured. When a fire occurred, an insurer's fire-fighting brigades put out only those fires in the buildings belonging to their policyholders.

The earliest recorded instance of litigation over a trademark of a deceased artisan involved a court decision in England in 1452. A widow of a London bladesmith was awarded the use of a particular mark that formerly belonged to her husband. The first actual reference to the infringement of a trademark in English law took place in 1618 in a court case where a clothier sued another clothier who used the same mark on "his ill-made cloth on purpose to deceive." It was not, however, until the nineteenth century when the concept of a trademark was considered to be a valuable piece of property and worthy of legal protection, as well as being transferable like other property. Only then did English trademark law begin to develop.

THE UNITED STATES

Like those in England, the first U.S. trademarks were primarily proprietary marks and used for such purposes as branding cattle and serving as distributor's marks that appeared on dairy product bottles. The earliest trademark case on state record in America was decided in Massachusetts in 1837. Then, in 1845, the first federal court trademark case was decided, also in Massachusetts, when an English manufacturer accused U.S. citizens of infringing his trademark. By 1870, only 62 total trademark cases had been decided in the United States. In 1871, the U.S. Supreme Court decided its first trademark case.

It was not until after these early court decisions that both England and the United States enacted national legislation. Keep in mind that although England had local ordinances and merchants' associations regulating the use of trademarks, the British Parliament did not pass a comprehensive trademark registration statute until 1875. In this country, it was as early as 1791 when Renaissance man Thomas Jefferson, serving as secretary of state, petitioned, along with others, to the Second Congress for the exclusive rights to use certain marks on sailcloth. Jefferson urged enactment of a federal trademark statute based on the interstate commerce power of the U.S. Constitution. While Congress was not persuaded at the time, it enacted the first federal trademark statute nearly 80 years later in 1870, and much of what Jefferson had recommended was then incorporated into the new law. Three years later, however, the Supreme Court struck it down as unconstitutional on the grounds that the law was not expressly limited to acts taking place in either interstate or foreign commerce, and therefore did not fall under the jurisdiction of Congress to enact. To replace the 1870 Act, the Act of 1881 was appropriately limited and passed by Congress. It continued in effect until it was replaced by the 1905 Act, which was based on the theory that the ownership of a trademark is acquired by adoption and use; it was often observed that registration under the act simply affected procedural rights. The 1905 Act was supplemented in 1920 and later replaced by the currently existing Trademark Act of 1946, referred to as the Lanham Act. The current Act has been amended several times since.

Today, a trademark constitutes a symbol by which the source of goods is identified. As you can see, it was not until the middle of the nineteenth century when mass production and distribution of consumer goods began to grow that the use and true value of trademarks became vital to commerce. Today, a trademark represents to customers that all goods bearing the mark will be uniform in quality because their quality is controlled by the same company. U.S. Supreme Court Justice Felix Frankfurter referred to trademarks as "commercial magnetism" to draw customers to the article or commodity on which the "congenial symbol" appears. It is interesting to note how our modern trademark practices stem directly from medieval days, particularly in respect to the goodwill associated with the reputation of an enterprise. In 1870, under the first federal act, 121 trademarks were registered. By 1970, a century later, there were 23,447 federal registrations granted and 33,326 applications filed. By the end of 1989, over 1,560,000 federal registrations had been issued, although many are now abandoned or canceled. The widespread use of trademarks has become an essential part of modern business.

PATENTS

II

WHAT IS A PATENT?

4

Patents serve a dual purpose in the United States. Not only does a patent provide incentive for the inventor, but society benefits by gaining knowledge of new technology and making investment in its marketing more attractive. Actually, a patent is a 17-year monopoly granted to an inventor by the federal government in exchange for a complete and thorough description of his or her invention.

In general, monopolies go against the grain of our American free enterprise system, because they can generate abundant profits to the detriment of society. A monopoly creates the unfair advantage of the ability to restrict the supply of goods or services in the marketplace, or to withhold the supply from particular buyers, both of which consequently result in higher prices. When the government, under statute, grants a patent, it does indeed permit a monopoly to exist, but unlike other monopolies, it creates something beneficial to society. Instead of only taking something away from citizens, the issuance of a patent guarantees the disclosure of new and useful information that serves as a stepping stone for further advancements in the art by others. If patents did not exist, an inventor would be tempted to keep the knowledge a carefully guarded secret. There would be little or no incentive to disclose it. After new knowledge is uncovered so that a patent may be granted, the public document issued kindles the fire for future inventions and additional technology—consequently, everyone benefits.

A patent is sometimes referred to as a contract between the inventor and the public. It is as if the government says to an inventor, "Give us your disclosure, and we will give you a limited monopoly." The inventor receives a 17-year headstart,

27

and during this time enjoys the opportunity to market, experiment with, or do nothing with the product. Competitors are prevented from profiting from the individual's creativity. If the inventor chooses not to manufacture the device, some or all of the patent rights may be assigned, sold, or licensed in return for royalties. The monopoly is a fair arrangement because the inventor has invested time and money into research and development and, once the product is created, the usual pain and suffering associated with the risky venture of entering the marketplace must be endured.

The main advantage that a patent offers to the inventor is the right to stop others from copying his invention. Not only is it easier for him to sell the product, but he has a decisive edge in attracting investors to fund his enterprise. Of course, the prestige associated with owning a patent is also present. The disadvantages of obtaining a patent are that there is a cost, and the limited monopoly expires in 17 years. The alternative to patenting a product is to keep it a secret and risk having others figure it out and copy the invention. If the secret is well kept, the exclusivity of the product could exist for a long period without being revealed. For example, if Coca-Cola ® had patented its famed formula, other companies would have had the opportunity to come out with an identical product after its first 17 years in business (the only difference would be the name, since Coca-Cola is a trademark). One can see that under certain circumstances some inventors might opt to take the risk of not patenting an invention.

There are three basic kinds of patents issued in the United States. The most common is a "utility" patent for mechanical, electrical, or chemical inventions covering processes, machines, articles of manufacture, or compositions of matter, as well as improvements of the same. As examples, the first page of each of six patents is appended to this chapter. Second are "design" patents that protect the aesthetic or ornamental external appearance of articles of manufacture. Two examples of this type are also appended to this chapter. Third are "plant" patents that may be granted to someone who invents or discovers and asexually reproduces any new variety of plant, including trees, shrubs, and flowers. Exceptions to this general rule are tuber-propagated plants and plants found in an uncultivated state.

Anyone, regardless of age, may obtain a patent in the United States, even somebody who is not a citizen. Employees of the U.S. Patent Office, however, are not eligible, although other people employed by the government are. The true inventor is the only person who may apply for a patent, and he or she must sign the application and execute an oath. Procedures exist, however, for filing a patent application if the true inventor is deceased, cannot be found, or refuses to sign.

A SOCIETY WITHOUT PATENTS

At first blush, some people may say, "In a free enterprise system, patents should not be granted since they create monopolies." If patents did not exist, would the best interest of the public be served? We do not think so.

If every invention was fair game to be copied, inventors would likely lose incentive to pursue an idea. An inventor would know that once the invention was brought to the marketplace and customers were educated of its value, bigger or well-established companies could then invest large sums of money in the same product, and coupled with their large distribution capacities, they would cause the inventor severe difficulty in surviving the competition. Hence, the number of small technology companies and innovative individuals who would bother to pursue their inventions would decrease, and considerably fewer innovations would be available to consumers. Technology would eventually be diminished and concentrated in the hands of a few big businesses. While big corporations make important contributions and are able to do some things that small businesses cannot, small businesses also make important contributions and can do things that large businesses cannot. In fact, under our present system, small companies do many things that otherwise would never get done, and in doing so they often grow into competing big companies. Xerography is just one example of something that would not have found its way to the marketplace when it did had there not been a patent system. So it is for good reason that the United States and the vast majority of other nations have patent laws that allow this kind of a monopoly to exist. With patents, we live in a better world.

IS IT PATENTABLE?

To be patentable, an invention must be one of the kinds of things that the patent statute permits to be patented. A so-called inventive idea must relate to new processes, machines, manufactures, compositions of matter, plants, or designs. Basically, it is the physical embodiments of science or the physical manipulation of things for useful purposes that are patentable.

A *process* is an art, process, or method of producing a useful industrial result. The means that produce a certain product may properly be the subject of a valid patent, as may the method and the product itself. However, an invention does not have to be, and rarely is, entirely new. It may be an improvement on an existing system, or a correlation of old systems in a novel manner that is beyond the skill of the mere routinist. This can mean a change in sequence or timing, or some other critical factor that is novel and inventive, or it could be a new unity of effort in all steps. A process includes a new use of a known process, machine, manufacture, composition of matter, or material.

A *machine* is an apparatus that performs a function and produces a definite result or effect. For example, it receives force and transmits, multiplies, or transforms such force. It could range from a simple device to a complicated combination of many parts.

A *manufacture* is an article that is produced and has a usefulness in trade, and can be produced either by hand labor or machinery.

Compositions of matter include chemical compounds and mixtures such as drugs, insecticides, and paints.

A *plant* is simply a plant as that term is commonly understood, but some types of plants, such as those that are tuber propagated or sexually propagated, cannot be patented.

A *design* is the ornamental, aesthetic, nonfunctional appearance of a useful object. Ordinary craftsmanship, however, does not qualify for a patent. Unlike utility patents, design patents are granted for a 14-year term.

On the other side of the coin, some things cannot be patented, such as phenomena of nature and results. For example, an 1862 court case decided that the idea of inhaling ether to produce insensitivity to pain was not patentable. Likewise, had you invented the first printing machine, the machine itself would be patentable, but you could not make the claim, "I patent all machines to print books." No inventor can patent a result. That would provide a monopoly to restrict others from competing in all other ways to get the same result as the patented invention.

Similarly, ideas or abstract principles cannot be patented. To put it simply, mental processes are not patentable because such a law would be, in effect, a prohibition against people's thinking. Then too, patenting an aggregation of two or more structures is not allowed by the U.S. Patent Office if each of the old structures continues to operate the same as it did before with no new cooperation between the two. For this reason, a person could not obtain a patent for an invention that combined a pencil and an eraser by attaching them because each still does what it did before and there is no new cooperation between the two. At least that is what the U.S. Supreme Court held many decades ago. Also, no patent would be granted for something in which the only novelty is in the arrangement of printed matter. The patent office would also disallow a patent for a business system, such as a bookkeeping system or a hotel checking system. Although such ideas may be valuable and creative, they are entirely intellectual and do not come within any of the previously described categories of the kinds of things that can be patented. However, physical objects used to implement such a system and methods for manipulating a computer to implement such a system are among the kinds of things that can be patented. Interestingly, there is a statute that denies an invention if it is useful only for making atomic weapons. Perhaps this statute exists because atomic weapons are not something our society wants to encourage. Additionally, national security requires that the government be free to use such inventions.

While many patents today represent improvements of an existing invention, the following are considered nonpatentable unless they actually change the operation of the device:

1. Improvements that only substitute one construction material for another, for example, to strengthen an already known device.

2. Improvements that merely change a size or dimension, for example, to enlarge or make smaller something already known. This would void an invention that merely made a television screen larger or a tape recorder smaller.

3. Improvements that only change a shape are not patentable.

4. Improvements that change the location of a device's parts, or reverse such parts without any change in operation or function. Remember that an invention must be a product of inventive facilities.

5. Improvements that substitute new parts for old parts without changing the operation or results achieved. Yet you can receive a patent if you simplify a device and change its mode of operation but obtain the same result just as or more efficiently.

NEW, USEFUL, AND NONOBVIOUS

Three principal requirements written in the patent statute are that an invention must be *new, useful, and nonobvious.*

First, an invention must be "new." New is the requirement of novelty—something different than what has been done before. If an invention has previously been patented or sold or a publication has appeared that shows the same thing, it is not patentable.

Second, an invention must be "useful," which means it must have some utility. For example, in the chemical field, a new chemical may be discovered that has never existed before. But simply being new is not sufficient. Chemical companies sometimes discover or invent a new chemical compound in the laboratory and, once known, they try it for every imaginable use in order to find the utility necessary to receive a patent. They might try to remove paint, kill bugs, or protect coatings, as well as make endless other attempts to figure out something useful to do with it. An attempt is made to get a patent issued, as the compound could be of value to the company for some later-discovered, still different purpose.

Third, and perhaps the most critical issue in patent law, is the interpretation of what is meant by "nonobvious." To understand the meaning of nonobvious as it applies to patents, it is necessary to mentally create or imagine a hypothetical person who existed at the time that the invention was made. Supposedly, this individual has the ordinary skill in the particular art. The person is not unusually skilled and does not lack skill or intelligence. This imaginary person has been educated and applies the ordinary principles of the technical field or art in a routine manner, and could be expected to do ordinary work in this field.

Once this hypothetical person is created, it is necessary to examine the closest prior art, such as other previous patents, all prior printed publications that can be found, and the available data existing on whatever has been sold. Everything is then presented to the person for review. The question is asked: "What is the difference between the proposed invention and what has previously existed?" Then the most critical question is asked: *"Would it have been obvious to this hypothetical person at the time when the invention took place to have made those differences?"* Plainly, this requires an extremely subjective judgment. If the answer is that it would have been obvious for the hypothetical person exercising normal skill to make those changes, the patent would be denied. On the other hand, if the invention has differences that are above and beyond the exercise of ordinary skill, it is entitled to a patent. Inventive skills have indeed been exerted, not just normal, routine skills.

The telephone is an excellent example of an invention that had been subjected to the "nonobvious test." On March 7, 1876, Alexander Graham Bell's patent was granted covering "the method of, and apparatus for, transmitting vocal or other sounds telegraphically...by causing electrical undulations, similar in form to the vibrations of the air which constitute the vocal or other sounds." However, although the telephone had not previously existed, people already knew that sound is waves, undulations, or vibrations that go through the atmosphere. Thus, a hot debate occurred as to whether the waves of electrical current transmitted through the wires of Bell's invention were nonobvious from sound waves through atmosphere.

THE UNITED STATES PATENT OFFICE

In 1925, the U.S. Patent Office was transferred from the Department of the Interior to the Department of Commerce and remains under its jurisdiction today. It is the job of the office to administer the laws pertaining to the granting of patents in the United States. It has published and kept extensive records of all patents granted in this country since 1836. The president appoints the commissioner of patents who supervises the office that includes more than 1400 examiners. Basically, it is the patent office's responsibility to process all patent and trademark applications, and on examining and sometimes reexamining these applications, to determine which ones should be issued as patents or trademark registrations.

Due to the existence of several different technical fields in science, patent examiners specialize in certain areas of technology such as chemistry or electronics and in more specific fields within those areas. Examiners spend a large portion of their time in the large Library of Patents, which is segregated into U.S. patents and foreign patents. The library is open to anyone who wishes to search for information on any patent that has been granted in the United States since 1836. There are more than 40,000 bound volumes of scientific periodicals and over 35,000 volumes of technical books. By and large, the examiners are friendly and are available to answer questions and help with a patent search. However, the U.S. Patent and Trademark Office cannot give legal advice.

Information concerning both patents and trademarks can be obtained by writing: Commissioner of Patents and Trademarks, Washington, D.C. 20231. However, the patent office is physically located at 2021 Jefferson Davis Highway, Arlington, Virginia 22202. You may contact the patent office by calling: (703) 557-INFO or (703) 305-HELP.

PATENT INFRINGEMENT

As stated earlier, when an inventor receives a patent, he or she is granted a monopoly for a 17-year period. If another party without authority makes, uses, or sells the invention within the United States during the term of the patent, that person is thereby liable for infringement. In some instances, the use of a patented process outside the United States and importation of a resulting product into the United States is also an infringement. Incidentally, patent law prohibits anyone from making a patented article (other than the patent owner, of course), *even for self-use*. If the patented article were made for one's home use, for instance, some people think that they would not need the permission of the inventor. They are mistaken. They would still be infringing on the patent owner's rights.

Of course, it is not always possible as a patent owner to know when somebody is infringing on your rights. Certainly it is difficult to discover when another person is making and using your product for personal use within the confinement of his or her home. Even in many business instances where your invention is being copied to be used in an industrial process, you cannot readily find out about it. After all, you cannot police every manufacturing and warehouse facility throughout the country. Nor, for that matter, can you enter the premises of suspected infringers. On the other hand, if your patented invention is being sold in the marketplace, it is probable that you will know about it and take appropriate action. Then all you have to do is purchase the other person's goods and compare the product with your patent. Once you know of infringement, keep in mind that the burden of establishing proof is your responsibility. There is no government body or other institution that will go out into the commercial world on your behalf to see if somebody is conducting activities that infringe your patent. You must protect your patent rights yourself.

Once you have gathered what you consider reasonable information to convince yourself that your patent has been infringed, you should evaluate the impact that the infringing activities have on you or your company. Not only is the economic impact you suffer a factor, but so is the effect that it has on your reputation. Then, too, will others be tempted to do the same? Failure to do anything can be interpreted as consent and can ruin your chances to win a future infringement suit. A court may then decide, "You sat on your hands for too long, and there is nothing that the court will do now." So, not only must you police the marketplace, but you must act when infringement exists.

Ordinarily, your patent attorney is the person to consult first in determining whether an infringement actually exists. If you suspect the owner of another patent, such as an improvement on your patented product, your attorney will probably want to review the other patent's records at the U.S. Patent and Trademark Office. If the attorney's review indicates that the improvement would infringe, or if it is an out-and-out case of someone without a patent simply copying your invention, a letter usually should be sent immediately to the infringer informing of your patent and demanding that the individual stop the infringement. However, such a letter can give the recipient a right to sue you to get a court decision on whether there is infringement. Hopefully a reasonable settlement can be reached to avoid the cost of litigation in the U.S. District Courts. All appeals in U.S. infringement suits now go to the Court of Appeals for the Federal Circuit (CAFC). Whether litigation is appropriate often depends on the business and economic factors involved with the infringement. The human characteristics and personalities of the individuals involved on each side are also important factors. If a settlement cannot be reached and if the commercial injury justifies it, a patent infringement suit may · have to be instituted against the infringer.

In such a suit, you, as the patent owner or the exclusive licensee, must prove that the offending product is infringing. The defendant is likely to attempt to prove that your patent is invalid because it should not have been issued by the patent office.

On finding infringement for you, the claimant, the court awards damages adequate to compensate for the infringement, but in no event less than a reasonable royalty for the use made of the invention by the infringer, together with interest and costs as fixed by the court. When damages are not found by a jury, the court assesses them, and in either event, the court may increase the damages up to three times the amount found or assessed. In exceptional cases, the court may award reasonable attorney fees to the prevailing party.

Through 1988, the CAFC upheld more than half of the patents that came before it and affirmed trial court holdings of patent validity more than 80 percent of the time. Awards of "lost profits" of 60 percent of infringing sales were routinely approved by the CAFC and damages based on a "reasonable royalty" of 15 percent to 25 percent were even awarded. In one case, the CAFC stated that a "reasonable royalty" was more than the selling price of the infringing machine.

While some awards have been high, the injunction normally granted to the successful patent owner is often the remedy most feared by a defendant. This is particularly true when a trial court refuses to stay the injunction pending appeal. Such an injunction can abruptly close down the defendant's factory or production line, as was the result of Kodak's 1986 loss of an infringement judgment in favor of Polaroid. The loss that could occur when large sums of money are invested in manufacturing and maintaining inventories can be staggering.

The risks taken when a company disregards or miscalculates a patent can be prohibitive. This is particularly true when damage awards are doubled or tripled because the defendant, after being told about the patent, manufactured goods without first obtaining an opinion of qualified counsel that the patent was invalid.

For obvious reasons, we strongly recommend seeking the advice of a patent attorney when the issue of infringement arises.

PATENT SUBJECT MATTER

The following copies of the first page from several patents illustrate some of the kinds of things that can be patented.

Mechanical devices are illustrated by a drive linkage for a Stirling Engine in patent 4,546,663 and a hot dog turner in patent 4,633,772.

Patent 4,645,696 illustrates a chemical manufacturing process and product. Many chemical patents are based on considerably more complex chemistry. Typically, chemical inventions have no drawings.

An electrical, computer-oriented invention is illustrated by patent 4,794,369.

Patents for ornamental designs are illustrated by patents Des. 281,844 and Des. 286,724.

United States Patent [19]

Wood

[11]	Patent Number: **4,546,663**
[45]	Date of Patent: **Oct. 15, 1985**

[54] **DRIVE LINKAGE FOR STIRLING CYCLE AND OTHER MACHINES**

[75] Inventor: James G. Wood, Athens, Ohio

[73] Assignee: Sunpower, Inc., Athens, Ohio

[21] Appl. No.: 906,313

[22] Filed: Jun. 21, 1985

[51] Int. Cl.⁴ F16H 21/32
[52] U.S. Cl. 74/40; 60/520; 62/6; 74/44
[58] Field of Search 74/40, 43, 44, 45; 62/6; 60/520

[56] **References Cited**

U.S. PATENT DOCUMENTS

1,656,601	1/1928	Novick	74/40
2,035,222	3/1936	Curtis	74/40
2,653,484	9/1953	Zecher	74/40
2,830,455	4/1958	Harmon	74/40
3,482,457	12/1969	Wallis	74/44
3,964,523	6/1976	Benedict	74/40

Primary Examiner—Ronald C. Capossela
Attorney, Agent, or Firm—Frank H. Foster

[57] **ABSTRACT**

An improved linkage which is advantageously used in linking the crank of a Stirling machine to its coaxially reciprocating pistons. A swing lever having at least three spaced pivot axes is connected at one of its pivot axes to the machine housing and at a second pivot axes to one of the pistons. A bell crank, also having at least three pivot axes which are triangularly arranged, is rotatably connected at one of its pivot axes to the crank throw pin and pivotally connected at a second one of its pivot axes to the other piston. The bell crank is pivotally connected at its third pivot axis to the third pivot axis of the swing lever.

12 Claims, 13 Drawing Figures

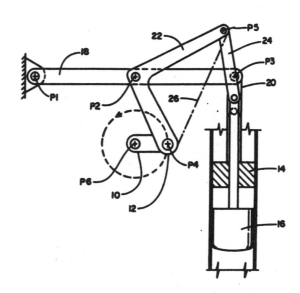

United States Patent [19]

Bowden et al.

[11]	Patent Number: **4,633,772**
[45]	Date of Patent: **Jan. 6, 1987**

[54] **GRIDDLE MOUNTED HOT DOG TURNER WITH LIFT OFF DETACHABLE DRIVE UNIT**

[75] Inventors: John E. Bowden, Ostrander; Roy E. Hook, Orient; E. Craig Miller, Powell, all of Ohio

[73] Assignee: Wendy's International, Inc., Dublin, Ohio

[21] Appl. No.: 790,886

[22] Filed: Oct. 24, 1985

[51] Int. Cl.⁴ A47J 37/04

[51] Int. Cl.^{4} A47J 37/04
[52] U.S. Cl. 99/332; 99/344; 99/423; 99/425; 99/441; 403/407.1
[58] Field of Search 99/423, 425, 332, 344, 99/441; 426/523; 403/253, 254, 349, 375, 407.1

[56] **References Cited**

U.S. PATENT DOCUMENTS

2,584,061 1/1952 Stilphen .... 99/441 X
2,631,525 3/1953 Finizie 99/423
3,298,303 1/1967 Waller 99/423
3,732,468 5/1973 Witt .

Primary Examiner—Billy J. Wilhite
Attorney, Agent, or Firm—Frank H. Foster

[57] **ABSTRACT**

An apparatus for automatically turning hot dogs upon a conventional griddle which has an easily attachable and detachable motor drive unit and continuously turns the hot dogs and cooks them properly on the griddle. The turner has a grid which slidably rests upon the griddle and has a plurality of laterally elongated openings for receipt of the hot dogs. A portable, detachable drive unit rests upon a surface which is adjacent to the griddle. A releasable coupling means drivingly, but detachable connects the drive unit to the grid for driving the grid in longitudinal reciprocation so that the hot dogs are rotated in alternate directions for even cooking.

9 Claims, 9 Drawing Figures

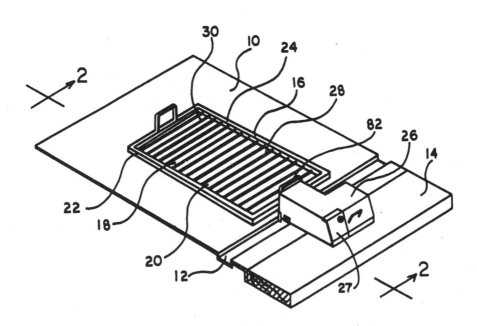

United States Patent [19]

Rood

[11] **Patent Number:** **4,645,696**

[45] **Date of Patent:** **Feb. 24, 1987**

[54] **TREATMENT FOR IMPROVING CELLULOSIC INSULATION**

[76] Inventor: Leonard D. Rood, 5764 Flintlock La., Columbus, Ohio 43213

[21] Appl. No.: 810,565

[22] Filed: Dec. 6, 1985

Related U.S. Application Data

[63] Continuation of Ser. No. 474,790, Mar. 14, 1983, abandoned, which is a continuation-in-part of Ser. No. 412,318, Aug. 27, 1982, abandoned, which is a continuation of Ser. No. 265,029, May 18, 1981, abandoned.

[51] Int. Cl.⁴ A62C 1/00; A62D 1/00; B27N 9/00

[52] U.S. Cl. 428/35; 252/2; 252/3; 252/5; 252/7; 252/62; 252/300; 252/607; 428/921

[58] Field of Search 252/300, 607, 2, 3, 252/5, 7, 62; 428/921, 35

[56] **References Cited**

U.S. PATENT DOCUMENTS

3,944,702	3/1976	Clark	428/391 X
4,182,681	1/1980	Gumbert	252/62 X
4,184,311	1/1980	Rood	428/35
4,386,119	5/1983	Draganov	252/62 X
4,430,380	2/1984	Honel et al.	428/288 X

OTHER PUBLICATIONS

McCutcheon's Functional Materials, The Manufacturer's Confectioner Publishing Co., 1980 Annual, pp. 24-28.

Primary Examiner—John E. Kittle
Assistant Examiner—Mukund J. Sham
Attorney, Agent, or Firm—Frank H. Foster

[57] **ABSTRACT**

In connection with the manufacture of cellulosic insulation of the type utilizing shredded newspaper which is treated with a fire retardant chemical composition and used for the thermal insulation of building structures, an anti-static agent is mixed and adhered to the fire retardant agent prior to depositing the fire retardant agent on the shredded cellulosic material. The anti-static agent may also be introduced into the finished product with desirable but not as significant improvements in the insulation and its manufacture.

16 Claims, No Drawings

United States Patent [19]

Haferd

[11] Patent Number: **4,794,369**

[45] Date of Patent: **Dec. 27, 1988**

[54] **MULTI-FUNCTION ELECTRICITY METERING TRANSDUCER**

[75] Inventor: James E. Haferd, Columbus, Ohio

[73] Assignee: Scientific Columbus, Inc., Columbus, Ohio

[21] Appl. No.: 660,380

[22] Filed: Oct. 12, 1984

Related U.S. Application Data

[63] Continuation of Ser. No. 352,106, Feb. 25, 1982, abandoned.

[51] Int. Cl.⁴ H03M 1/00
[52] U.S. Cl. 341/166; 324/141; 324/142; 358/138; 328/151; 364/178; 364/483; 341/123; 341/118
[58] Field of Search .... 340/347 M, 347 AD, 347 CC, 340/347 M, 347 C; 364/483, 178, 179; 324/142, 141; 358/138; 328/151

[56] **References Cited**

U.S. PATENT DOCUMENTS

3,244,808	4/1966	Roberts	358/133
3,484,591	12/1969	Trimble	364/734 X
3,914,760	10/1975	Logue	340/347 M X
3,984,829	10/1976	Zwack	340/347 C
4,213,134	7/1980	Chen	307/353 X
4,276,605	6/1981	Okamoto et al.	364/481 X
4,345,311	8/1982	Fielden	324/142 X

OTHER PUBLICATIONS

Kerchner et al., Alternating–Current Circuits, J. Wiley & Sons, Inc., 1938, pp. 52–55; 187–189.
The Engineering Staff of Federal Scientific Corp., Dithering Increases Dynamic Range . . . . , 8/1973, pp. 1–8.
Gray et al., Companded Pulse–Code Modulation Voice Codec . . . . , IEEE Journal of Solid–State Circuits, 12/1975, pp. 497 and 498.
Millman et al., Pulse and Digital Circuits, McGraw-Hill Book Co., Inc., 1956, pp. 323–335.

Primary Examiner—T. J. Sloyan
Attorney, Agent, or Firm—Frank H. Foster

[57] **ABSTRACT**

An electricity metering transducer is disclosed which samples voltages and currents at an innerconnection terminal of an electrical energy distribution system, converts those samples to digital form and computes selected electricity metering quantities. In a multiphase system current and voltage signals are multiplexed to a pair of codecs, one for current signals and one for voltage signals. The period of the signals being sampled is detected and used to generate a substantially nonsynchronous sampling signal so that a sample migration system is created which provides a large number of samples of a composite wave form. The steps of a digitally generated stepwise approximation of a sawtooth waveform are summed with the sequential analog samples and then removed from the digital value of each sample by software operation in order to increase the resolution of the digital to analog conversion.

4 Claims, 5 Drawing Sheets

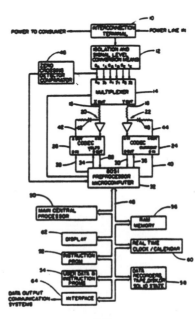

United States Patent [19]

Waldeck

[11] **Patent Number:** **Des. 281,844**

[45] **Date of Patent:** ** **Dec. 24, 1985**

[54] **COUNTERTOP SHOWCASE**

[76] Inventor: William D. Waldeck, 801 18th St., Parkersburg, W. Va. 26101

[**] Term: **14 Years**

[21] Appl. No.: **432,696**

[22] Filed: **Dec. 15, 1982**

[52] U.S. Cl. D6/472

[58] Field of Search D6/432, 436, 396, 441, D6/443, 449, 470, 471, 472, 473, 474, 467, 468; 312/114, 116, 117, 126

[56] **References Cited**

U.S. PATENT DOCUMENTS

D. 63,369	11/1923	Katzman	D6/472 X
D. 93,636	10/1934	Sawin et al.	D6/467
D. 112,149	11/1938	Kleinwachter	D6/436
D. 119,285	3/1940	Siersma	D6/468
D. 149,966	6/1948	Newman	D6/472 X
392,125	10/1888	King	312/114
557,974	4/1896	Conlin et al.	D6/472 X
629,672	7/1899	Fadum	D6/471 X
2,123,394	7/1938	Anderson	312/114 X

Primary Examiner—Carmen H. Vales
Attorney, Agent, or Firm—Frank H. Foster

[57] **CLAIM**

The ornamental design for a countertop showcase, as shown and described.

DESCRIPTION

FIG. 1 is a front perspective view of a countertop showcase showing my new design;

FIG. 2 is a rear perspective view thereof; the bottom shelf showing another tray embodiment; and

FIG. 3 is a bottom perspective view thereof; the trays have been removed for convenience of illustration.

United States Patent [19]

Whang

[11] **Patent Number:** **Des. 286,724**

[45] **Date of Patent:** ** **Nov. 18, 1986**

[54] **DRINKING MUG**

[75] Inventor: **Young K. Whang,** Seoul, Rep. of Korea

[73] Assignee: **Frank Strafella,** Powell, Ohio

[**] Term: **14 Years**

[21] Appl. No.: **490,836**

[22] Filed: **May 2, 1983**

[30]   **Foreign Application Priority Data**

Nov. 15, 1982 [KR]   Rep. of Korea 10122
[52] U.S. Cl. D7/9
[58] Field of Search D7/9, 10, 7, 3

[56]   **References Cited**
U.S. PATENT DOCUMENTS

D. 228,273   9/1973   Refsgaard D7/9

OTHER PUBLICATIONS

Hall China Company catalog–Service China, p. 3, top row, #1316 Coffee Mug—center col.
HFD–Retailing Home Furnishings, 2-9-81, p. 31, top right of page, Vandor Heart Mug.
Country Gourmet, vol. 52, p. 6, Loving Cup with Double Heart Handle, right col. #576.

Primary Examiner—Winifred E. Herrmann
Attorney, Agent, or Firm—Frank H. Foster

[57]   **CLAIM**

The ornamental design for a drinking mug, as shown.

DESCRIPTION

FIG. 1 is a bottom front perspective view of a drinking mug showing my new design;
FIG. 2 is a top rear perspective view thereof;
FIG. 3 is a bottom rear perspective view thereof;
FIG. 4 is a top front perspective view thereof;
FIG. 5 is a right side elevational view of FIG. 4; and,
FIG. 6 is a top plan view thereof.

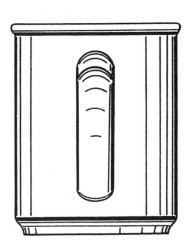

HOW TO PROTECT YOURSELF *BEFORE* SEEKING A PATENT

5

Although the granting of your patent represents protection under the umbrella of a 17-year monopoly, there are several things you should do and other things you must avoid doing *beforehand* in order to ensure your future rights. Most importantly, you must anticipate future possibilities. We recommend that you read this chapter carefully, because failure to comply with the proper procedures in the beginning stages of your invention could later come back to haunt you.

Under U.S. patent law, the first person to think of an invention is generally entitled to obtain a patent. However, this rule does not apply if the first inventor abandons efforts to either build a working model or file a patent application. Remember that there is always the possibility another person could think of the same invention you did, so it is highly desirable for you to accumulate proof of when you first thought about it and afterwards of your making diligent efforts either to file a patent application or build a working model.

DOCUMENTING YOUR INVENTION

Under certain circumstances, it could be essential for you to provide evidence to the U.S. Patent Office or a court demonstrating when you actually made your invention. In the event that you must do this, some documentation will be necessary to prove when you had your earliest observations and made experiments. For this reason, at the outset, you should routinely record everything you do in your own handwriting in a multipaged bound book. We emphasize the use of a *bound* book because the pages cannot easily be torn out or others substituted. Be sure to write a thorough account of your thoughts of the invention, how it works, what it does, what its physical parts are (if it has any), how the parts interrelate to each other, how they are shaped, and how they are made. When possible, you should use sketches and diagrams, although it is not necessary to have professional drawings. You should chronologically record your thoughts about the invention as they occur, and be sure to include dates for every entry. Sign and date each entry.

The log book is often referred to as a laboratory notebook, and is one of the most cost-effective systems for creating and maintaining suitable records. In the majority of cases, a system of this nature is used by the major research organizations, and most of them have their own printed bound books that contain mostly blank numbered pages and legends indicating the information that should be recorded. There are also books that can be purchased for this purpose.

Figure 5.1 is a sample log book page that can be duplicated. Record ideas and observations as they occur directly in the book in ink, and continue to make such entries on the next available page(s). Include favorable and unfavorable observations and changes. Don't erase—instead, make new entries. The log book is a record of the progression of events as they happen, not a manuscript being prepared for publication. Humans make mistakes and change their minds. The more detail, the better. Remember, if it's not here, a court or the Patent Office may conclude that it didn't exist or didn't happen, even if you remember that it did.

Most importantly, you should have two trustworthy witnesses sign all of your entries. Generally, the witnesses will be colleagues within your own company. It is essential for the witnesses to be able to testify that (1) they understood what you were doing, (2) they understood what the invention was and how it operated, and (3) what you wrote down was actually witnessed on the exact date entered in your book. Of course, this means that you must take the time to explain the invention to your witnesses.

Remember that evidence is like money—the more you have, the better off you are. Remember also to get into the habit of making your entries on a routine basis. Novice inven-

FIGURE 5.1 Sample Log Book Page

LABORATORY NOTEBOOK   PAGE _____

Project Title: _____

Sketches and explanations in ink of ideas, experiments, and observations, whether favorable or unfavorable. Give details of
structure, function, and result.

Inventor: _____ Coinventors (if any): _____
Date of idea or observation: _____
Recorded by: _____ Date of above entry: _____
Other co-workers or observers: _____
The above was explained to and understood by me on the date after
my name:

Witness 1: _____ date witnessed: _____

Witness 2: _____ date witnessed: _____

tors sometimes tend to wait until they have finished working
on their product and then attempt to complete a notebook, and
then it is too late to obtain witnesses with dated signatures.
By waiting, you can diminish your chances of getting your
patent, because, in the event that you need to submit your
book to the patent office, you may fail to meet the requirement of independent corroboration. The patent office wants
somebody besides yourself to say, "Yes, this is true." It is anticipated that every inventor is going to say what is in his or her
best interests. If there is a court proceeding, a judge is more apt

to rule favorably when an independent person is available to speak on your behalf.

In order for you to get the benefit of the actual date you thought of the invention, you must thereafter make diligent efforts to actually build one that works or file a patent application. If you abandon your efforts or just put the idea on the "back burner," your date of invention will become the date you resume your diligent efforts. Someone who thought of it after you did but before you resumed your efforts, continued working diligently, and did not abandon the invention may have the right to get the patent instead of you.

A progressive research organization is likely to have routine procedures for every employee to follow. The employee should be instructed on what to do with a new idea. Who should be told about it and when? Should experimentation come first? Should the idea first be discussed with colleagues or taken to the supervisor? Should a screening committee be set up? Depending on the organization, the procedure may be informal or formal. Perhaps an immediate conversation is needed, supplemented by the laboratory notebook, or perhaps a more formal approach is needed, with a form to be completed and submitted to a committee.

RECORDING YOUR INVENTION WITH THE PATENT OFFICE

An alternative or additional way to provide evidence is to file your invention with the U.S. Patent Office. To do this, you write down the kind of information about your invention as described above, have it witnessed by two qualified people, and send it to the patent office with a $10 fee. Send them two copies with a stamped, self-addressed envelope. One copy will be returned to you with the U.S. Patent Office's stamp on it; this copy represents proof of the date when you filed your idea. A separate paper must be included, signed by the inventor, stating that he or she is the inventor and requesting that the material be received for processing under the Disclosure Document Program. In turn, the patent office will keep this disclosure document for two years. Later you can file your patent application and tell the office to put your disclosure document in the patent application file.

Even though a well-prepared laboratory notebook is adequate proof, we recommend this procedure as an extra precaution. It is well worth the small cost, and is an especially good idea for the novice inventor who does not have the experience in keeping a formal laboratory notebook. Remember, however, that it is not a patent application. The complete patent office rules for this Disclosure Document Program are reproduced in Figure 5.2.

HAVING AN EMPLOYER/EMPLOYEE AGREEMENT

When a person is hired mainly for the purpose of inventing, it is reasonable for the employer to retain full ownership of the patented invention. On the other hand, and much less common, an employee can be given full ownership of the invention especially when it is unrelated to the employer's business. In between these two extremes is what is referred to as *shop right*, where the employer has some rights in the invention, but not to such extent as to completely extinguish the inventor's rights. This means that the employer can practice the invention but cannot grant a license to anyone else. Furthermore, under the *shop right* doctrine, an employee who leaves the employer has the right to practice the invention as well as license somebody else. In this case, both parties are permitted to practice the invention.

In a 1960 decision, the limits of the shop right doctrine have been defined as follows:

> *Where an employee (1) during his hours of employment, (2) working with his employer's materials and appliances, (3) conceives and (4) perfects an invention for which he obtains a patent, he must accord his employer a nonexclusive right to practice the invention. United States v. Dubilier Condenser Corp. 289 U.S. 178, 188, 17 USPQ 154, 158.*

Agreements between employers and employees should be in writing beforehand to safeguard inventions and ensure that ownership is where the employer and employee intend it to be. Of course, from a practical point of view, ownership of an invention should be always predetermined. First, no one wants to spend money to get a patent for someone else. Second, if a company should own the invention, the inventor, except under unusual circumstances, must sign papers. If ownership is

FIGURE 5.2   Description of Disclosure Documents

1706   Disclosure Documents [R-11]

The Patent and Trademark Office accepts and preserves, for a limited time, "Disclosure Documents" as evidence of the dates of conception of inventions.

THE PROGRAM

A paper disclosing an invention and signed by the inventor or inventors may be forwarded to the Patent and Trademark Office by the inventor (or by any one of the inventors when there are joint inventors), by the owner of the invention, or by the attorney or agent of the inventor(s) or owner. It will be retained for two years and then be destroyed unless it is referred to in a separate letter in a related application within two years.

The Disclosure Document is not a patent application, and the date of its receipt in the Patent and Trademark Office will not become the effective filing date of any patent application subsequently filed. However, like patent applications, these documents will be kept in confidence by the Patent and Trademark Office until a patent is granted.

This program does not diminish the value of the conventional witnessed and notarized records as evidence of conception of an invention, but it should provide a more credible form of evidence than that provided by the popular practice of mailing a disclosure to one self or another person by registered mail.

A Disclosure Document is available to the public when an application which refers to it issues as a patent.

CONTENT OF DISCLOSURE DOCUMENT

Although there are no restrictions as to content and claims are not necessary, the benefits afforded by the Disclosure Document will depend directly upon the adequacy of the disclosure. Therefore, it is strongly urged that the document contain a clear and complete explanation of the manner and process of making and using the invention in sufficient detail to enable a person having ordinary knowledge in the field of the invention to make and use the invention. When the nature of the invention permits, a drawing or sketch should be included. The use or utility of the invention should be described, especially in chemical inventions.

PREPARATION OF THE DOCUMENT

The Disclosure Document must be limited to written matter or drawings on paper or other thin, flexible material, such as linen or plastic drafting material, having dimensions or being folded to dimensions not to exceed 8 1/2 by 13 inches (21.6 by 33 cm.). Photographs also are acceptable. Each page should be numbered. Text and drawings should be sufficiently dark to permit reproduction with commonly used office copying machines.

OTHER ENCLOSURES

In addition to the fee described below, the Disclosure Document must be accompanied by a stamped, self-addressed envelope and a separate paper in duplicate, signed by the inventor, stating that he or she is the inventor and requesting that the material be received for processing under the Disclosure Document Program. The papers will be stamped by the Patent and Trademark Office with an identifying number and date of receipt, and the duplicate request will be returned in the self-addressed envelope together with a notice indicating that the Disclosure Document may be relied upon only as evidence and that a patent application should be diligently filed if patent protection is desired. The inventor's request may take the following form:

"The undersigned, being the inventor of the disclosed invention, requests that the enclosed papers be accepted under the Disclosure Document Program, and that they be preserved for a period of two years."

DISPOSITION

The Disclosure Document will be preserved in the Patent and Trademark Office for two years and then will be destroyed unless it is referred to in a separate letter in a related patent application filed within the two-year period. The Disclosure Document should be referred to in a separate letter filed in a pending application by identifying the Document by its title, number, and date of receipt. Acknowledgment of receipt of such letters is made in the next official communication or in a separate letter from the Patent and Trademark Office. Unless it is desired to have the Patent and Trademark Office retain the Disclosure Document beyond the two-year period, it is not required that it be referred to in a patent application.

ACKNOWLEDGMENT

When a paper referring to a Disclosure Document is filed in a patent application within two years after the filing of a Disclosure Document, the group clerk either prepares (1) a memorandum indicating that a reference to Disclosure Document No. — — has been made in application Serial No., — —, or (2) a copy of the paper filed in the application referring to the Disclosure Document. The memorandum or copy is forwarded to the Head of the Correspondence and Mail Division.

Upon receipt, the Correspondence and Mail Division prepares a retention label (PTO-150) and attaches it to the Disclosure Document, indicates on the forwarded memo or copy that the retention label has been applied and returns the memo or copy to the group. The returned memo or copy is stapled to the inside left flap of the file wrapper so that the examiner's attention is directed to it when the next Office action is prepared. If prosecution before the examiner has been concluded, a separate letter indicating that the Disclosure Document will be retained should be sent to the applicant by the group clerk.

After the acknowledging letter is mailed, the paper in the application file referring to the Disclosure Document is noted with the paper number of the acknowledgment. The returned memo or copy is stapled to and retained with the original paper in the file wrapper referring to the Disclosure Document.

FEE

A fee of $>6 (37 CFR 1.21(c))< is charged for filing a Disclosure Document. Payment must accompany the Disclosure Document when it is submitted to the Patent and Trademark Office

WARNING TO INVENTORS

The two-year retention period should not be considered to be a "grace period" during which the inventor can wait to file his patent application without possible loss of benefits. It must be recognized that in establishing priority of invention an affidavit or testimony referring to a Disclosure Document must usually also establish diligence in completing the invention or in filing the patent application since the filing of the Disclosure Document.

Inventors are also reminded that any public use or sale in the United States or publication of the invention anywhere in the world more than one year prior to the filing of a patent application on that invention will prohibit the granting of a patent on it.

If the inventor is not familiar with what is considered to be "diligence in completing the invention" or "reduction to practice" under the patent law, or if he has other questions about patent matters, the Patent and Trademark Office advises him to consult an attorney or agent registered to practice before the Patent and Trademark Office. A Directory of Registered Patent Attorneys and Agents Arranged by States and Counties titled ATTORNEYS AND AGENTS REGISTERED TO PRACTICE BEFORE THE U.S. PATENT AND TRADEMARK OFFICE [1982] is available from the Superintendent of Documents, U.S. Government Printing Office, Washington, D.C. 20402. Patent attorneys and agents may be found in the telephone directories of most major cities. Also, many large cities have associations of patent attorneys which may be consulted.

uncertain because there is no written agreement, the inventor may refuse to sign the papers, which will cause considerable problems down the road.

Under U.S. patent law, all inventions begin by being owned by the inventor, a natural person. The inventor remains the owner unless there is a reason for ownership to belong to another party. One common reason for transferring ownership is a sale. The inventor may also agree with an employer to assign future inventions to the employer in return for wages or salary. With a written agreement beforehand (generally in an employment agreement), an employee is likely to cooperate and sign the necessary papers. However, if ownership is not clear, the employee might wish to claim sole ownership and refuse to sign the papers. In that event, a legal dispute will arise and result in legal expenses to both parties, which could possibly lead to making a payment to the inventor to secure settlement of the matter and get the necessary signature.

Bear in mind that if an ownership agreement is not in writing, an employer may still be the owner if the employee was hired to innovate or invent in the technical field in which the invention was made. It is best to avoid future disputes by putting the agreement in writing in the employment contract. This is also a good place to protect the employer's trade secrets. A trade secret is information that is not known to others and that provides a competitive advantage. While trade secrets are not incorporated into patent law, the courts will prevent their unlawful use by others. In order to keep something a trade secret, an effort must be made on the part of the owner to maintain secrecy from outsiders. Although it is permissible to disclose a trade secret to an employee for the purpose of carrying out duties, public disclosure destroys the right to stop others (including a former employee) from using the trade secret. The employment agreement should contain a provision in which the employee promises not to disclose trade secrets to others and not to use them for personal commercial benefit.

While there are many kinds of employment agreements that could be executed to protect the rights of an employer and an inventor, an example follows. Please note, however, that the subject of employment agreements is a complicated area of law and there may be particular facts that could render this agreement unenforceable. In addition, an extensive diversity of terms might be applicable in your agreement, so you are advised to seek the counsel of an attorney who is knowledgeable in the area of patents, trade secrets, and employment agreements. We recommend counseling in order to have an agreement properly prepared to meet your particular needs. Keep in mind that some employment agreements can be held unenforceable if they are signed in the course of employment without both the employer and the employee getting something as a result.

Employment Agreement

As part of the consideration of my employment or continued employment with XYZ Corporation, I hereby agree with the XYZ Corporation as follows:

1. All inventions, improvements, or discoveries which, during the period of my employment, I shall conceive or make, either alone or jointly with others, shall be the exclusive property of the employer if either (a) they were made or conceived while I was engaged in any work for the employer or with the use of facilities or materials of the employer, or (b) which relate to any product, process, development, research work, or any other business of the employer.

2. I further agree that all records relating thereto shall be the sole property of the employer and will be promptly and fully disclosed to the employer. Additionally, I will, at the expense of the employer, sign and otherwise fully execute and deliver to the employer all patent applications of the United States or any foreign country on such improvements, inventions, or discoveries and will further sign and otherwise fully execute assignments to the employer of the entire right, title, and interest in them and will give the employer such reasonable assistance as may be requested of me in securing, enforcing, and protecting the applications and patents at the employer's expense. In the event that I am no longer employed by the employer, I shall be paid a reasonable compensation for time devoted to such efforts and will be reimbursed for expenses necessarily incurred.

3. I recognize that as a result of and during my employment I may acquire confidential information, including trade secrets and proprietary data, regarding

the business of the employer. I agree to hold such matter in confidence during and following my employment and will not divulge it to anyone without the express written authorization of the employer, so long as it remains confidential and proprietary. I further agree that if my employment ceases I will not take with me any drawings, blueprints, documents, compilations of technical data, specifications, or any other record of any nature belonging to the employer or any reproductions thereof.

_____

Employee Signature

_____

Date of Signature

_____

Witness

JOINT INVENTORS

The inventor is the person who thinks of the invention, not somebody who merely builds something described by another party. If an idea arises as a result of a discussion among several people, all those who contributed to the resulting invention are joint inventors. As mentioned earlier, the patent office requires the inventor to be an individual (a corporation is not an individual), so more than one inventor can sign the patent application. A patent can also be granted to two or more people.

Here, too, unless the joint inventors will assign the invention to another, we recommend that you get an agreement between the joint inventors in writing early in the game to avoid future problems. You and your partner(s) should resolve such matters as how the product will be marketed, how the business will be funded, who is responsible for what duties, how profits will be distributed (including royalties and licensing fees), how licensing will be handled, and so on. In the absence of an agreement, in the event that joint owners do not see eye-to-eye, each is free to go his or her own way and actually compete against the other(s). Thus, a competitive bidding situation may develop where each owner is undercutting a former partner. Without an agreement stating otherwise, each owner also has the right to license a third party and personally keep all the licensing fees. For obvious reasons, it is in the best interest of all partners to have a written agreement that spells out every contingency before any problems arise.

DON'T MAKE IT PUBLIC *BEFORE* YOU FILE YOUR PATENT APPLICATION

In most countries, a common patent law provision is that, if you publish a description of your invention or otherwise disclose it publicly anywhere in the world before you file your patent application, you lose your right to have your invention patented. Your own publication or disclosure is viewed as prior art because it is identical to your invention. Hence, if this happens, your invention is no longer deemed as something new. For this reason, if you plan to do business in foreign countries, make sure you do not publish anything on your invention before you have filed here at home. Note that the vast majority of countries other than the United States abide by this rule.

In the United States, an inventor is granted a one-year grace period after the first commercial sale or first publication, during which time the inventor must file or lose the rights for a patent forever. It is thus possible to get a U.S. patent but destroy your right for one in other countries. The thinking behind U.S. patent law is to allow a person to "test the waters" and actually attempt to market the invention before having to undergo the cost of filing a patent application. Then too, one may be able to generate enough sales (and profit) to cover these expenses. Keep in mind that, while publishing the invention will definitely destroy your rights in the majority of foreign countries, selling your product beforehand will also ruin your chances in many countries, but not in as many countries as publication does. We also want to emphasize that a simple piece of paper containing directions sold with the product could be construed as published material. It is not restricted to publication in the ordinary sense, such as periodicals or newspapers, although this, too, would certainly constitute published material and disallow the opportunity for a patent in foreign countries.

It is important to keep in mind that you have only a one-year grace period in this country. During this time you can publish and/or sell all you want and not destroy your U.S. patent rights—as long as you file your application here within one year following your first sale or first publication. Many small businesspersons do not aspire to do business outside the United States and, as long as they understand this, their decision to enter the marketplace before applying for a patent is a sensible one. If and when they do get a U.S. patent, foreign inventors with the same product cannot infringe on their rights in this country.

If nothing is made public before filing in the United States, you may still be able to get a patent in most foreign countries, even if you make it public right after you file in the United States. To do this, you must take other actions within the first year after you filed in the United States.

PATENT PENDING

As the words indicate, patent pending means that an application has been filed with and is pending in the patent office, but the invention has not yet been granted a patent. Since it presently takes approximately 18 months for an application to be processed by the patent office, putting the words "patent pending" on a product is a formal way to inform the public that an application for a patent is pending in the patent office. Putting this on a product that is being marketed also serves as a way to attempt to scare off competitors. While patent pending has no legal consequence, it does give notice to others that they should consider not competing with your product because if your patent is granted, they might later be enjoined from marketing it. If so, their investment may go down the drain. Of course, during the time that your patent is pending, or in the event that it is not granted, others have the right to compete against you. However, if a patent application has been filed and someone begins copying your invention, the U.S. Patent and Trademark Office has a procedure for speeding up the examination of your patent application.

HAVING A CONFIDENTIAL DISCLOSURE AGREEMENT

Sometimes an individual may have an idea for an invention and lack the financial and marketing resources to enter the marketplace. For this reason, one may choose to approach a leading company for the purpose of having it handle the invention. Generally, an inventor's decision to take this route may be because she wants to have the company manufacture, distribute, and promote the invention and, in turn, the inventor will participate in future profits. From a negotiating point of view, this position will be strengthened if the inventor has a patent application on file. In fact, some companies insist on this for their own protection. This way, the inventor cannot later come back and claim that the idea is something different than what was originally presented. This is important to prevent the company from being accused of "stealing" the idea when, in fact, it already had the same or a similar invention in the works. Of course, filing a patent application is the most expensive way to protect the inventor, but like most things that cost the most, it is also the best.

If a patent application is not yet filed, the next best thing is to approach a company and have it sign a confidential disclosure agreement. This agreement should essentially state that the company will not tell anyone about your invention, and that the company will not use it for commercial purposes without your written permission. An example of an agreement of this nature follows. Again, we advise you that this is a proposed form of a general nature. Its language may not be directed to the particular facts, intentions, or expectations with regard to your specific situation. It is highly advisable that you consult an attorney who is knowledgeable in patent and trade secret law about your particular case.

Confidential Disclosure Agreement Letter

I am in the possession of certain confidential ideas and information relating to _____ (insert a short title describing the subject matter of the information) which I refer to as my trade secrets. It is my wish, as well as yours, that I disclose these trade secrets to you so that you may evaluate them to determine whether you wish to discuss a business relationship for our mutual benefit. It is my desire to convey the trade secrets to you if you will treat it as valuable proprietary trade secret information and maintain it in confidence.

Thus, I am willing to disclose the information and I understand you wish to have the opportunity to evaluate it on the following basis.

You agree not to disclose this confidential, proprietary, trade secret information to anyone other than those who reasonably need to know of it for purposes of making your evaluation. Furthermore, you agree that you will at no time disclose these trade secrets to anyone outside of your organization and will not use this information for commercial purposes, except for your evaluation, unless you have my express written consent, or unless the trade secrets have already, or at any time in the future, become part of the public domain or been publicly disclosed by someone having a right to make such a public disclosure or information has been or is in the future disclosed to you by a third party who is lawfully in possession of the trade secrets and has a right to disclose them to you.

_____   _____

Date of Signature

_____   _____

Date of Signature

Many companies will refuse to sign an agreement of this nature and, in fact, they might insist that the inventor first sign an agreement that states no confidential arrangement exists. Usually such an agreement also says that, in the event that you do get patent rights, the company will negotiate with you if there is an interest on its part.

Often, it boils down to how good a salesperson you are in presenting your idea. You must convince the company that you are a reputable, competent individual, and that your invention will benefit the company. If you are convinced that you are dealing with an honest company, and we think that the majority of companies are reputable, you might still wish to pursue your discussion with it on these terms. You must understand that when a company reacts this way, it probably means that it is conservatively trying to protect itself from future lawsuits.

If you do not have a patent, it is still important to preserve some evidence that the company learned about your idea from you. We recommend that you start by saving copies of all correspondence, travel receipts (airfare, gasoline, car rentals, lodging, meals, etc.), and long-distance telephone calls made to the company. When you meet with company representatives, take along a written description of your invention and ask to have it signed. Most companies are willing to sign a paper that states that you told them what the invention is.

Sometimes an individual will take to a company an idea that is not patentable, but is one that has merit and will give the company a head start on its competition. In such a situation, what you are selling still has value, even though the company realizes that its competitors will start selling it too in the not-too-distant future. Still, a confidential disclosure agreement is recommended (a modified version of the one previously appearing). Most companies are willing to pay an inventor for a useful idea even if it is not patentable. Note that people sometimes have an overinflated view of how good their idea is, and it might not be as valuable as they think. Again, good salesmanship is an important factor in negotiating the best deal.

Another situation where a confidential disclosure agreement may be in order is with a supplier. Here, an individual may have a product that may or may not be patentable. While testing the waters, the person may contract with a third party to manufacture one or more parts, if not the entire product. In such a case, the inventor does not want the public to know certain things about the activities involved, and certainly does not want the supplier to pass on confidential information to competitors, or for that matter, go into the business itself as competition. Thus, it is important to have the third party sign some form of a confidential disclosure agreement. Here again, we recommend that you consult an attorney; you also do not want to enter an agreement that is an antitrust violation and therefore not enforceable.

SEEKING AN ATTORNEY

One of the first things to do before you seek a patent is to select the right attorney. While it is possible to get your own patent without legal advice, it is rare and we do not recommend it. Even if you get the patent, it will probably have little legal strength. Keep in mind that the purpose of this book is not to encourage you to "do it yourself," but instead to give you a basic knowledge about patents, copyrights, and trademarks so that when you *do* work with a lawyer, you will have a better understanding of what is going on.

The first step in selecting the right attorney is to find one who specializes in patent law. After all, we live in an age of specialization. You would not go to an ophthalmologist to take out your gall bladder, would you? Nor would you choose an attorney who specializes in bankruptcy law to handle your patent. However, if you have or know an attorney who is not a patent attorney, it could be very helpful to ask for a recommended patent attorney.

Second, the more clearly a lawyer understands the technology about your invention, the better the job that will be done for you. Most patent attorneys also have some kind of technical degree in such fields as chemical engineering, electrical engineering, and so on. We recommend that you find one who has a clear understanding about your invention—this background knowledge will be needed to do the patent search and file the patent application.

Finally, in the event that you are considering applying for a patent without an attorney, it certainly is possible for you to do it, but be prepared to spend a lot of time and effort. Like most things in life, when you do them for the first time, they are always more time consuming and difficult. It is like putting together a bicycle—the first time, even with the instructions, it is difficult. The second time around, however, you can whiz right through the procedure. If you have some time to spare, it may make perfectly good sense to patent your invention without the advice of an attorney. However, if you place a premium on your time, then you are probably better off employing a patent attorney. In the following chapter, you will get a clear picture of how a patent search is made, and this information may help you decide on whether you want to go the route with an attorney or do it by yourself.

The greatest risk of not having a patent attorney is that you may think things are going well and later discover that something necessary was not done. You may discover that often it is too late to correct it, with the result that you thought you had something and later discover you have nothing.

THE PATENT SEARCH

6

On the way to the patent office to do a search, it would be appropriate for an attorney to say to the client, "Aren't you going to wish me bad luck?" Because if a thorough search does not find a previous patent or publication that shows the proposed invention, it is good news.

A patent search is a library-type investigation made prior to the filing of a patent application. Its purpose is to find disclosures of the proposed invention or similar inventions in publications of technology in order to determine if a great enough difference exists between the proposed invention and what has been published that a patent will be granted. Accomplishing this with the absolute degree of accuracy would require a search of the entire body of technology for everything that has ever been published throughout the entire world. Obviously, such a complete search is not possible because there are just too many publications and it would be too expensive to search it all.

So where does one even begin to start a patent search? Perhaps the best place is at your local library, because it is close and easy and if you come across what you are looking for immediately, there is no need to look any further. In this event, you save the expense of a trip to the U.S. Patent and Trademark Office, or the cost of a patent search by a patent attorney, which is the next most cost-efficient method to use when doing a search.

It is important to realize that while the patent office library is a wonderful resource in which to do a patent search, there may be occasions when the search should focus on available published literature. Keep in mind that it takes approximately 18 months from the date that a patent application is filed for a patent to be granted, and there is some further time lag until the patent office gets it out on the shelves in order for it to be available to show up in your search. Published literature is apt to be more current, particularly in certain fields such as computer technology and genetic engineering technology. The fast-changing fields of today's modern world often demand that a search concentrate on published matter.

Generally, the inventor is the best qualified person to know the most recently published technical literature in his or her field of expertise, and this person can be expected to be familiar with what is in various periodicals pertaining to the invention. Usually, it is the inventor who is on the edge of the technology and, for the most part, it is up to him or her to assist the patent attorney in this end of the search.

CONDUCTING THE SEARCH AT THE U.S. PATENT LIBRARY

Like any library search, the first place to begin at the U.S. Patent Office is by using the searching aids. All patents are arranged in technological classes and subclasses. There are five broad classifications: (1) Electrical, (2) Mechanical, (3) Chemical, (4) Plant, and (5) Design. It is important to identify the right class of technology, and then remember that each of these broad categories is subdivided into other classes. These are illustrated at the end of the chapter (pages 73–86). All in all, there are roughly 400 classifications and over 100,000 subclassifications. An example showing the Elevator class is shown in Figure 6.1. All these classes and their subclasses are listed in the front of a searching aid volume entitled *The Manual of Classification*. The list is reproduced at the end of this chapter. There is also an index that indicates to which classes and subclasses you should refer. For instance, there are subclassifications for "Hoops," "Fire Extinguishers," "Earth Boring Devices," "Perfume," and "Mouse Traps" in class No. 43. Under "Corpses" there are subclasses for "Body," "Carriers," "Coolers," "Cremating Furnaces," and "Undertaking." "Brassieres" is a subclassification under "Surgical Supports." A sample page is given

FIGURE 6.1   The Elevator Class of Patentable Items

CLASS 187   ELEVATORS

DECEMBER 1986

1 R	MISCELLANEOUS
1 A	..Tension equalizers
2	BUILDING MATERIAL
3	DUMB-WAITER TYPE
4	.Mail
5	.Locked car
6	EXTERIOR WALL
7	.Lateral movement
8	.Car brake
8.41	ROADWAY VEHICLE TYPE
8.43	.With jack superimposed on elevator
8.45	.With adjustable integral elevating unit
8.47	.With safety device
8.49	..Locking means or additional support
8.5	...Rack and detent (e.g., pawl and ratchet) lock
8.52	..Wheel chocks or stops
8.54	.Convertible, "run-on" to and from "freewheel"
8.56	.Vehicle operated
8.57	.Expansible quadrilateral bar type
8.59	.Four-poster type
8.61	.With attached floor section
8.62	.With pit closure operator
8.64	.With rotation limiting means
8.65	.With floor contacting guides
8.67	.Adaptable to vehicles of different gauge
8.69	.Gearing type elevating unit
8.71	.Lever or linkage type elevating unit
8.72	..Expansible quadrilateral type
8.74	.Axle-engaging type
8.75	..Adjustable
8.77	.Loading guides
9 R	PORTABLE
9 E	..Extensible mast
10	.Inclined
11	.Winding drum
12	INCLINED
13	.Cable-controlled brakes
14	..Rail gripping
15	SHIFTABLE WEIGHT
16	SUPERPOSED CARS
17	MOTOR MECHANISM
18	.Lazy tongs
19	.Rack and pinion
20	.Rope drive
21	..Hand-rope operated
22	..Tensioning feature
23	..Differential sheave
24	.Screw
25	..Traveling rotary element
26	.Traveling sheave
27	.Winding drum
28	CONTROL MECHANISM
29 R	.Electric
29 A	...Hydraulic - electrically controlled
29 B	....Having speed control
29 C	...Electric propelled - hydraulic contrl
29 D	...All electric - manual control
29 E	....With leveling and speed control
29 F	....With leveling only
29 G	....With speed only
29 H	....Having manual start, automatic stop
29 J	.....With stopping by hall or car buttons
29 K	...Combined manual or automatic
29 L	....Noninterference push buttons
29 M	....With speed control
29 N	....Advance push buttons
29 P	....Having leveling means
29 Q	....Having high call reverse
29 S	...Automatic push-button all electric contrl
29 T	....Noninterfering push-button
29 SB	....With speed control
29 V	....With leveling
29 W	....With return to home station

29 SE	....With call storing, high call reverse
29 Y	...Electric control, two or more cars
29 AB	....With dispatching
29 AC	....Quota
29 AD	...Manual start, automatic stop, bank call cancelling
29 AE	....Zones
29 AF	...Overtaken car loses its zone
29 AG	....Transferring or bypassing
29 AH	.....With quota
29 AJ	...Manual or automatic, plural cars, call cancelling
29 AK	....With zones
29 AL	.....With bypassing
29 AM	......With high call reversing
29 AN	.......With quota
29 AP	...Automatic push-button, plural cars, call cancelling
29 AQ	....Having zones
29 AS	.....Overtaken car loses its zone
29 AT	.....Means to transfer calls to second car
29 AV	......Return cars to terminal
30	.Door actuated
31	..Electric
32	.Landing stops
33	.Lock
34	.Limit
35	..Electric
36	.Carrier actuated
37	...Deflected rope
38	.Speed controlled
39	..Electric
40	.Well obstruction
41	..Electric
42	.Operator actuated
43	..Electric
44	..Rope controllers
45	...Running rope
46	.Controller locks
47	.Door actuated
48	...Electric
49	...Locked door
50	....Electric
51	DOOR MECHANISM
52 R	.Motor actuated
52 LC	...Landing and car doors operatively coupled
53	..Common motor shaft
54	..Separate motors
55	.Flexible screens
56	.Sliding doors
57	.Locked door
58	..Vertical movement
59	...Locked door
60	...Sliding coupler
61	.Locks
62	HATCH MECHANISM
63	.Lever opener
64	.Sliding coupler
65	.Direct contact
66	.Vertically slidable hatch
67	WELL-END CUSHIONS
68	FLUID GOVERNORS
69	.Car-supported pump
70	.Counterweight
71	EMERGENCY CABLES
72	CABLE RELEASERS
73	CAR BRAKES AND CATCHES
74	.Door controlled
75	.Landing chairs
76	..Car supported
77	.Driven catch devices
78	..Rotating gear
79	.Well supported
80	.Car supported
81	..Cable controlled
82	...Positive

60

FIGURE 6.1 *(continued)*

CLASS 187   ELEVATORS

```
      CAR BRAKES AND CATCHES
      .Car supported
      ..Cable controlled
      ...Positive
83    ....Rail side
84    ....Sliding
85    ...Rail face
86    ...Rail side
87    ....Eccentric
88    ....Wedge
89    ..Speed controlled
90    ...Rail side
91    ....Vertically pivoted
92    ..Operator controlled
93    ...Rail side
94    COUNTERBALANCES
95    GUIDES
96    .Mine crossheads
97    RAILWAY-CAR LOCKS
98    WELL-OBSTRUCTION DEVICES

      DIGEST

DIG 1 Safety edge
```

in Figure 6.2. There are definitions of the classes and subclasses in multiple volumes to help you identify which is most applicable to your invention. All these searching aids are available for public use in the U.S. Patent and Trademark Office.

If you need assistance, there are government employees specially hired to assist you with your inquiries. Not only will they tell you where to look, but they will show you how to do it. This is their job—you are not interrupting them by asking for their help. They are accessible and friendly. These people are normally available at the drop of a hat. It is only on particularly busy days that you might have a brief 5- or 10-minute wait until somebody can assist you.

The length of time to do a search depends on several factors. Obviously, it will take longer for the novice inventor versus somebody with searching experience. Of course, the nature of your invention will also determine the degree of difficulty you will have during your search, and so will the way that the patent office has the related technology categorized. An experienced searcher will typically conduct a satisfactory search in two to four hours. It may take the novice as many as one to four days to cover the same ground.

A major concern with doing your first patent search is knowing whether you found the closest prior technology that exists. The more you search and do not find it, the more

FIGURE 6.2 Sample from Index of the Manual of Classification
(pictured on the opposite page)

you are apt to struggle, wondering if you have looked in the right place. Of course, if you quickly find an existing patent that shows your invention, there is no need to continue the search. If you do not, and you are uncertain about how thorough your search has been, you might want to consult one of the patent examiners who is more knowledgeable with your area of technology than the assistant whom you might have asked for help earlier. A patent examiner can put you on the right track if you started off in the wrong class or subclass.

What it often confusing to the novice is when the search is begun in a category that is close to what is needed, *but not close enough*. Lack of experience can result in spending hours and hours (or perhaps days) searching in the wrong classes or subclasses. Sometimes, the novice may be off the track and consequently conclude that a patent does not exist when, in fact, it does. Though even an experienced patent searcher may commit this error, the probability of the novice doing it wrong is considerably greater.

The odds are high that a patent search will reveal that an invention is not patentable, so an experienced searcher who uncovers prior art will generally not need the assistance of an examiner. One is more apt to ask for guidance when nothing shows up but there is still some uncertainty about whether something might have been missed (especially if one is not familiar with the technology of the invention). Then, like the novice, the professional is concerned about having looked in the right places.

SHOULD I DO THE PATENT SEARCH MYSELF?

First, many people are capable of doing a patent search at the U.S. Patent Library if they take enough time. The question you must ask yourself is: "Is it feasible to do it or should I pay somebody else with experience to do it?" Again, it depends on your individual circumstances and the risks you want to take. If you have a lot of time, it may be economical to do it yourself. However, if you are a busy person and have more profitable ways to occupy your time, or if you do not want to risk making a mistake that a good patent attorney probably would not make, you may want to pay a professional to do the search. There are also people who want to do a patent search themselves because it is a challenge as well as an enjoyable experience.

From a strictly dollars-and-cents standpoint, you should take into consideration what out-of-pocket expenses you will incur if you do it yourself. These expenses include round-trip transportation to Washington, D.C., lodging, meals, and so forth. Naturally, if you live in the vicinity of the District of Columbia, your expenses will be less.

You can also consider hiring a patent searcher to do it for you. There are many full-time, nonlawyer searchers listed in the Washington, D.C., telephone book who specialize in doing patent searches. In fact, most patent attorneys hire these people in lieu of traveling to the patent office themselves, although others prefer to personally conduct the search because it gives them "a good hands-on feel" for the invention (this will be helpful in filing the actual patent application). Please note that "jobbing out this work" is strictly a personal preference and should not influence your selection of the right patent attorney. If you employ a nonlawyer patent searcher to do your search, however, you will be unable to obtain a legal opinion on whether you are likely to be able to get a patent. As a point of interest, the vast majority of people in the search room of the patent office are likely to be full-time searchers and attorneys—not inventors.

The actual cost of having a patent attorney do your search will vary, depending on the technology, ranging from approximately $500 to $1,500. Of course, if more than the usual search effort is needed, more cost could be required. Always discuss fees before instructing your lawyer to proceed. It is better for both of you.

Finally, and once again, the need for having an experienced person do your patent search is so you can feel assured knowing that if nothing like your invention is found, it is probably because no other information actually exists. As a novice, it is doubtful that you will have peace of mind because you will not know what stones may have been left unturned.

SHOULD A SEARCH BE DONE?

A question often asked is: "Since the patent office will do its own search after the patent application is filed, why is a patent search necessary at all?"

First, the cost of filing a patent application is considerably higher than the cost of a patent search. So if your invention is not likely to be patentable, it is simply good business to invest in the cost of the search to determine if a patent application is likely to result in a patent. Ordinarily you would not want to spend the money on a patent application if you did not have more than a ghost of a chance that the patent will be granted. Keep in mind that the cost of a patent application typically falls in the $3,000 to $6,000 range, which includes attorney fees (considerably more than double the cost of most searches). The cost can be greater for highly technical inventions. With this in mind, you will get your money's worth on the search in the event it convinces you not to file an application for a patent.

Another reason for doing a search is to accumulate information that will be beneficial to use if you do file your patent application. By knowing what inventions have already been patented or published, you have a better understanding about how your application should be written. This information can be used by your attorney to help focus on the exact new improvements your invention offers over the previously patented invention(s). Then, your application can emphasize only the new part(s) and you do not have to explain what has already been patented. Additionally, you might refer in your patent application to what has previously been done, point out its shortcomings, and state where your invention is different. Then, too, a separate document can be filed with the patent office that cites a few of the most relevant patents and tells the examiner how your invention differs.

Yet a patent search is not always done, and for good reason. First, a company may bring out a new product that required a large investment. With a lot of research and development costs, the expense of the patent application may represent a relatively minor part of the total cost. So the company takes the position, "Let's try to get a patent, and if we don't get exactly what we want, at least we may get something. In view of what we've put into this project, let's see what comes of it and try to get the best protection we can." In the meantime, the company can put patent pending on its product, which may tend to discourage other companies from investing large sums of money in copying, manufacturing, and marketing a similar product for fear of infringement and the possibility of getting caught with an inventory they will be prohibited from selling.

THE INFRINGEMENT SEARCH

It is sometimes worthwhile for a company to try to find out in advance if a product on the drawing board may infringe on someone else's patent. The reason to do an infringement search of this nature is to avoid a patent infringement suit. Rather than taking the risk of making a significant investment in bringing a new product to the marketplace and then being enjoined by a court from selling it, an infringement search is in order. In general, an infringement search is considerably more expensive than a standard patentability search and is justified only when a particular product has a large investment such as in R&D, building an inventory, or marketing. Such a search is more expensive because the claims of other patents must be studied and often many more technical areas must be searched. For example, this type of patent search might involve a machine with many different parts, and you must determine whether a patent exists on each of them.

Patent infringement suits are brought in the federal courts. All appeals for patent infringement suits now go to the Court of Appeals for the Federal Circuit (CAFC), which is upholding more than half of the patents that come before it and 80 percent of the time has affirmed trial court holdings of patent validity. In recent years, U.S. courts have been awarding patent owners much higher damages than ever before. Awards of "lost profits" of 60 percent of the infringing sales have been approved by the CAFC. Additionally, damages based on a "reasonable royalty" of 15 to 25 percent of sales have been awarded. The patent statute says that damages for patent infringement shall not be less than a reasonable royalty.

In several recent cases, damage awards were doubled and tripled because the defendant manufactured infringing goods without first obtaining an opinion of qualified counsel that there was no infringement or that the patent was invalid. Some recent awards include Hughes Tool receiving $120 million for infringement of its drill bit patent; Pfizer Inc.'s Shiley Inc. unit receiving $45 million on sales of $143 million for infringement on its blood oxygenator patent; and Schering Corporation receiving $3.8 million on a contact lens that generated sales less than $1.4 million. In another case, the CAFC stated that a reasonable royalty could be more than the selling price of the infringing machine.

It is important to note that the injunction normally granted to the successful patent owner is also a feared remedy that the infringing defendant could suffer. In its infringement suit with Polaroid, an injunction forced Kodak to abruptly close down its production line.

DOING A FOREIGN SEARCH

The U.S. Patent Office has only limited information about patents that exist outside the United States. In fact, sometimes there is little or no data on them. What does exist at the patent office is incomplete, and if you depend on what is there, you may discover down the road that foreign patents or publications that make your invention not patentable exist or, if you make or sell in a foreign country, that you have infringed on a patent already granted in another country. Of course, if the foreign inventor did not get it patented here, then you have the right to market it in this country, but without the monopoly of a patent—even if one is granted to you, it could turn out to be invalid—others could compete directly against you in the United States. Depending on the timing of a publication of his product, the foreign inventor may or may not have destroyed the rights to get a U.S. patent. As you can see, the same risk exists with a foreign patent search that you take when your search does not reveal technical literature showing an invention in another country. Maybe the closest patent was not found. Although such incidences are unusual, they do occur, which means that there is no guarantee that any search, even a highly reliable search, is ever absolutely complete.

It is difficult and expensive to conduct a worldwide patent search, and unreasonable for the vast majority of inventors. As a point of interest, the creation of the European Patent Office has caused a recent drop in the filing of patent applications in European countries, so the Swedish patent office is doing patent searches in European literature for inventors and companies. For more information, we advise you to contact the patent office in Sweden or your patent attorney.

FIGURE 6.3   Patent Office Manual of Classification

CLASSES WITHIN THE U.S. CLASSIFICATION SYSTEM

Arranged by Related Subjects

Main Groups

I.   CHEMICAL AND RELATED ARTS

II.   COMMUNICATIONS, DESIGNS, RADIANT ENERGY,
        WEAPONS, ELECTRICAL, AND RELATED ARTS

III.   BODY TREATMENT AND CARE, HEATING AND
        COOLING, MATERIAL HANDLING AND TREATMENT,
        MECHANICAL MANUFACTURING, MECHANICAL
        POWER, STATIC, AND RELATED ARTS

Note: In the following lists, classes preceded by an asterisk
(e.g., *364) appear more than once. Subject titles used may differ from official class titles.

FIGURE 6.3 (*continued*)

December 1992   I. CHEMICAL AND RELATED ARTS   I-6

Class	Subject
505	SUPERCONDUCTOR TECHNOLOGY – APPARATUS, MATERIAL, PROCESS (Over 30° K)
503	RECORD RECEIVER HAVING PLURAL LEAVES OR A COLORLESS COLOR FORMER, METHOD OF USE OR DEVELOPER THEREFOR
428	STOCK MATERIAL OR MISCELLANEOUS ARTICLES
437	SEMICONDUCTOR DEVICE MANUFACTURING: PROCESS
156	ADHESIVE BONDING AND MISCELLANEOUS CHEMICAL MANUFACTURE
8/94.1-142	BLEACHING AND DYEING: FLUID TREATMENT AND CHEMICAL MODIFICATION OF TEXTILES AND FIBERS
147-159	(See also Group III, Class 8, Manipulative fluid treatment; Class 68, Textiles, Fluid Treating Apparatus)
427	COATING PROCESSES (See also Group III, Classes 101 and 118 for printing and coating apparatus)
419	POWDER METALLURGY – PROCESSES
420	ALLOYS OR METALLIC COMPOSITIONS
75	SPECIALIZED METALLURGICAL PROCESSES, COMPOSITIONS FOR USE THEREIN, CONSOLIDATED METAL POWDER COMPOSITIONS, ETC.
148	METAL TREATMENT
65	GLASS MANUFACTURING
264	PLASTIC AND NONMETALLIC ARTICLE SHAPING OR TREATING: PROCESSES (See also Group II, Class 264 for treating of explosive or radioactive material)

Class	Subject
424 and 514	DRUG, BIO–AFFECTING AND BODY TREATING COMPOSITIONS
426	FOOD OR EDIBLE MATERIAL: PROCESSES, COMPOSITIONS AND PRODUCTS (See also Group III, Class 99 for treating apparatus)
430	RADIATION IMAGERY CHEMISTRY – PROCESS, COMPOSITION OR PRODUCT
162	PAPER MAKING AND FIBER LIBERATION
512	PERFUME COMPOSITIONS
252	COMPOSITIONS (Miscellaneous) (In some instances, compositions specialized to a particular art are classified with that art; e.g., Class 51, etc.)
507	COMPOSITIONS OR METHODS OF PREPARATION OR MERE METHODS OF USING SAID COMPOSITIONS OR A COMPOUND, FOR EARTH BORING, ETC.
502	CATALYST, SOLID SORBENT, OR SUPPORT THEREFOR, PRODUCT OR PROCESS OF MAKING
71	CHEMISTRY, FERTILIZERS
48	GAS, HEATING AND ILLUMINATING
44	FUEL AND RELATED COMPOSITIONS
*210/ 500.1+	LIQUID PURIFICATION OR SEPARATION (Filter Material)
*51/293+	ABRADING (Material) (See also Group III, Class 51 for abrading machines and processes)
520 – 528	CHEMISTRY, SYNTHETIC RESINS OR NATURAL RUBBERS
106	COMPOSITIONS, COATING OR PLASTIC
501	COMPOSITIONS: CERAMIC
436	CHEMISTRY: ANALYTICAL AND IMMUNOLOGICAL TESTING
435	CHEMISTRY: MOLECULAR BIOLOGY AND MICROBIOLOGY

FIGURE 6.3 *(continued)*

Class	Subject
429	CHEMISTRY, ELECTRICAL CURRENT PRODUCING APPARATUS, PRODUCT, AND PROCESS
136	BATTERIES, THERMOELECTRIC AND PHOTOELECTRIC
204	CHEMISTRY, ELECTRICAL AND WAVE ENERGY
205	ELECTROLYSIS: PROCESSES, COMPOSITIONS USED THEREIN AND METHODS OF PREPARING THE COMPOSITIONS
423	CHEMISTRY, INORGANIC
518	CHEMISTRY, FISCHER-TROPSCH PROCESSES; OR PURIFICATION OR RECOVERY OF PRODUCTS THEREOF
*260 and 530–585	CHEMISTRY, CARBON COMPOUNDS
208	MINERAL OILS: PROCESSES AND PRODUCTS
196	MINERAL OILS: APPARATUS
127	SUGAR, STARCH, AND CARBOHY-DRATES (See notes to the definitions of Class 422 for distribution of this art.)
134/1–42	CLEANING AND LIQUID CONTACT WITH SOLIDS (See also Group III, Class 134 for apparatus)
422	PROCESS DISINFECTING, DEODORIZING, PRESERVING OR STERILIZING, AND CHEMICAL APPARATUS
55	GAS SEPARATION
261	GAS AND LIQUID CONTACT APPARATUS
201	DISTILLATION: PROCESSES, THERMOLYTIC
202	DISTILLATION: APPARATUS
203	DISTILLATION: PROCESSES, SEPARATORY

Class	Subject
159	CONCENTRATING EVAPORATORS
210	LIQUID PURIFICATION OR SEPARATION
588	HAZARDOUS OR TOXIC WASTE DESTRUCTION OR CONTAINMENT
935	GENETIC ENGINEERING: RECOMBINANT DNA TECHNOLOGY, HYBRID OR FUSED CELL TECHNOLOGY AND RELATED MANIPULATIONS OF NUCLEIC ACIDS (Cross–Reference Art Collection)
930	PEPTIDE OR PROTEIN SEQUENCE (Cross–Reference Art Collection)

FIGURE 6.3 *(continued)*

Class	Subject
505	SUPERCONDUCTOR TECHNOLOGY – APPARATUS, MATERIAL, PROCESS (See subclass 1 involving material superconducting above 30° Kelvin and Subclasses 800–933 for art collections on superconductor technology.)
376	INDUCED NUCLEAR REACTIONS, SYSTEMS AND ELEMENTS
380	CRYPTOGRAPHY
340	COMMUNICATIONS, ELECTRICAL
358	PICTORIAL COMMUNICATION; TELEVISION
382	IMAGE ANALYSIS
342	COMMUNICATIONS, DIRECTIVE RADIO WAVE SYSTEMS AND DEVICES (E.G., RADAR, RADIO NAVIGATION)
343	COMMUNICATIONS, RADIO WAVE ANTENNAS
370	MULTIPLEX COMMUNICATIONS
381	ELECTRICAL AUDIO SIGNAL PROCESSING SYSTEMS, AND DEVICES
379	TELEPHONIC COMMUNICATIONS
178	TELEGRAPHY
375	PULSE OR DIGITAL COMMUNICATIONS
455	TELECOMMUNICATIONS
341	CODED DATA GENERATION OR CONVERSION
367	COMMUNICATIONS, ELECTRICAL: ACOUSTIC WAVE SYSTEMS AND DEVICES
334	TUNERS
332	MODULATORS
329	DEMODULATORS
116	SIGNALS AND INDICATORS
	CALCULATORS, COMPUTERS OR DATA PROCESSING SYSTEMS
371	ERROR DETECTION/CORRECTION AND FAULT DETECTION/RECOVERY

Class	Subject
*364/737	ARITHMETICAL ERRORS
*235/375	REGISTERS (Systems Controlled by Data Bearing Records)
400	(Ordnance or Weapon System Computers) (Record Controlled Calculators)
364	ELECTRICAL COMPUTERS AND DATA PROCESSING SYSTEMS
395	INFORMATION PROCESSING SYSTEM ORGANIZATION
377	ELECTRICAL PULSE COUNTERS, PULSE DIVIDERS OR SHIFT REGISTERS: CIRCUITS AND SYSTEMS
902	ELECTRONIC FUNDS TRANSFER
*235/61	REGISTERS (Mechanical Calculators)
	INFORMATION STORAGE
369	DYNAMIC INFORMATION STORAGE OR RETRIEVAL
360	DYNAMIC MAGNETIC INFORMATION STORAGE OR RETRIEVAL
365	STATIC INFORMATION STORAGE AND RETRIEVAL
*235/435	REGISTERS (Coded Sensors)
346	RECORDERS
	MEASURING, TESTING, PRECISION INSTRUMENTS (See also Group I, Class 436, Chemistry: Analytical and Immunologoical Testing)
73	MEASURING AND TESTING
324	ELECTRICITY, MEASURING AND TESTING
*250/250	WAVEMETERS
356	OPTICS, MEASURING AND TESTING
368	HOROLOGY: TIME MEASURING SYSTEMS OR DEVICES
374	THERMAL MEASURING AND TESTING
177	WEIGHING SCALES
33	GEOMETRICAL INSTRUMENTS
*250	RADIANT ENERGY (See also Group I, Class 204, Chemistry, Electrical and Wave Energy)

71

Class	Subject	Class	Subject
	RADIANT ENERGY – (con.)	388	ELECTRICITY, MOTOR CONTROL SYSTEMS
378	X-RAY OR GAMMA RAY SYSTEMS OR DEVICES	187/29	ELEVATORS (electric control) (See also Group III, Class 187, Elevators Structure)
*250/ 316.1–319, 330–334, 338–353	INFRARED RAY	320	ELECTRICITY, BATTERY AND CONDENSER CHARGING AND DISCHARGING
372	COHERENT LIGHT GENERATORS	331	OSCILLATORS
385	OPTICAL WAVEGUIDES	330	AMPLIFIERS
359	OPTICS, SYSTEMS (INCLUDING COMMUNICATION) AND ELEMENTS	328	MISCELLANEOUS ELECTRON SPACE DISCHARGE DEVICE SYSTEMS
351	OPTICS, EYE EXAMINING, VISION TESTING AND CORRECTING	*307/400– 430	MISCELLANEOUS NONLINEAR REACTOR SYSTEMS
352	OPTICS, MOTION PICTURES	*307/200+	MISCELLANEOUS NONLINEAR SOLID STATE DEVICE CIRCUITS
354	PHOTOGRAPHY (Note: Class 430, Photographic Chemistry, Processes and Material, in Group I)	333	WAVE TRANSMISSION LINES AND NETWORKS
355	PHOTOCOPYING	363	ELECTRIC POWER CONVERSION SYSTEMS
353	OPTICS, IMAGE PROJECTORS	323	ELECTRICITY, POWER SUPPLY, OR REGULATION SYSTEMS
362	ILLUMINATION	315	ELECTRIC LAMP AND DISCHARGE DEVICES, SYSTEMS
84	MUSIC (See also Class 116, Horns, Whistles, Sirens, Bells, Compressional Wave Generators, Signals and Indicators, subs. 137 to 172; Class 340, Communications, Electrical, subs. 384+)	314	ELECTRIC LAMP AND DISCHARGE DEVICES, CONSUMABLE ELECTRODES
		322	ELECTRICITY, SINGLE GENERATOR SYSTEMS
181	ACOUSTICS		ELECTRICITY, HEATING
361	ELECTRICITY, ELECTRICAL SYSTEMS AND DEVICES (Nonelectrical device with electrical operation or control is classified with nonelectrical device)	*307	MISCELLANEOUS SYSTEMS
		313	ELECTRIC LAMP AND DISCHARGE DEVICES
219	ELECTRIC HEATING (Nonelectric Heating, in Group III)	357	ACTIVE SOLID STATE DEVICES, E.G., TRANSISTORS, SOLID STATE DIODES
392	ELECTRIC RESISTANCE HEATING DEVICES	310	ELECTRICAL GENERATOR OR MOTOR STRUCTURE
373	INDUSTRIAL ELECTRIC HEATING FURNACES	335	ELECTRICITY, MAGNETICALLY OPER-ATED SWITCHES, MAGNETS AND ELEC-TROMAGNETS (See also Class 200, Electricity, Circuit Makers and Breakers, below, for mechanically actuated switches in general, and Class 337, Electricity, Electrothermally or Thermally Actuated Switches, below, for thermally actuated switch structures)
290	PRIME-MOVER DYNAMO PLANTS (See also Group III, Power Plants and Nonelec-tric Motors)		
318	ELECTRICITY, MOTIVE POWER SYSTEMS		

FIGURE 6.3 *(continued)*

Class	Subject
	ELECTRICITY, HEATING – (con.)
337	**ELECTRICITY, ELECTROTHERMALLY OR THERMALLY ACTUATED SWITCHES** (See also Class 200, Electricity, Circuit Makers and Breakers, below, for mechanically actuated switches in general, and Class 335, Electricity, Magnetically Actuated Switches, Magnets and Electromagnets, above, for magnetically actuated switch structures)
336	**INDUCTOR DEVICES**
361/433 +	**ELECTROLYTIC DEVICES** (See also Group I, Classes 136, Batteries and 204, Chemistry, Electrical and Wave Energy)
361/271 +	**CAPACITOR DEVICES**
338	**ELECTRICAL RESISTORS**
200	**ELECTRICITY, CIRCUIT MAKERS AND BREAKERS** (See also Class 335, Electricity, Magnetically Operated Switches, Magnets and Electromagnets, above, for magnetically actuated switches, and Class 337, Electricity, Electrothermally or Thermally Actuated Switches, above, for thermally actuated switches)
174	**ELECTRICITY, CONDUCTORS AND INSULATORS**
	AMMUNITION, WEAPONS
89	**ORDNANCE** (See also Group III, Class 124, Mechanical Guns and Projectors)
244/14	**AIRCRAFT, TORPEDOES** (See also Group III, Class 244, Aircraft Structure)
114/20–25	**SHIPS** (See also Group III, Class 114, Ship Structure)
42	**FIREARMS**
102	**AMMUNITION AND EXPLOSIVES**
149	**EXPLOSIVE AND THERMIC COMPOSITIONS OR CHARGES**
86	**AMMUNITION AND EXPLOSIVE CHARGE MAKING**
D–1 to D–99	**DESIGNS**

FIGURE 6.3 (continued)

Class	Subject
505	SUPERCONDUCTOR TECHNOLOGY – APPARATUS, MATERIAL, PROCESS (See subclass 1 involving material superconducting above 30° Kelvin and Subclasses 800–933 for art collections on superconductor technology)
	BODY TREATMENT CARE, ADORNMENT (See also Group I, Class 424, Drug, Bio–Affecting and Body Treating Compositions)
433	Dentistry
623	Prosthesis (i.e., Artificial Body Members), Parts Thereof or Aids and Accessories Therefor
128	Surgery
600	Surgery
602	Surgery: Splint, Brace, or Bandage
604	Surgery
606	Surgery
132	Toilet
63	Jewelry
27	Undertaking
	APPAREL AND RELATED ARTS
2	Apparel
223	Apparel Apparatus
450	Foundation Garments
36	Boots, Shoes and Leggings
12	Boot and Shoe Making
69	Leather Manufactures
112	Sewing
	PLANT AND ANIMAL HUSBANDRY (Note: See Class 100, Presses, for balers; Class 289, Knots and Knot Tying; Class 460, Crop Threshing or Separating)
PLT	Plants
449	Bee Culture
452	Butchering

Class	Subject
	PLANT AND ANIMAL HUSBANDRY – (con.)
43	Fishing, Trapping and Vermin Destroying
47	Plant Husbandry
119	Animal Husbandry
54	Harness
168	Farriery
231	Whips and Whip Apparatus
	TEACHING
434	Education and Demonstration (See also Group II for navigation and radar)
40	Card, Picture and Sign Exhibiting
472	AMUSEMENT DEVICES
273	Amusement Devices, Games
446	Amusement Devices, Toys
124	Mechanical Guns and Projectors
482	Exercise Devices
99/275–450	FOOD PREPARING AND TREATING APPARATUS (See also Group I, Food Compositions and Processes)
	HEATING, COOLING (See also Group II, Electric Heating)
62	Refrigeration (See also Group I, Liquified Gas)
237	Heating Systems
236	Automatic Temperature and Humidity Regulation
432	Heating
122	Liquid Heaters and Vaporizers
126	Stoves and Furnaces
431	Combustion
110	Furnaces (Solid or Combined Fuels)
165	Heat Exchange

FIGURE 6.3 *(continued)*

Class	Subject

BUILDINGS

135	Tents, Canopies, Umbrellas and Canes
109	Safes, Bank Protection and Related Devices
52	Static Structures, e.g., Buildings
14	Bridges
404	Road Structure, Process and Apparatus
182	Fire Escapes, Ladders, Scaffolds

220 RECEPTACLES

312	Supports, Cabinet Structures
190	Trunks and Hand Carried Luggage
206	Special Receptacle or Package
215	Bottles and Jars
229	Envelopes, Wrappers and Paperboard Boxes
150	Purses, Wallets, and Protective Covers
383	Flexible Bags
217	Wooden Receptacles

248 SUPPORTS

5	Beds
297	Chairs and Seats
211	Supports, Racks
108	Horizontally Supported Planar Surfaces

CLOSURES, PARTITIONS, PANELS
(Building and receptacle classes for other closures, partitions, and panels)

*267	Spring Devices (Support Type)
49	Movable or Removable Closures
160	Closures, Partitions and Panels, Flexible and Portable
256	Fences

TEXTILES

8/147–159	Bleaching and Dyeing; Fluid Treatment and Chemical Modification of Textiles and Fibers (See also Group I for processes and compositions)
245	Wire Fabrics and Structure
289	Knots and Knot Tying
28	Textiles, Manufacturing
26	Textiles, Cloth Finishing
66	Textiles, Knitting
87	Textiles, Braiding, Netting and Lace Making
139	Textiles, Weaving
57	Textiles, Spinning, Twisting and Twining
19	Textiles, Fiber Preparation

EARTH WORKING AND AGRICULTURAL MACHINERY

405	Hydraulic and Earth Engineering
299	Mining or In Situ Disintegration of Hard Material
166	Wells
175	Boring or Penetrating the Earth
111	Planting
171	Unearthing Plants or Buried Objects
37	Excavating
56	Harvesters
172	Earth Working

194 CHECK-ACTUATED CONTROL MECHANISMS

DISPENSING
(For the distribution of this art, see notes to definitions of Class 222, Dispensing, and Class 220, Receptacles)

453	Coin Handling
141	Fluent Material Handling, with Receiver or Receiver Coacting Means

FIGURE 6.3 *(continued)*

Class	Subject	Class	Subject
	DISPENSING– (con.)		VEHICLES – (con.)
169	Fire Extinguishers	440	Marine Propulsion
291	Track Sanders	191	Electricity, Transmission to Vehicles
239	Fluid Sprinkling, Spraying and Diffusing	104	Railways
222	Dispensing	246	Railway Switches and Signals
221	Article Dispensing	105	Railway Rolling Stock
232	Deposit and Collection Receptacles	238	Railways, Surface Track
414	MATERIAL OR ARTICLE HANDLING	280	Land Vehicles (e.g., chassis and running gear)
258	Railway Mail Delivery	298	Land Vehicles, Dumping
186	Merchandising	180	Motor Vehicles
406	Conveyors, Fluid Current	296	Land Vehicles, Bodies and Tops Parts
212	Traversing Hoists		(Mechanisms and Machine Elements, below)
198	Conveyers, Power–Driven	301	Land Vehicles, Wheels and Axles
*187	Elevators (See also Group II, Electric control)	295	Railway Wheels and Axles
		152	Resilient Tires and Wheels
193	Conveyers, Chutes, Skids, Guides and Ways	305	Wheel Substitutes for Land Vehicles
224	Package and Article Carriers	213	Railway Draft Appliances
294	Handling, Hand and Hoist–Line Implements (Class 81, Tools)	278	Land Vehicles, Animal Draft Appliances
		293	Vehicle Fenders
*901	Robots *Accepts No Applications (Cross–Reference Art Collection)	*267/2–68, 140.1–141.7	Spring Devices
137	FLUID HANDLING	410	FREIGHT ACCOMMODATION ON FREIGHT CARRIER
454	Ventilation		MOTORS, ENGINES, PUMPS (See also Group II, Electricity, for electric motors)
4	Baths, Closets, Sinks and Spittoons		
138	Pipes and Tubular Conduits	60	Power Plants (See also Group I for chemical reaction motors)
251	Valves and Valve Actuation		
	VEHICLES	123	Internal–Combustion Engines
244	Aeronautics (See Group II for aerial torpedoes)	417	Pumps
		91	Motors, Expansible Chamber Type
114	Ships (See Group II for torpedoes)	415	Rotary Kinetic Fluid Motors or Pumps
441	Buoys, Rafts, and Aquatic Devices	416	Fluid Reaction Surfaces (i.e., Impellers)

FIGURE 6.3 *(continued)*

Class	Subject

MOTORS, ENGINES, PUMPS – (con.)

185	Motors, Spring, Weight and Animal Powered
418	Rotary Expansible Chamber Devices
92	Expansible Chamber Devices

COATING, PRINTING, AND PRINTED MATERIAL; STATIONARY, BOOKS

118	Coating Apparatus (See also Group I, Class 427, Coating Processes)
184	Lubrication
101	Printing
400	Typewriting Machines
199	Type Casting
276	Type Setting
401	Coating Implements with Material Supply
281	Books, Strips and Leaves
462	Books, Strips and Leaves for Manifolding
283	Printed Matter

MANUFACTURING, ASSEMBLING, INCLUDING SOME CORRELATIVE MISCELLANEOUS PRODUCTS

164	Metal Founding
266	Metallurgical Apparatus
*29/1– 25.42, 81–91.8, 560, 560.1	Metal Working (General Manufacturing)
412	Bookbinding: Process and Apparatus
53	Package Making
59	Chain, Staple and Horseshoe Making
76	Metal Tools and Implements, Making
79	Button Making

MANUFACTURING, ASSEMBLING, INCLUDING SOME CORRELATIVE MISCELLANEOUS PRODUCTS – (con.)

493	Manufacturing Container or Tube from Paper; or Other Manufacturing from a Sheet or Web
131	Tobacco
147	Coopering
157	Wheelwright Machines
163	Needle and Pin Making
227	Elongated–Member–Driving Apparatus
270	Sheet–Material Associating
300	Brush, Broom and Mop Making
445	Electric Lamp or Space Discharge Component or Device Manufacturing
*29/ 148.3–179, 400–426.6, 428–559, 569–623.5, 631, 825–885	Metal Working (Methods)
*29/700–824	Metal Working (Assembling Apparatus)
*29/650	Plural Diverse Manufacturing Apparatus

CUTTING, COMMINUTING, AND MACHINING

483	Tool Changing
234	Selective Cutting (e.g., Punching)
460	Crop Threshing or Separating
241	Solid Material Comminution or Disintegration
470	Threaded, Headed Fastener, or Washer Making: Process and Apparatus
*29/26–80 561–568	Metal Working (Miscellaneous Machining)
407	Cutters, For Shaping
30	Cutlery
51	Abrading
408	Cutting by Use of Rotating Axially Moving Tool

77

FIGURE 6.3 (continued)

December 1992   III.   BODY TREATMENT AND CARE, HEATING AND COOLING,   I-15
                                    MATERIAL HANDLING AND TREATMENT, MECHANICAL
                                    MANUFACTURING MECHANICAL POWER, STATIC, AND
                                    RELATED ARTS

Class	Subject	Class	Subject
	CUTTING, COMMINUTING, AND MACHINING – (con.)		**HANDLING OR STORING SHEETS, WEBS, STRANDS, AND CABLE**
82	Turning	402	Binder Device Releasably Engaging Aperture or Notch of Sheet
83	Cutting		
409	Gear Cutting, Milling, or Planing	226	Advancing Material of Indeterminate–Length
125	Stone Working		
144	Woodworking	242	Winding and Reeling
142	Wood Turning	*254/ 199–417	Implements or Apparatus for Applying Pushing or Pulling Force (Cable Hauling or Strand Placing)
225	Severing by Tearing or Breaking		
	PLASTIC DEFORMATION, PRESSING, OR TREATING (See also Group I, Plastics)	271	Sheet Feeding or Delivering
72	Metal Deforming	74	**MACHINE ELEMENTS AND MECHANISMS**
425	Plastic Article or Earthenware Shaping or Treating: Apparatus (See also Group I, Class 264, Plastic and Nonmetallic Article Shaping or Treating: Processes)	475	Planetary Gear Transmission Systems and Components
		474	Endless Belt Power Transmission Systems and Components
100	Presses		
413	Sheet Metal Container Making	*29/110– 132	Metal Working (Rolls)
140	Wireworking		
228	Metal Fusion Bonding	464	Rotary Shafts, Gudgeons, Housings and Flexible Couplings for Rotary Shafts
249	Static Molds		
	MISCELLANEOUS TREATING (See Group I for chemical treatment and physical separation)	384	Bearings
		173	Tool Driving or Impacting
494	Imperforate Bowl, Centrifugal Separators	188	Brakes
209	Classifying, Separating and Assorting Solids	192	Clutches and Power–Stop Control
366	Agitating	*254/ 1–134.7 418,427	Implements or Apparatus for Applying Pushing or Pulling Force (Force Multipliers)
*134	Cleaning and Liquid Contact with Solids (See also Group I for cleaning processes)	269	Work Holders
34	Drying and Gas or Vapor Contact With Solids	303	Fluid–Pressure Brake and Analogous Systems
68	Textiles, Fluid Treating Apparatus	*16/1–220	**MISCELLANEOUS HARDWARE**
38	Textiles, Ironing or Smoothing	70	Locks
15	Brushing, Scrubbing and General Cleaning	*267	Spring Devices

78

FIGURE 6.3 *(continued)*

Class	Subject
	TOOLS
7	Compound Tools
*29/213–283	Metal Working (Assembling Devices)
81	Tools
403	JOINTS AND CONNECTIONS
439	Electrical Connectors
285	Pipe Joints or Couplings
*16/221–392	Miscellaneous Hardware (Hinges)
279	Chucks and Sockets
277	Joint Packing
	FASTENINGS
292	Closure Fasteners
24	Buckles, Buttons, Clasps, etc.
411	Expanded, Threaded, Driven, Headed, Tool–Deformed, or Locked–Threaded Fastener

FIGURE 6.3 *(continued)*

Class 260 is being reclassified in steps by forming new classes from parts of it. The new class numbers are in numerical order according to the hierarchy of the whole system. For subject matter that has not been reclassified, 260 appears in the "Class" column.

CLASS	SUBJECT MATTER
260	Miscellaneous
518	Fischer–Tropsch reactions
520	Synthetic Resins and Natural Rubbers
521	. Ion Exchange Resins; Cellular Products (Foams)
522	. Prepared By Wave Energy
523, 524	. With Nonreactive Additives
525	. Mixed Synthetic Resins, Block or Graft Copolymers; Chemical Modification of Solid Synthetic Resins (e.g., unsaturated + preformed resin)
526	. Reaction Zone Features
	. Polymers from Unsaturated Monomers
527	. Polymers from Specialized Reactants (e.g., proteins, carbohydrates)
528	. Condensates (from various starting materials, e.g., phenols)
530	Natural Resins, Proteins, Peptides or Lignins
532	Has no patents presently. Definitions contain a glossary of terms used in 532–570 Series of Classes.
534	. Noble gas, Radioactive Metal or Rare Earth Metal containing; Azo–type Compounds
536	. Carbohydrates
540	. Heterocyclic Compounds
	. . Seven or more ring members with at least one hetero nitrogen; Steroids; Beta–lactams such as Cephalosporins and Penicillins
544	. . Six–membered ring with two or more ring heteros, at least one hetero nitrogen
546	. . Six–membered ring with one hetero nitrogen and five carbons
548	. . Five–, Four–, or Three–membered ring with at least one hetero nitrogen
549	. . Hetero Sulfur or Oxygen
552	. Azides, Triphenylmethanes
260	. Carbocyclic or Acyclic
552	. . Anthrones, Anthranols, Quinones, Steroids,
554	. . Fatty Acids, Salts, Esters, or Amides
556	. . Heavy Metal, Aluminum, or Silicon containing
558, 560	. . Esters
562	. . Organic Acids, Acid Halides, Acid Anhydrides, Selenium or Tellurium Compounds
564	. . Urea Adducts, Amino Nitrogen Compounds
568	. . Boron, Phosphorus, Sulfur or Oxygen containing
260	. . C–metal (light metal bonded directly to carbon)
570	. . Halogen containing
585	Hydrocarbons

APPLYING FOR A PATENT

7

If your search indicates that obtaining a patent is feasible, your next step is to apply for a patent. This is a more complicated process than the search and requires a great deal of professional knowledge and skill based on training and experience. Again, though it is possible for you to do it yourself, we recommend using a patent attorney, because an inventor who personally prepares and files an application takes the risk of endangering the chances of obtaining a good patent. Just the same, you should have a general understanding of this procedure, as it will be immensely helpful to your attorney.

There is not an actual document that can give you step-by-step instructions on how to complete a patent application, because a patent application is not just a form to be filled out. You can, however, request information about the filing procedure from the patent office.

Do not be concerned about the danger that any information in your application will be revealed to anyone. The U.S. Patent Office maintains the strictest secrecy until the patent is issued. If it is not issued, the file is kept secret and is eventually destroyed. Of course, in the event that your patent is issued, the application and all correspondence leading up to its issuance are made available in the patent office for inspection by anyone. As we mentioned earlier, one purpose of a patent is to have an inventor disclose the invention in return for a 17-year monopoly so the general public can later practice it. Copies of all files of a patented invention may be purchased from the patent office or may be made by a member of the public in the patent office.

It is not necessary for you or your attorney to visit the patent office to transact business concerning patent matters. Most business is conducted by correspondence, and some by telephone, although personal interviews with examiners pertaining to pending applications can be arranged and are often helpful. Although there are some 1,500 examiners, the backlog of applications is currently running at approximately one year. Once your filed application has been assigned to the appropriate division of the patent office and is ready for examination, an examiner searches prior patents and such publications as deemed pertinent. The examiner's job is to allow or disallow the claims of your application depending on whether your invention, as precisely defined by your claims (discussed later in this chapter), is sufficiently different from prior technology. Usually the examiner applies the test of obviousness that was documented in Chapter 4. Some or all of the claims may be rejected, and in that case, the examiner will cite those prior patents or publications believed to anticipate the invention expressed in such claims and will send a copy for you to study. With this information, you may then decide on what course of action you wish to take. You may continue to pursue your patent or abandon it. The patent office will answer all inquiries on the status of your application as to whether it has been rejected, allowed, or is awaiting action. You, or your attorney on your behalf, may explain to the examiner how your invention is different from the prior technology and why you should get a patent. You can make some changes in your application. However, the patent office will correspond either to you or your attorney. Ordinarily, all comments about your application will be sent to your attorney unless you tell your attorney or the patent office otherwise.

There is a series of fees that must be paid with the filing of a patent application. The fee schedule is structured to be lower for an invention that is owned by an individual, a small business entity, or a university than for a large entity with 500 or more employees. While we will not go into details, the small inventor pays approximately 50 percent of the fee charged to the large enterprise. Patent office regulations and forms, as well as the fee schedule, which is frequently changed, are reproduced at the end of this chapter (Figures 7.1–7.3).

THE APPLICATION

A patent application is not one that typically requires you to complete a form and answer questions in the appropriate blank spaces. If filling out a questionnaire was all that was necessary, you would not require legal advice. There are usually five main parts of the application: (1) the Formal Papers, (2) the Specification, (3) the Claims, (4) the Filing Fee, and (5) the Drawings. The specification, claims, and drawings are printed in the issued patent. An issued patent is reproduced on pages 84–94 so you may see examples of the parts that we describe.

The formal papers include a petition, a power of attorney, and an oath or declaration as well as small entity papers if you are entitled to pay the lower fees. Patent office forms for these papers are reproduced at the end of this chapter. Often an assignment is included. Only these formal papers have any resemblance to an ordinary application form. In this part, you must complete your name, address, and so forth. The petition is addressed to the commissioner of patents and trademarks, asking that a patent be issued to you as the inventor. The oath or declaration must be signed with your statement that you believe yourself to be the first inventor and stating other facts you believe to be true. It usually includes a standard power of attorney that, in this case, gives permission to your lawyer or agent to sign other documents concerning your patent as your representative. By giving this power of attorney, you are consenting to the fact that all further correspondence from the U.S. Patent Office will be directed to your lawyer rather than you. Attached to these formal papers are the specification, drawings, and claims, which are more complicated.

The specification has several parts. First, as shown in the sample patent, it begins with a title that names your invention. Secondly, it briefly describes what has been done before in the technical field in which you have made an improvement (see the portion entitled "Background Art"). Thirdly, it provides a detailed description of the invention, explaining how it is constructed and how it operates (see the sample portion entitled "Detailed Description"). While it is not always necessary to have drawings, most patent applications do because they are helpful in explaining an invention. The description should make reference to the drawings when it is appropriate and necessary. A patent application for a mechanical invention, for example, would require drawings, and, similarly, an electrical invention would have circuit diagrams shown in the drawings. Drawings are not always feasible, however. For example, drawings are only sometimes used in the field of chemistry. In fact, the Goodyear patent for vulcanization of rubber does not contain a single drawing. A plant patent application contains photographs of the plant. Of course, a design patent would have drawings of the actual design, which would also act as the description. There is essentially no written description of a design.

Patent law requires that the specification provide a description sufficiently full and clear so that it could teach a person of

United States Patent [19]

Williams et al.

[11] **Patent Number:** 4,538,709

[45] **Date of Patent:** Sep. 3, 1985

[54] **WHEELED GARMENT BAG**

[75] Inventors: **Marvin E. Williams,** Worthington; **David B. Chaney,** Columbus; **Donald J. Rebele,** Worthington, all of Ohio

[73] Assignee: **The Huntington National Bank,** Columbus, Ohio

[21] Appl. No.: **512,734**

[22] Filed: **Jul. 11, 1983**

[51] Int. Cl.³ **A45C 5/14; A45C 13/26; A45C 13/30; A45C 13/38**

[52] U.S. Cl. .... **190/18 A;** 190/115; 206/287.1; 248/188.5; 280/37; 280/47.17

[58] Field of Search .... 190/18 R, 18 A, 115, 190/39; 206/287.1; 280/34, 47, 17, 47.26, DIG. 3; 248/188.5

[56] **References Cited**

U.S. PATENT DOCUMENTS

1,215,369	2/1917	Hart	248/188.5 X
2,427,841	9/1947	Dichter	248/188.5 X
2,581,417	1/1952	Jones	190/18 A X
2,689,631	9/1954	Marks	206/287.1 X
2,957,187	10/1960	Raia	248/188.5 X
3,522,955	8/1970	Warner, Jr.	190/18 A X
3,559,777	2/1971	Gardner	190/111 X
3,606,372	9/1971	Browning	190/115 X
3,891,230	6/1975	Mayer	190/18 A X
3,934,895	1/1976	Fox	190/18 A X
4,030,768	6/1977	Lugash	190/18 A X
4,036,336	7/1977	Burtley	190/18 A
4,062,429	12/1977	Tabor et al.	190/18 A
4,256,320	3/1981	Hager	280/37
4,262,780	4/1981	Samuelian	190/18 A

FOREIGN PATENT DOCUMENTS

0021918	1/1981	European Pat. Off.	190/18 A
2056657	5/1972	Fed. Rep. of Germany	190/18 A
2359229	6/1975	Fed. Rep. of Germany	190/18 A
1301349	4/1969	France	280/47.17

Primary Examiner—William Price
Assistant Examiner—Sue A. Weaver
Attorney, Agent, or Firm—Frank H. Foster

[57] **ABSTRACT**

A multipurpose piece of luggage with wheels and a collapsible handle having a garment enclosure in which large articles of clothing may be hung and lesser enclosures for storage of small articles. The invention also serves as a cart for other luggage. Its handle may be collapsed, support feet retracted and garment enclosure folded to give it the appearance and utility of a normal suitcase.

4 Claims, 12 Drawing Figures

Fig. 1A

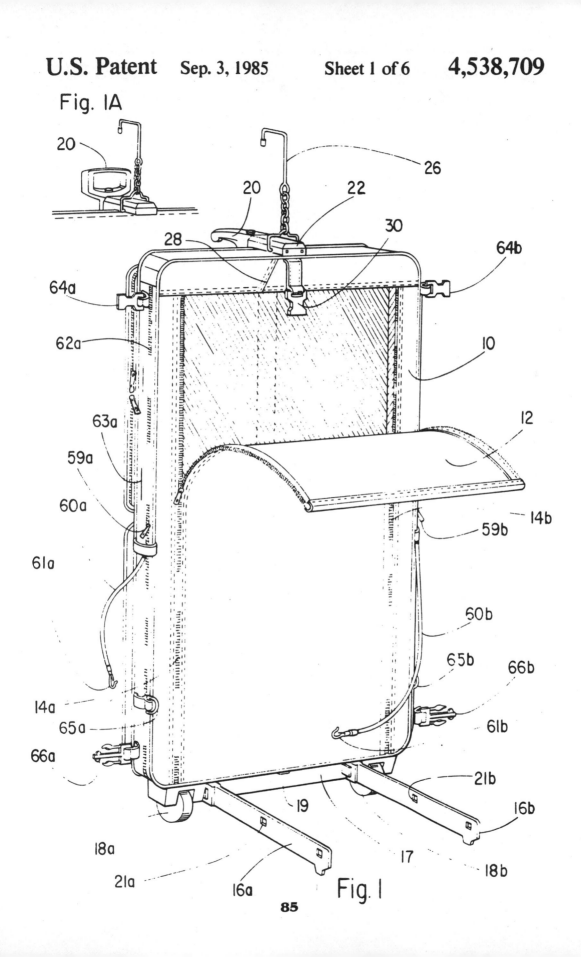

Fig. 1

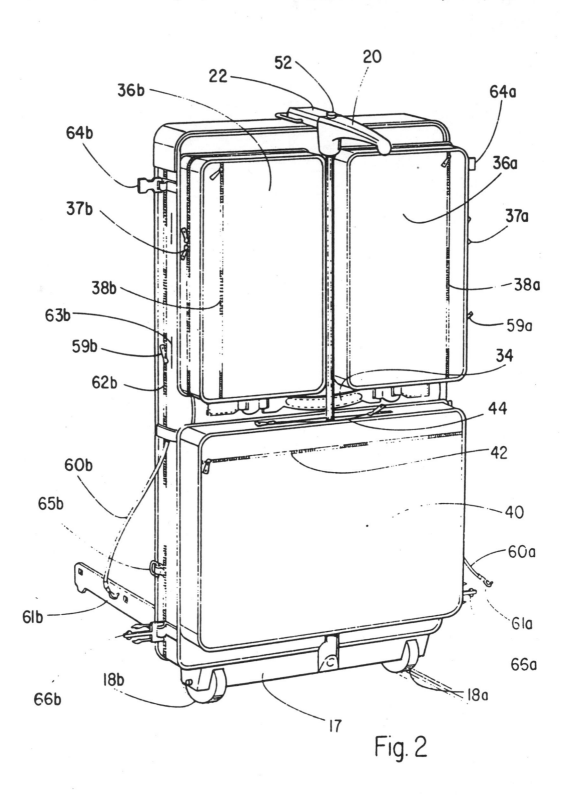

Fig. 2

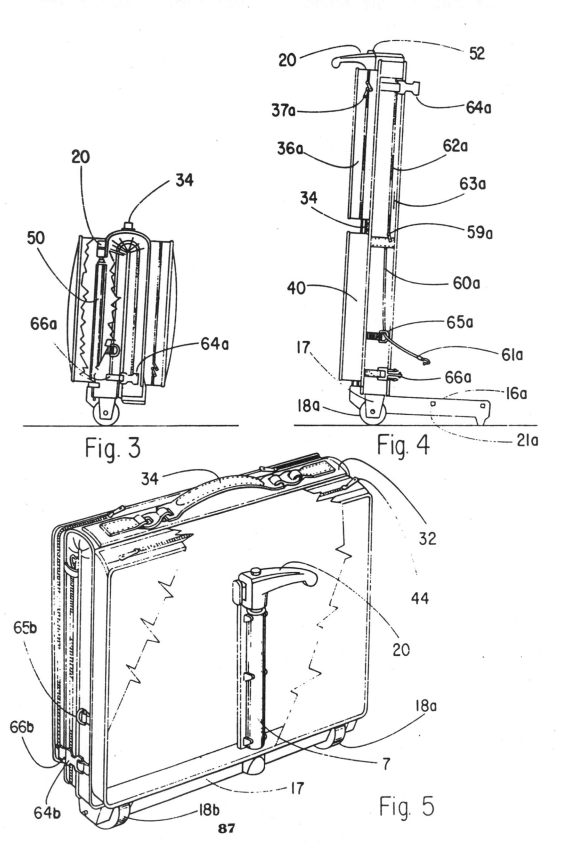

Fig. 3

Fig. 4

Fig. 5

87

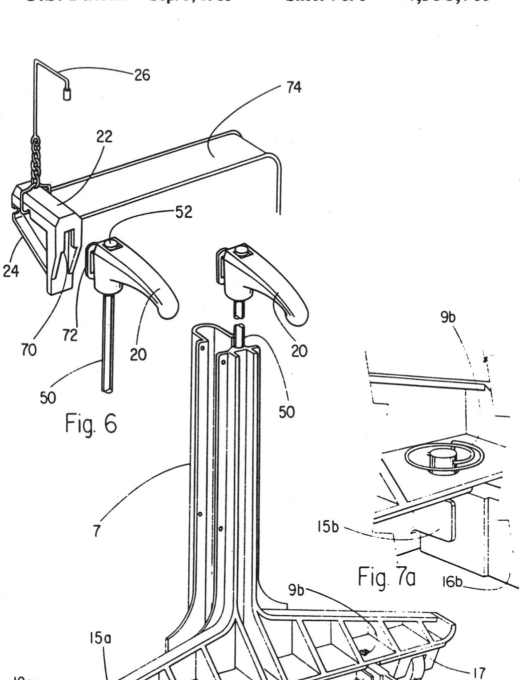

Fig. 6

Fig. 7a

Fig. 7

Fig. 8

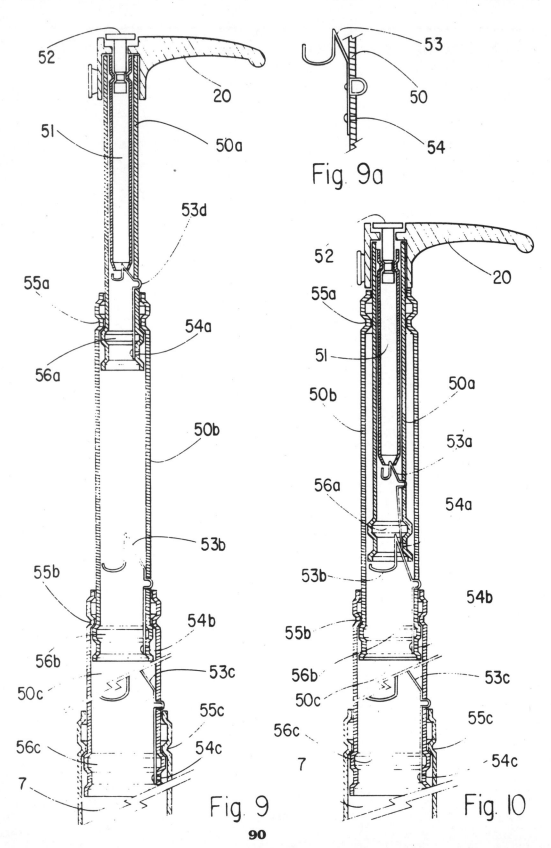

Fig. 9a

Fig. 9

Fig. 10

1

WHEELED GARMENT BAG

TECHNICAL FIELD

The present invention relates to wheeled, hand-held luggage suitable for airline carry on use. In particular, the present invention relates to multipurpose, collapsible luggage capable of performing as a cart for additional bags and as a self-supporting garment bag.

BACKGROUND ART

Traditionally the traveller has had a choice of hand-held luggage consisting of suitcases, lightweight "carry on" bags, and garment bags. Suitcases can carry an ample amount of articles, but clothing such as dresses, coats, or suits must be folded and thereby wrinkled when placed inside. The resultant package is generally heavy and cumbersome. Wheels and handles have been added to suitcases in prior inventions, but the luggage, though more mobile, does not leave a traveller's clothing looking fresh. The suitcase is not generally fit for the "business" traveller, who only needs to carry one or two days worth of clothing and would prefer to transport all his needs in a single piece of carry on luggage in order to save time otherwise spent waiting for his luggage to be unloaded from aircraft. The business traveller gains the added benefit of not risking the loss of his luggage when he is able to store all his needs in a single carry on piece of luggage.

Lightweight carry on bags do not allow a traveller to store longer articles of clothing without their being folded and, thus, wrinkled. Secondly, when lightweight carry on bags are used in conjunction with other luggage they must be carried separately adding to the traveller's burdens and causing him to have to pick up, position, and put down all his luggage between each time he is required to use his hands.

Garment bags are usually bulky and cumbersome. When carried over one's arms the articles of clothing are still subject to folding and wrinkling. Any smaller items carried in a garment bag, such as folded shirts or toiletry articles, usually fall to the bottom of the bag in a disorderly manner. Attempts to make the garment bags more like a big suitcase have resulted in a large rigid piece of luggage, which, when in conjunction with a number of other bags, only adds to the difficulties of a traveller attempting to carry all his luggage and intermittently stop and use his hands. For example, the wheeled garment bag disclosed in Lugash U.S. Pat. No. 4,030,768 provides a rigid, mobile bag capable of carrying long pieces of clothing without folding. It even provides for a hook to temporarily hold a lightweight bag, such as a brief case, but the invention disclosed still only compounds a traveller's problems when he attempts to transport the garment bag in conjunction with two or more suitcases.

BRIEF DISCLOSURE OF THE INVENTION

The preferred embodiment of the present invention has a base support unit. Assembled to this unit are wheels and spring loaded, retractable support feed. Affixed to the upper portion of the base support unit is a telescoping pole attached to a handle.

The garment enclosure is manufactured from a durable, flexible material. Within the enclosure is a hanger bar. The enclosure is large enough to hang a number of suits or dresses. The garment enclosure, when in an operable position is held rigid from its lower portion to

its center by the base support unit. The upper portion of the enclosure may be folded over or held in an upright position against the extended telescoping pole. In either position the invention may be pushed or pulled along by using the handle attached to the extended telescoping pole. When the garment enclosure is folded over and the telescoping pole collapsed, both the pole and its handle are concealed within a zippered lining. An auxiliary handle affixed to the center of the garment enclosure may be used to carry the invention when it is in the folded position.

Retractable, spring loaded support feet may be extended to have additional luggage rested upon them. Regardless of the position of the garment enclosure, the invention serves as a free standing luggage cart.

Fashioned to the outer wall of the garment enclosure are smaller, additional enclosures suitable for carrying articles of lesser size.

An object of this invention is to provide a traveller with a piece of multipurpose luggage capable of hanging large articles of clothing without folding them while providing separate storage for smaller articles.

An object of this invention is to provide a traveller with a multipurpose piece of luggage that also doubles as a cart for smaller pieces of luggage.

Another object of this invention is to provide a soft-sided carry on garment enclosure that may be hung for storage and with the handle and telescoping tube support collapsed into the bag it can be folded to be stored in tight places.

An additional object of this invention is to provide a piece of luggage with wheels and a handle that may act as a garment bag and is free standing.

BRIEF DESCRIPTION OF THE DRAWINGS

FIG. 1 is a perspective view showing the inward side of the garment enclosure and the retractable support feet extended and with two handle designs.

FIG. 2 is a perspective view of a preferred embodiment of the outward side of the garment enclosure with an arrangement of smaller enclosures.

FIG. 3 is a side elevation with the telescoping pole collapsed and the garment enclosure folded.

FIG. 4 is a side elevation with the garment enclosure in an upright position.

FIG. 5 is a top perspective view of the garment enclosure in a folded position with the handle collapsed.

FIG. 6 is a perspective view of the garment enclosure's bracket assembly and corresponding handle clip device.

FIGS. 7 and 7a are a front perspective view of the base support unit with the garment enclosure removed illustrating the wheel and retractable foot support assemblies and including a blow up of one spring assembly.

FIG. 8 is a perspective view of the invention in its operable position while being pushed and carrying a brief case.

FIGS. 9 and 9a are a side elevation of the preferred embodiment of the telescoping pole in an extended position with portions broken away to illustrate the interrelationship of the interior parts and including a blow up of alternative spring clip designs.

FIG. 10 is a side elevation of the preferred embodiment of the telescoping pole illustrating the interrelationship of the interior parts when the first section is partially collapsed.

3

In describing the preferred embodiment of the invention, which is illustrated in the drawings, specific terminology will be resorted to for the sake of clarity. However, it is not intended that the invention be limited to the specific terms so selected and it is to be understood that each specific term includes all technical equivalents which operate in a similar manner to accomplish a similar purpose.

DETAILED DESCRIPTION

Referring to FIG. 1 a base support unit 17 having wheels 18a and 18b holds the invention upright by means of support feet 16a and 16b. The inward side of the garment enclosure 10 is illustrated. Access to the inner portion of the garment enclosure 10 is achieved by opening flap 12 with the use of the flap zippers 14a and 14b. An optional strap 30 may be used to assist in holding flap 12 closed. Large articles of clothing on hangers may be suspended within the garment enclosure 10 by use of an inner hanger bar 24 (FIG. 6). In the preferred embodiment this bar is designed to slant downward such that the first articles of clothing hung inside the garment enclosure 10 slide downward and into the enclosure away from the flap 12. When upright the entire invention may itself be hung in a closet or onto some other device by the use of hanger hook 26. A hook pocket 28 is provided to store the hanger hook 26 when it is not in use.

In FIG. 2 the outward side of the garment enclosure 10 is illustrated in the upright position and shows a alternative handle design. This preferred embodiment illustrates an arrangement for two small enclosures 36a and 36b and one medium enclosure 40. The small enclosures 36a and 36b are designed in the preferred embodiment to accomodate a number of folded shirts or similar garments. In an alternative, less expensive embodiment of the invention, the two small enclosures are absent and storage is provided by a pocket in the lining of the garment enclosure. Access to the small enclosures 36a and 36b is through access zipper 37a and 37b respectively. Access to the medium enclosure is through access zipper 42. An additional feature of the preferred embodiment is a storage pocket for papers provided in the linings of small enclosures 36a and 36b with access through zipper 38a and 38b respectively. The pockets provide quick storage and retrieval for items such as newspapers or airplane tickets. The fashioning of the small and medium enclosures to the exterior of the garment enclosure overcomes drawbacks found in prior art. By providing compartmentalized storage space outside of the garment enclosure smaller items may be packed or removed without first having to remove the large articles of clothing stored within the garment enclosure. Additionally, small bulky items such as shoes are not pressed directly against suits or dresses, thereby not causing those items to be wrinkled, torn or soiled.

As indicated in FIGS. 3 and 5 the garment enclosure 10 may be folded over to form a piece of luggage approximately the same size as a normal carry on bag. The preferred embodiment when folded is designed to fit neatly into tight spaces. Even when the invention is in a folded position it will function as a cart for additional luggage which may be rested upon the support feet 16a and 16b. A telescoping pole 50 with an attached handle 20 locks into an extended position and provides a means for the traveller to push or pull the bag without having to stoop or bend over to pick up the handle.

4

As indicated in FIGS. 1, 3 and 4 male clasps 66a and 66b and female clasps 64a and 64b are provided to retain the garment enclosure 10 in a folded position. FIG. 1 and FIG. 4 demonstrate the provisions in the preferred embodiment for rings 65a and 65b to be used for strapping additional luggage to the invention. Also provided in the preferred embodiment are stretch cords 60a and 60b with terminal hooks 61a and 61b for use in securing additional luggage to the invention. These cords may be used in three positions to secure additional luggage to the invention. For large pieces of luggage the cords may simply be extended around the luggage and attached to one another by their respective hooks 61a and 61b. Secondly, for smaller parcels, the cords may be extended downward through the rings 65a and 65b and then joined together by their respective hooks. Lastly, the hooks may be attached to holes 21a and 21b in the support legs 16a and 16b to brace very large items. These stretch cords 60a and 60b with their respective hooks 61a and 61b may be stored out of sight within tubular pockets 63a and 63b. A non-opening zipper 62a or 62b keeps the tubular pockets 63a or 63b closed when the zipper glides 59a and 59b, that are attached to an end of stretch cords 60a or 60b, are used to pull or extend the stretch cords 60a or 60b into or out of the tubular pockets 63a or 63b.

In FIG. 5 the top of the invention is illustrated with the support feet 16a and 16b retracted out of sight and the garment enclosure 10 in a folded position. Telescoping pole 50 has been collapsed and concealed along with handle 20 in a compartment beneath the zipper 44. When the invention is in this position it assumes the size and appearance of a normal suitcase. Auxiliary handle 34 is used to carry the invention. Auxiliary handle 34 in the preferred embodiment is affixed to a support shoulder 32 that, when the invention is in the folded position, acts it's spine and provides lateral dimension to the invention.

In FIG. 6 the handle 20 is illustrated in two embodiments with a button snap 72 and the telescoping pole 50 almost fully extended. The garment enclosure 10 is in the upright position. A bracket assembly 22 has a notched receptacle 70. As the telescoping pole 50 is being fully extended the notched receptacle 70 receives the button snap 72. Once the telescoping pole 50 is fully extended it locks itself automatically in the extended position. The notched receptacle 70 of the bracket assembly 22 thereby is held rigidly in an upright position. The bracket assembly 22 supports the end of the garment enclosure 10 in a lateral dimension by use of an inner shoulder support 74. When the garment enclosure 10 is to be folded on the telescoping pole 50 and its handle 20 stored, a release button 52 on the handle 20 is depressed and the locking mechanism of the telescoping pole 50 releases. The button snap 72 will then slide down and out of the notched receptacle 70 allowing the garment enclosure 10 to be folded. Regardless of the design of the handle, the function of button snap and the release button remain the same and either version allows the invention to be comfortable pushed along.

Referring to FIG. 7 the base support unit 17 is illustrated in detail. Support feet 16a and 16b are movably attached to be base support unit 17 by hinges 15a and 15b respectively. The support feet 16a and 16b automatically rotate outward from a folded position because of the tension supplied by springs 9a and 9b. A plastic tab hook 19 attached to the base support unit 17 in the preferred embodiment snaps on top of the support feet

5

and retains them in their folded position. The preferred embodiment of the invention, when the garment enclosure 10 is folded, will sit in an upright position with the support feet 16a and 16b extended or folded. When the traveller desires to extend the support feet 16a and 16b he may do so by using his foot to unsnap the tab hook 19 from the support feet 16a and 16b. The support feet 16a and 16b will then spring to an extended position.

FIG. 7 also illustrates another feature of the preferred embodiment of the base support unit 17. A durable sleeve 7 provides a protective shell around the telescoping tube 50. When the telescoping tube is collapsed and stored inside of the concealment zipper 44 this sleeve will protect the telescoping pole 50 from being bent by objects either contained or outside of the invention.

FIG. 8 illustrates an alternative embodiment of the invention with a medium size enclosure 40, but no small enclosures 36a or 36b. This version of the invention may be made less expensively than the preferred embodiment, but does not lack any of the significant features of the invention. A pocket may be fashioned in the lining of the invention in place of the small enclosures in order to allow for storage of some additional articles such as folded shirts or trousers. In this view alternative handle design 20 is shown.

FIG. 9 represents the telescoping pole 50 in the extended, locked position. The pole consists of three tubular sections 50a, 50b and 50c. These three sections telescope one at a time with section 50a sliding into section 50b, then these two into section 50c, and finally all three into the protective cover 7 of the base support unit 17. Regardless of the version of the handle used when the telescoping pole is fully collapsed the handle will rest upon the upper portion of the protective cover inside the concealment zipper 44 completely out of sight.

Within the preferred embodiment the first tubular section 50a is an inner tube 51. Atop tube 51 rests the release button 52 which protrudes from the handle. Tube 51 rests upon a spring clip 53a. The spring clip is fashioned to provide tension against tube 51 which in turn pushes against the release button 52. The spring clip 53a is affixed to the tubular section 50a by a rivet 54a or another suitable means of fastening. A portion of the spring clip 53a protrudes through a hole in tubular section 50a and locks this section into the extended position on top of tubular section 50b. A bulbous ring 56a fashioned into the lower portion of tubular section 50a prevents this section from being pulled past the upper lip 55a of the second tubular section 50b. Tubular sections 50b and 50c have like spring clips 53b and 53c with rivets 54b and 54c respectively. These two sections also have bulbous rings 56b and 56c to prevent tubular section 50b from being pulled past lip 55b of tubular section 50c and to prevent tubular section 50c from being pulled past lip 55c of the protective cover 7 of the base support unit 17. Other styles of spring clips may be suitable for use in this invention. Suitable embodiments include clips fashioned in a "u" shape and also clips having attached bullets to protrude from the tubular sections of the telescoping pole.

FIG. 10 illustrates the telescoping pole with its first tubular section 50a collapsed. When release button 52 is depressed the inner tube 51 is pushed against the tension of spring clip 53a causing its portion protruding through the hole in tubular section 50a and resting upon lip 55a to be retracted. When retracted the tension of the spring clip 53a still urges the inner tube 51 against release button 52 to keep that button protruding out of

6

the handle. A secondary embodiment of the invention which is less expensive to manufacture does not have an inner tube or release button. Instead an alternative actuation of the collapsing feaure of the telescoping pole is utilized. In this version the operator directly depresses the portion of the clip protruding through the tubular section or may depress a button positioned above the protruding portion of the clip which causes that portion to retract.

When the spring clip 53a is retracted tubular section 50a may be slid into tubular section 50b. When the lower portion of tubular section 50a engages the second spring clip 53b that clip will be retracted and tubular section 50b may then be slid into tubular section 50c. As can be seen each tubular section as it is collapsed engages a corresponding spring clip thus allowing the next tubular section to be collapsed until the telescoping pole is fully collapsed and within the protective cover 7 of the base support unit 17.

One embodiment of the invention includes an article of luggage, as described, sold with additional, but separate bags that are designed to fit on the support feet 16a and 16b and compliment the design of the invention.

While certain preferred embodiments of the present invention have been disclosed in detail, it is to be understood that various modifications in its structure may be adopted without departing from the spirit of the invention or the scope of the following claims.

We claim:

1. A luggage device comprising:
(a) a base support unit having wheels extending downward upon which it may roll;
(b) a garment enclosure which, when in an operable position, has its lower portion attached to said base support unit and its upper portion either folded downwardly or raised upwardly;
(c) a linearly extensible, telescoping pole including means for releasably locking it in an extended position, means for attaching said pole at one end to said base support unit, said pole extending upwardly through only said lower portion of said garment enclosure and having a handle near its other end, means for releasably attaching said handle to the top of said upper portion for supporting said garment enclosure when said pole is extended; and
(d) one or more retractable support feet assembled to said base support unit to hold said luggage device upright and to carry additional luggage rested upon them when they are extended outward from said base support unit.

2. A luggage device in accordance with claim 1 wherein a rigid protective sleeve is fixed to said base support unit and extends upward around said telescoping pole.

3. A luggage device in accordance with claim 1 further comprising at least one stretch cord mounted in a tubular pocket formed in said garment enclosure and attached to a slide which slides longitudinally along said pocket between a retracted storage position and an extended position for securing other objects to the luggage device.

4. A luggage device as recited in claim 1 wherein said means for releasably locking said telescoping pole includes a plurality of tubular sections which are locked into said extended position by a plurality of spring clips, a portion of which protrude through holes which are aligned in registration in the tubular section and are

7

8

retracted by engagement of a relatively interior tubular section, wherein an inner tube is slideably mounted at the upper end of said pole and resiliently biased away from the uppermost spring clip, said tube being con-

nected to a button formed on said handle which may be depressed to move the interior tube against the uppermost spring clip and retract it.

* * * * *

5

10

15

20

25

30

35

40

45

50

55

60

65

ordinary skill in the art to make and use the invention without undue experimentation. After all, this is the principal purpose for the federal government to grant a patent, so here the inventor must fulfill the obligation of disclosure. The specification also provides the background that enables a reader to understand the next and most important part of the application, the claims.

The claims define your invention in concise language. They must distinguish your invention from prior technology (in the example see the numbered paragraphs beginning at column 6, line 30). The claims must be accurate and must distinctly define the improvement or combination or whatever else is the inventive subject matter of the application. In other words, the claims define what constitutes an infringement of your patent by establishing the boundaries of your patent rights. This is the most critical part of the application—and certainly the most delicate. Claims require the most knowledge and experience in patent law. If the claims are limited to unimportant incidental features, other persons may be able to use the important features without infringing on your rights merely by making simple changes to eliminate those incidental features. In order for it to give you the most protection, the application should claim your invention in language broad enough to include all the different ways to make your invention. Yet, if you state your claims so broadly that the claims describe prior technology or something that is obvious from prior technology, your patent will not be allowed. The difficulty is in finding the feature(s) that distinguish your invention from earlier ones, and preparing claims that define it in language broad enough to provide proper protection without overstating your case by claiming too much. This is the principal reason that someone who is not a patent attorney or agent is unable to adequately protect your invention. The most important parts of the patent office regulations describing the requirements for patent applications are appended to the end of this chapter in Figure 7.1.

CITATION OF ART

A citation of art should be filed along with or within three months after filing the patent application. The Patent Office rules now clearly impose a duty of candor and good faith upon the inventor, attorney, and any assignee. They are required to disclose information of which they are aware that is material to examination of the application. The information is submitted in an Information Disclosure Statement and includes any public disclosure, such as a publication, use, or sale, and any test data that shows the invention does not work. This disclosure statement should be filed, along with a list of and a copy of each cited publication, within three months of filing the application, although it can be filed later in some circumstances when accompanied by a fee.

It is imprudent to not disclose the closest prior art of which you are aware. There is no duty to search for such information, but if you know of it and fail to tell the Patent Office about it, your patent rights could be seriously jeopardized, and you could even be required to pay attorney fees to someone you sue for patent infringement.

It is also desirable to include a statement describing the relevance of each cited prior patent or publication, including what you believe are the differences between your invention and the prior technology and why you believe your invention is patentable. This part of a citation of art can be included in the background part of the patent application.

Submitting all this information complies with the requirements of the rules, prevents later accusations that you fraudulently withheld important information, and strengthens your patent. If the examiner considers this prior art and allows your patent, your patent is more likely to stand up in court. Judges are predisposed to rely on the judgment of a patent examiner.

THE GREATEST HAZARDS

The most difficult part of the application is knowing what to put down in the claims. The other difficult part is to be sure to include all the information that will be needed long after the application is filed. As we previously discussed, the publication or sale of your product in the United States more than one year before you file your application can destroy your patent rights. The danger you, as a novice inventor, may fail to realize is that by not including important information, you jeopardize your patent application, because you will not be able to go back at some later date and add new information. While it is possible for you to have an otherwise patentable invention, you could conceivably prepare an inadequate application that would cause the patent to be rejected. In the meantime, if you commercially sell or publish your invention, and many months expire since originally filing your application, you may not be able to get a patent. Although there are procedures that permit you to add a new disclosure, anything new receives a new filing date. It does not matter that you originally had a filing date within one year after you sold your product—if the new filing date is more than a year after your first sale or publication, the newly disclosed portion of your invention has lost its right to be the basis for a patent.

In your haste to get your product into the marketplace, you must be careful (as a novice inventor) not to unwittingly think that, just because you filed your application within one year after it was first sold or published, there was no danger of having those sales or publishing activities destroy your patent rights. Of course, if your application is filed properly with a full disclosure, you have nothing to worry about. But filing your own application without the counsel of an attorney increases the chances of an inadequate application—and, if you are like most inventors, you will probably take your product to the marketplace as soon as possible. Therein lies the danger of jeopardizing your patent rights. Again you are reminded of the long time lag, often more than a year, that follows the filing of an application before it is acted on.

CONTINUATION-IN-PART

The procedure for adding new information is to refile an application with new information added to it. This application is called a continuation-in-part application. It must be filed before the original application becomes abandoned or issues as a patent. The new application becomes the sum total of the old plus the new. What is old and appeared in the original application maintains its original filing date, and what is new is given a new filing date.

To illustrate what can happen with a new and an old date, let us suppose you file a continuation-in-part 20 months after your first application. The invention had parts A, B, and C in the original application, and the patent was rejected.

On reviewing your application with its examiner, you say, "There's also a part D that should have been included, and with this addition, I feel that my invention warrants a patent."

"But you didn't have D in your application," the examiner states.

"I know," you add, "but I should have."

"You should have put it in," the examiner says.

"I didn't think it was important," you reply.

In the meantime, since you were already selling the product and part D has a new application date, it is nonpatentable because the one-year grace period has terminated.

Occasionally, an inventor does not include some important information to prevent public awareness of it. This is a serious mistake, as the example mentioned above demonstrated.

ABANDONMENT DUE TO FAILURE TO RESPOND TO PATENT OFFICE COMMUNICATION

After the examiner conducts a patent search, he or she will send a letter to you or your attorney. On hearing from the examiner, you may wish to write, call, or visit to discuss why your application should be allowed. Each time the patent office sends a written communication, it gives you a certain time limit within which you must respond and comply with whatever happens to be the next procedure. If you fail to act within the allotted time, your application will be abandoned. Ordinarily, you will have three months from the date it was mailed to respond to the examiner's communication.

You may obtain an extension of time, and there are fees for this that vary according to how much time you pay for, usually up to an additional three-month period. For a large entity, this fee may cost several hundred dollars for a full three-month period. If you fail to respond because you never received communication or for some other reason that made your failure unavoidable, you may file a petition for an extension and include a statement explaining why you did not respond.

DISAGREEING WITH AN UNFAVORABLE RULING

After doing a search, an examiner may refuse to grant your patent. If so, you are permitted to respond in writing and to contact this person to discuss why you believe the decision is not valid. You and/or your attorney can either come to the patent office or call the examiner on the phone for a discussion, but something must be submitted in writing. There is room for negotiation; for instance, your attorney may choose to narrow the application's claims. Then, after again considering your application, the examiner renders a second opinion. After that, if you are still convinced that you are unable to change the examiner's mind and believe your patent should be granted, you can appeal the decision.

Now you can take your case to the Board of Patent Appeals and Interferences at the patent office. This procedure can take several months, even years; it involves both you and the examiner, filing a brief explaining the position that each of you took. The board generally consists of three former patent examiners, and, if you choose, you or your attorney can appear before the board and present your arguments in person instead of relying on your filed written brief. Keep in mind that only a small percentage of applicants go through this appeal process, because of its expense, and only about 20 percent of the examiners' decisions are ever reversed by the board.

If the board turns your application down, and you want to take your case to the court system, you have two choices. The first is to appeal to the U.S. District Court of the District of Columbia, a federal court, and present evidence to a judge for a decision. If you are still not satisfied, you can go to the Court of Appeals. From there, your final recourse is the U.S. Supreme Court. Only one patent case every few years goes this far, but it is possible that a highly important case might. Your alternative route is to appeal from the board to the Court of Appeals for the Federal Circuit, a court that specializes in certain areas of law, one of which is patents. This court will review the decision made by the board and decide on the merits of your patent. Theoretically, you can appeal the board's decision to the U.S. Supreme Court, but the chances are quite slim that the highest court in the land will hear it.

INTERFERENCE

An interference occurs when two applications by different inventors for the same invention are pending at the patent office. An interference also occurs when the invention is already patented by someone else in an unexpired patent. When this happens, this patent office procedure must determine the earlier inventor, who is, in turn, entitled to the patent. The main issue to be determined is priority, although other considerations are originality, laches, abandonment, and estoppel.

The patent office is more apt to favor the earliest filed application, assuming it has priority, and a later applicant is given the burden of proving the contrary.

Where a patent was already issued, the applicant in the later application must complete an affidavit stating the invention was made in the United States before the filing date of the patentee. The subject of interference is excessively complicated, and we highly recommend that you consult a patent attorney to learn more about it.

Chapter 600 Parts, Form and Content of Application

601 Content of Application [R-14]

35 U.S.C. 111. Application for patent

Application for patent shall be made, or authorized to be made, by the inventor, except as otherwise provided in this title, in writing to the Commissioner. Such application shall include (1) a specification as prescribed by section 112 of this title; (2) a drawing as prescribed by section 113 of this title; and (3) an oath by the applicant as prescribed by section 115 of this title. The application must be accompanied by the fee required by law. The fee and oath may be submitted after the specification and any required drawing are submitted, within such period and under such conditions, including the payment of a surcharge, as may be prescribed by the Commissioner. Upon failure to

FIGURE 7.1 (continued)

submit the fee and oath within such prescribed period, the application shall be regarded as abandoned, unless it is shown to the satisfaction of the Commissioner that the delay in submitting the fee and oath was unavoidable. The filing date of an application shall be the date on which the specification and any required drawing are received in the Patent and Trademark Office.

37 CFR 1.51 General requisites of an application.

(a) Applications for patents must be made to the Commissioner of Patents and Trademarks. A complete application comprises:

(1) A specification, including a claim or claims, see §§ 1.71 to 1.77.

(2) An oath or declaration, see §§ 1.63 and 1.68.

(3) Drawings, when necessary, see §§ 1.81 to 1.88.

(4) The prescribed filing fee, see § 1.16.

(b) Applicants are encouraged to file an information disclosure statement, See §§ 1.97 **>and 1.98<.

(c) Applicants may desire and are permitted to file with, or in, the application an authorization to charge, at any time during the pendency of the application, any fees required under any of §§ 1.16 to 1.18 to a deposit account established and maintained in accordance with § 1.25.

GUIDELINES FOR DRAFTING A MODEL PATENT APPLICATION

The following guidelines illustrate the preferred layout and content of patent applications. These guidelines are suggested for the applicant's use.

Arrangement and Contents of the Specification

The following order of arrangement is preferable in framing the specification and, except for the title of the invention, each of the lettered items should be preceded by the headings indicated.

(a) Title of the Invention.

(b) Cross-References to Related Applications (if any).

(c) Statement as to rights to inventions made under Federally-sponsored research and development (if any).

(d) Background of the Invention.

1. Field of the Invention.

2. Description of related art including information disclosed under §§ 1.97**>and 1.98<.

(e) Summary of the Invention.

(f) Brief Description of the Drawing.

(g) Description of the Preferred Embodiment(s).

(h) Claim(s).

(i) Abstract of the Disclosure.

Content

(a) *Title of the Invention*: (See 37 CFR 1.72(a).) The title of the invention should be placed at the top of the first page of the specification. It should be brief but technically accurate and descriptive preferably from two to seven words.

(b) *Cross-References to Related Applications:* (See 37 CFR 1.78 and MPEP § 201.11.)

(c) *Statement as to rights to inventions made under Federally sponsored research and development (if any):* (See MPEP § 310).

(d) *Background of the Invention:* The specification should set forth the Background of the Invention in two parts:

(1) Field of the Invention: A statement of the field of art to which the invention pertains. This statement may include a paraphrasing of the applicable U.S. patent classification definitions. The statement should be directed to the subject matter of the claimed invention. This item may also be titled "Technical Field".

(2) Description of the related art including information disclosed under 37 CFR 1.97 **>and 1.98<: A paragraph(s) describing to the extent practical the information known to the applicant, including references to specific documents where appropriate. Where applicable, the problems involved in the information disclosed which are solved by the applicant's invention, should be indicated. This item may also be titled "Background Information".

(e) *Summary of the Invention*: A brief summary or general statement of the invention as set forth in 37 CFR 1.73. The summary is separate and distinct from the abstract and is directed toward the invention rather than the disclosure as a whole. The summary may point out the advantages of the invention or how it solves problems previously existent in the art (and preferably indicated in the Background of the Invention). In chemical cases the summary should point out in general terms the utility of the invention. If possible, the nature and gist of the invention or the inventive concept should be set forth. Objects of the invention should be treated briefly and only to the extent that they contribute to an understanding of the invention. This item may also be titled "Disclosure of Invention".

(f) *Brief Description of the Drawing(s):* A reference to and brief description of the drawing(s) as set forth in 37 CFR 1.74.

(g) *Description of the Preferred Embodiment(s):* A description of the preferred embodiment(s) of the invention as required in 37 CFR 1.71. The description should be as short and specific as is necessary to adequately and accurately describe the invention. This item may also be titled "Best Mode for Carrying Out the Invention".

Where elements or groups of elements, compounds, and processes, which are conventional and generally widely known in the field to which the invention pertains, form a part of the invention described and their exact nature or type is not necessary for an understanding and use of the invention by a person skilled in the art, they should not be described in detail. However, where particularly complicated subject matter is involved or where the elements, compounds, or processes may not be commonly or widely known in the field, the specification should refer to another patent or readily available publication which adequately describes the subject matter.

(h) *Claim(s):* (See 37 CFR 1.75) A claim may be typed with the various elements subdivided in paragraph form. There may be plural indentations to further segregate subcombinations or related steps.

Reference characters corresponding to elements recited in the detailed description and the drawings may be used in conjunction with the recitation of the same element or group of elements in the claims. The reference characters, however,

FIGURE 7.1 *(continued)*

should be enclosed within parentheses so as to avoid confusion with other numbers or characters which may appear in the claims. The use of reference characters is to be considered as having no effect on the scope of the claims.

Claims should preferably be arranged in order of scope so that the first claim presented is the broadest. Where separate species are claimed, the claims of like species should be grouped together where possible and physically separated by drawing a line between claims or groups of claims. (Both of these provisions may not be practical or possible where several species claims depend from the same generic claim.) Similarly, product and process claims should be separately grouped. Such arrangements are for the purpose of facilitating classification and examination.

The form of claim required in 37 CFR 1.75(e) is particularly adapted for the description of improvement type inventions. Such a claim is to be considered a combination claim and should be drafted with this thought in mind.

In drafting claims in accordance with 37 CFR 1.75(e), the preamble is to be considered to positively and clearly include all the elements or steps recited therein as a part of the claimed combination.

(i) *Abstract of the Disclosure:* (See 37 CFR 1.72(b) and MPEP § 608.01(b).)

Oath or Declaration

(See 37 CFR 1.63, 1.68, and 1.69.) Where one or more previously filed foreign applications are cited or mentioned in the oath or declaration, complete identifying data, including the application or serial number as well as the country and date of filing, should be provided.

THE APPLICATION

The specification must be filed >in< or translated into the English language and must be legibly typewritten, written or printed in permanent ink or its equivalent in quality. See 37 CFR 1.52 and MPEP § 608.01.

The parts of the application may be included in a single document.

Determination of completeness of an application is covered in MPEP § 506 >and § 601.01<.

The specification and oath or declaration are secured together in a file wrapper, bearing appropriate identifying data including the serial number and filing date (MPEP § 717).

Note

Division applications MPEP § 201.06.
Continuation applications MPEP § 201.07.
Reissue applications MPEP § 1401.
Design applications, MPEP Chapter 1500.
Plant applications, MPEP Chapter 1600.

A model, exhibit or specimen is not required as part of the application as filed, although it may be required in the prosecution of the application (37 CFR 1.91-1.93, MPEP § 608.03).

37 CFR 1.59. Papers of application with filing date not returned.

Papers in an application which has received a filing date pursuant to § 1.53 will not be returned for any purpose whatever. If applicants have not preserved copies of the papers, the Office will furnish copies at the usual cost of any application in which either the required basic filing fee (§ 1.16) or the processing and retention fee (§ 1.21(l)) has been paid. See § 1.618 for return of unauthorized and improper papers in interferences.

See, however, MPEP § 201.14(c) and § 604.04(a).

The Patent and Trademark Office has initiated a program for expediting newly filed application papers through pre-examination steps. This program requires the cooperation of applicants in order to attain the desired result — a reduction in processing time.

Therefore, all applicants are requested to include a preliminary classification on newly filed patent applications. The preliminary classification, preferably class and subclass designations, should be identified in the upper right-hand corner of the letter of transmittal accompanying the application papers, for example "Proposed class 2, subclass 129."

This program is voluntary and the classification submitted will be accepted as advisory in nature. The final class and subclass assignment remains the responsibility of the Office.

601.01 Complete Application [R-14]

37 CFR 1.53 Serial number, filing date, and completion of application.

(a) Any application for a patent received in the Patent and Trademark Office will be assigned a serial number for identification purposes.

(b) The filing date of an application for patent >filed under this section< is the date on which: (1) A specification containing a description pursuant to § 1.71 and at least one claim pursuant to §1.75; and (2) any drawing required by §1.81(a), are filed in the Patent and Trademark Office in the name of the actual inventor or inventors as required by §1.41. No new matter may be introduced into an application after its filing date (§1.118). >If all the names of the actual inventor or inventors are not supplied when the specification and any required drawing are filed, the application will not be given a filing date earlier than the date upon which the names are supplied unless a petition with the fee set forth in §1.17(i)(1) is filed which sets forth the reasons the delay in supplying the names should be excused. A continuation or divisional application (filed under the conditions specified in 35 U.S.C. 120 or 121 and §1.78(a)) may be filed pursuant to this section, §1.60 or §1.62. A continuation-in-part application may be filed pursuant to this section or §1.62.<

(c) If any application is filed without the specification *>, drawing or name, or names, of the actual inventor or inventors< required by paragraph (b) of this section, applicant will be so notified and given a time period within which to submit the omitted specification *>,< drawing >, name, or names, of the actual inventor, or inventors,< in order to obtain a filing date as of the date of filing of such submission. >A copy of the "Notice of Incomplete Application" form notifying the applicant should accompany any response thereto submitted to the Office.< If the omission is not corrected within the time period set, the application will be returned or otherwise disposed of; the fee, if submitted, will be refunded less **>the< handling fee >set forth in §1.21(n).<

(d) If an application which has been accorded a filing date pursuant to paragraph (b) of this section does not include the appropriate filing

FIGURE 7.1 *(continued)*

601.01   MANUAL OF PATENT EXAMINING PROCEDURE

fee or an oath or declaration by the applicant, applicant will be so notified, if a correspondence address has been provided and given a period of time within which to file the fee, oath, or declaration and to pay the surcharge as set forth in § 1.16(e) in order to prevent abandonment of the application. A copy of the "Notice to File Missing Parts" form mailed to applicant should accompany any response thereto submitted to the Office. If the required filing fee is not timely paid, or if the processing and retention fee set forth in § 1.21(l) is not paid within one year of the date of mailing of the notification required by this paragraph, the application will be disposed of. No copies will be provided or certified by the Office of an application which has been disposed of or in which neither the required basic filing fee nor the processing and retention fee has been paid. The notification pursuant to this paragraph may be made simultaneously with any notification pursuant to paragraph (c) of this section. If no correspondence address is included in the application, applicant has two months from the filing date to file the basic filing fee, oath or declaration and to pay the surcharge as set forth in § 1.16(e) in order to prevent abandonment of the application; or, if no basic filing fee has been paid, one year from the filing date to pay the processing and retention fee set forth in § 1.21(l) to prevent disposal of the application.

(e) An application for a patent will not be placed upon the files for examination until all its required parts, complying with the rules relating thereto, are received, except that certain minor informalities may be waived subject to subsequent correction whenever required.

(f) The filing date of an international application designating the United States of America shall be treated as the filing date in the United States of America under PCT Article 11(3), except as provided in 35 U.S.C. 102(e).

[Paras. (b) & (c) amended, 54 FR 47518, Nov. 15, 1989, effective Jan. 16, 1990]

37 CFR 1.53 relates to application serial numbers, filing dates and completion of applications. 37 CFR 1.53(a) indicates that a serial number is assigned to any filed application for identification purposes, even if the application is incomplete or informal. 37 CFR 1.53(b) provides that a filing date is assigned to an application as of the date a specification containing a description and claim and any required drawing and the names of all inventors are filed in the Patent and Trademark Office. Failure to meet any of the requirements in 37 CFR 1.53(b) will result in the application being denied a filing date. The filing date to be accorded such an application is the date on which all of the requirements of 37 CFR 1.53(b) are met. Although the filing fee and oath or declaration can be submitted later, no amendments can be made to the specification or drawings which will introduce new matter. This practice is authorized by 35 U.S.C. 111 as amended by Pub. L. 97-247. 37 CFR 1.53(c) provides for notifying applicant of any application incomplete because the specification or drawing is missing and giving the applicant a time period to correct any omission. Applicant will also be notified if all the inventors are not named, such as by the use of "et al.". If the omission is not corrected within the time period given, the application will be returned or otherwise disposed of and a handling fee >set forth in 37 CFR 1.21(n)<** will be retained from any refund of a filing fee. 37 CFR 1.53(d) provides that, where a filing date has been assigned to a filed specification and drawing, the applicant will be notified if a correspondence address has been provided and be given a period of time in which to file the missing fee, oath or declara-

tion and to pay the surcharge due in order to prevent abandonment of the application. The time period usually set is one month from the date of notification by the Patent and Trademark Office, but in no case less than two months after the date of filing of the application. This time period is subject to the provisions of 37 CFR 1.136(a).

If the required basic filing fee is not timely paid, or the processing and retention fee set forth in 37 CFR 1.21(l) is not paid within one year of the date of mailing of the notification, the application will be disposed of. No copies will be provided or certified by the Office of an application which has been disposed of or in which neither the required basic filing fee nor the processing and retention fee has been paid. The notification under 37 CFR 1.53(d) may be made simultaneously with any notification pursuant to paragraph (c) of 37 CFR 1.63. If no correspondence address is included in the application, applicant has two months from the filing date to file the fee, oath or declaration and to pay the surcharge as set forth in 37 CFR 1.16(e) in order to prevent abandonment of the application or one year from the filing date to pay the processing and retention fee set forth in 37 CFR 1.21(l) to prevent disposal of the application. 37 CFR< 1.53(e) indicates that a patent application will not be forwarded for examination on the merits until all required parts have been received. 37 CFR 1.53(f) indicates that international applications filed under the Patent Cooperation Treaty which designate the United States of America are considered to have a United States filing date under PCT Article 11(3), except as provided in 35 U.S.C. 102(e), on the date the requirements of PCT Article 11(1) (i) to (iii) are met.

Effective February 27, 1983, in accordance with the provisions of 35 U.S.C. 111 and 37 CFR 1.53(b), a filing date is granted to an application for patent, which includes at least a specification containing a description pursuant to 37 CFR 1.71 and at least one claim pursuant to 37 CFR 1.75, and any drawing referred to in the specification or required by 37 CFR 1.81(a), which is filed in the Patent and Trademark Office and which names the actual inventor or inventors pursuant to 37 CFR 1.41(a). If an application which has been accorded a filing date does not include the appropriate filing fee or oath or declaration, applicant will be so notified and given a period of time within which to file the missing parts to complete the application and to pay the surcharge as set forth in 37 CFR 1.16(e) in order to prevent abandonment of the application.

Applicants should submit a copy of the notice(s) to file missing parts and the notice(s) of incomplete applications with the response submitted to the Patent and Trademark Office. Applicants should also include the application serial number on all correspondence to the Office. These measures will aid the Office in matching papers to applications, thereby expediting the processing of applications.

In order for the Office to so notify the applicant, a correspondence address must also be provided in the application. The address may be different from the Post Office address of the applicant. For example, the address of applicant's registered attorney or agent may be used as the correspondence address. If applicant fails to provide the Office with a correspondence address, the Office will be unable to provide applicant with notification to complete the application and to pay the surcharge as set forth in 37 CFR 1.16(e). In such a case, applicant will be considered to have constructive notice as of the filing date that the application must be completed and 37 CFR 1.53(d) gives applicant two months from the filing date in which to do so before abandonment occurs. >This time period may be extended pursuant to 37 CFR 1.136.<

The oath or declaration filed in response to such a notice under 37 CFR 1.53(d) must be executed by the inventors named on filing unless a petition for correction of inventorship complying with 37 CFR 1.48 is filed within the time period set.

The oath or declaration filed in response to such a notice must identify the specification and any amendment filed with the specification which is intended to be part of the original disclosure. If an amendment is filed with the oath or declaration filed after the filing date of the application, it may be identified in the oath or declaration but may not include new matter. No new matter may be included after the filing date of the application. See MPEP § 608.04(b). If the oath or declaration improperly refers to an amendment containing new matter, a supplemental oath or declaration will be required pursuant to 37 CFR 1.67(b), deleting the reference to the amendment containing new matter. If an amendment is filed on the same day that the application filed under 37 CFR 1.53 is filed and is referred to in the original oath or declaration filed with or after the application, it constitutes a part of the original application papers and the question of new matter is not considered. Similarly, if the application papers are altered prior to execution of the oath or declaration and the filing of the application, new matter is not a consideration since the alteration is considered as part of the original disclosure.

An amendment which adds additional disclosure filed with a request for a continuation-in-part application under 37 CFR 1.62 is automatically considered a part of the original disclosure of the application by virtue of the rule. Therefore, the oath or declaration filed in such an application must identify the amendment adding additional disclosure as one of the papers which the inventor(s) has "reviewed and understands" in order to comply with 37 CFR 1.63. If the original oath or declaration submitted in a continuation-in-part application filed under 37 CFR 1.62 does not contain a reference to the amendment filed with the request for an application under 37 CFR 1.62, the examiner must require a supplemental oath or declaration referring to the amendment.

37 CFR 1.63 requires that an oath or declaration "identify the specification to which it is directed." Since filing dates are now granted on applications with the oath or declaration being filed later with a surcharge, the question has arisen as to what information must be supplied in the oath or declaration to identify the specification to which it is directed and to comply with the rule.

The declaration form suggested by the Office includes spaces for filling in the names of the inventors, title of invention, application serial number, filing date, foreign priority application information and United States priority application information. While this information should be provided, it is not essential that all of these spaces be filled in in order to adequately identify the specification in compliance with 37 CFR 1.63.

The following combinations of information supplied in an oath or declaration are acceptable as minimums for identifying a specification:

    (1) name of inventor and application serial number;

    (2) name of inventor, attorney docket number which was on the application as filed, and filing date of the application;

    (3) name of inventor, title of invention and filing date;

    (4) name of inventor, title of invention and reference to a specification which is attached to the oath or declaration at the time of execution and filed with the oath or declaration; or

    (5) name of inventor, title of invention and a statement by a registered attorney or agent that the application filed in the PTO is the application which the inventor executed by signing the oath or declaration.

If the oath or declaration is filed with an "attached" specification as indicated in item (4) above, it must be accompanied by a statement that the "attached" specification is a copy of the specification and any amendments thereto which were filed in the Office in order to obtain a filing date for the application. Such statement must be a verified statement if made by a person not registered to practice before the Office.

Oaths or declarations which do not meet the requirements set forth above will not be accepted as complying with 37 CFR 1.63 for completing an application. Any variance from the above guidelines will only be considered upon the filing of a petition for waiver of the rules under 37 CFR 1.183 accompanied by a petition fee (37 CFR 1.17(h)). Supplemental oaths or declarations in accordance with 37 CFR 1.67 will be required in applications in which the oaths or declarations are not completely filled in but contain sufficient information to identify the specifications to which they apply as detailed above.

The periods of time within which applicant must complete the application may be extended under the provisions of 37 CFR 1.136. Applications which are not completed in a timely manner will be abandoned.

The following forms used by Application Branch to notify applicants of defects are reproduced on the following pages. "Notice to File Missing Parts of Application - Filing Date Granted'" form PTO-1533; "Notice to File Missing Parts of Application - No Filing Date "; form PTO-1532, "Notice of Informal Application'" form PTO-152; "Notice of Incomplete Application", form PTO-1123, and "Notice of Incomplete Application filed Pursuant to 37 CFR 1.60'" form PTO-1534.

FIGURE 7.1 *(continued)*

PARTS, FORM AND CONTENT OF APPLICATION   608

incorporated in the notice of allowance. This will be accomplished by placing an "X" in the designated box on the notice of allowance form and entering thereunder the title as changed by the examiner who should initial the face of the file wrapper.

However, if an examiner's amendment must be prepared for other reasons any change in title will be incorporated therein.

Inasmuch as the words "improved", "improvement of" and "improvement in" are not considered as part of the title of an invention, the Patent and Trademark Office does not include these words at the beginning of the title of the invention.

607 Filing Fee [R-14]

**>Patent application filing fees are set in accordance with 35 U.S.C.41 and are listed in 37 CFR 1.16.<

See MPEP § 608.01(n) for multiple dependent claims.
**

When filing an application, a basic fee ** entitles applicant to present 20 claims including not more than 3 claims in independent form. If claims in excess of the above are included at the time of filing, an additional fee ** is required for each independent claim in excess of three, and a * fee >is required< for each claim in excess of *20 claims (whether independent or dependent). **>Fees for a proper multiple dependent claim are calculated based on the numbers of claims to which the multiple dependent claim refers, 37 CFR 1.75(c)< and *>a fee is required< per application containing a proper multiple dependent claim **. For an improper multiple dependent claim>,< the fee **>charged is that charged for a single dependent claim<.

Upon submission of an amendment (whether entered or not) affecting the claims, payment of ** fees is required. **

The Application Branch has been authorized to accept all applications, otherwise acceptable, if the basic fee ** is submitted, and to require payment of the deficiency within a stated period upon notification of the deficiency.

Amendments before the first action, or not filed in response to an Office action, presenting additional claims in excess of the number already paid for, not accompanied by the full additional fee due, will not be entered in whole or in part and applicant will be so advised. Such amendments filed in reply to an Office action will be regarded as not responsive thereto and the practice set forth in MPEP § 714.03 will be followed.

The additional fees, if any, due with an amendment are calculated on the basis of the claims (total and independent) which would be present, if the amendment were entered. The amendment of a claim, unless it changes a dependent claim to an independent claim or adds to the number of claims referred to in a multiple dependent claim>,< and the replacement of a claim by a claim of the same type>,< unless it is a multiple dependent claim which refers to more prior claims, do not require any additional fees.

For purposes of determining the fee due the Patent and Trademark Office, a claim will be treated as dependent if it contains reference to one or more other claims in the application. A claim determined to be dependent by this test will be entered if the fee paid reflects this determination.

Any claim which is in dependent form but which is so worded that it, in fact>,< is not a proper dependent claim, as for example it does not include every limitation of the claim on which it depends, will be required to be canceled as not being a proper dependent claim; and cancellation of any further claim depending on such a dependent claim will be similarly required. The applicant may thereupon amend the claims to place them in proper dependent form, or may redraft them as independent claims, upon payment of any necessary additional fee.

After a requirement for restriction, nonelected claims will be included in determining the fees due in connection with a subsequent amendment unless such claims are canceled.

An amendment canceling claims accompanying the papers constituting the application will be effective to diminish the number of claims to be considered in calculating the filing fees to be paid.

The additional fees, if any, due with an amendment are required prior to any consideration of the amendment by the examiner.

Money paid in connection with the filing of a proposed amendment will not be refunded by reason of the nonentry of the amendment. However, unentered claims will not be counted when calculating the fee due in subsequent amendments. Amendments affecting the claims cannot serve as the basis for granting any refund.

See MPEP § 1415 for reissue application fees.

607.02 Returnability of Fees [R-8]

All questions pertaining to the return of fees are referred to the Refund Section of the Accounting Division of the Office of Finance. No opinions should be expressed to attorneys or applicants as to whether or not fees are returnable in particular cases. >Such questions may also be treated, to the extent appropriate, in decisions on petition decided by various Patent and Trademark Office officials.<

608 Disclosure [R-8]

In return for a patent, the inventor gives as consideration a complete revelation or disclosure of the invention for which protection is sought. All amendments or claims must find basis in the original disclosure, or they involve new matter. Applicant may rely for disclosure upon the specification with original claims and drawings, as filed. See 37 CFR 1.118 and >MPEP< § 608.04.

If during the course of examination of a patent application, an examiner notes the use of language that could be deemed offensive to any race, religion, sex, ethnic group, or nationality, he or she should object to the use of the language as failing to comply with the Rules of Practice. >37 CFR< 1.3 proscribes the presentation of papers which are lacking in decorum and courtesy. There is a further basis for objection in that the inclusion of such proscribed language in a Federal Government publication would not be in the public interest. Also, the inclusion in application drawings of any depictions or caricatures that might reasonably be considered offensive to any group should be similarly objected to, on like authority.

FIGURE 7.1 (*continued*)

The examiner should not pass the application to issue until such language or drawings have been deleted, or questions relating to the propriety thereof fully resolved.

For design application practice see >MPEP< § 1504.

608.01 Specification [R-14]

35 U.S.C. 22. Printing of papers filed.

The Commissioner may require papers filed in the Patent and Trademark Office to be printed or typewritten.

37 CFR 1.71 Detailed description and specification of the invention.

(a) The specification must include a written description of the invention or discovery and of the manner and process of making and using the same, and is required to be in such full, clear, concise, and exact terms as to enable any person skilled in the art or science to which the invention or discovery appertains, or with which it is most nearly connected, to make and use the same.

(b) The specification must set forth the precise invention for which a patent is solicited, in such manner as to distinguish it from other inventions and from what is old. It must describe completely a specific embodiment of the process, machine, manufacture, composition of matter or improvement invented, and must explain the mode of operation or principle whenever applicable. The best mode contemplated by the inventor of carrying out his invention must be set forth.

(c) In the case of an improvement, the specification must particularly point out the part or parts of the process, machine, manufacture, or composition of matter to which the improvement relates, and the description should be confined to the specific improvement and to such parts as necessarily cooperate with it or as may be necessary to a complete understanding or description of it.

>(d) A copyright or mask work notice may be placed in a design or utility patent application adjacent to copyright and mask work material contained therein. The notice may appear at any appropriate portion of the patent application disclosure. For notices in drawings, see § 1.84(o). The content of the notice must be limited to only those elements required by law. For example, "©1983 John Doe"(17 U.S.C. 401) and "*M* John Doe" (17 U.S.C. 909) would be properly limited and, under current statutes, legally sufficient notices of copyright and mask work, respectively. Inclusion of a copyright or mask work notice will be permitted only if the authorization language set forth in paragraph (e) of this section is included at the beginning (preferably as the first paragraph) of the specification.

(e) The authorization shall read as follows:

A portion of the disclosure of this patent document contains material which is subject to {copyright or mask work} protection. The {copyright or mask work} owner has no objection to the facsimile reproduction by anyone of the patent document or the patent disclosure, as it appears in the Patent and Trademark Office patent file or records, but otherwise reserves all {copyright or mask work} rights whatsoever.<

[Paras. (d) & (e) added, Nov. 28, 1988, 53 FR 47808, effective Jan. 1, 1989]

Certain cross notes to other related applications may be made. References to foreign applications or to applications identified only by the attorney's docket number should be required to be cancelled. See 37 CFR 1.78 and MPEP § 202.01.

37 CFR 1.52. Language, paper, writing, margins.

(a) The application, any amendments or corrections thereto, and the oath or declaration must be in the English language except as provided for in § 1.69 and paragraph (d) of this section, or be accompanied by a verified translation of the application and a translation of any corrections or amendments into the English language. All papers which are to become apart of the permanent records of the Patent and Trademark Office must be legibly written, typed, or printed in permanent ink or its equivalent in quality. All of the application papers must be presented in a form having sufficient clarity and contrast between the paper and the writing, typing, or printing thereon to permit the direct production of readily legible copies in any number by use of photographic, electrostatic, photo-offset, and microfilming processes. If the papers are not of the required quality, substitute typewritten or printed papers of suitable quality may be required.

(b) The application papers (specification, including claims, abstract, oath or declaration, and papers as provided for in §§ 1.42, 1.43, 1.47, etc.) and also papers subsequently filed, must be plainly written on but one side of the paper. The size of all sheets of paper should be 8 to 8 1/2 by 10 1/2 to 13 inches (20.3 to 21.6 cm. by 26.6 to 33.0 cm.) A margin of at least approximately 1 inch (2.5 cm.) must be reserved on the left-hand of each page. The top of each page of the application, including claims must have a margin of at least approximately 3/4 inch (2 cm.). The lines must not be crowded too closely together; typewritten lines should be 1 1/2 or double spaced. The pages of the application including claims and abstract should be numbered consecutively, starting with 1, the numbers being centrally located above or preferably, below, the text.

(c) Any interlineation, erasure, * cancellation or other alteration of the application papers filed *>should< be made before the signing of any accompanying oath or declaration pursuant to § 1.63 referring to those application papers and should be dated and initialed or signed by the applicant on the same sheet of paper. **>Application papers containing alterations made after the signing of an oath or declaration referring to those application papers must be supported by a supplemental oath or declaration under § 1.67(c)<. After the signing of the oath or declaration referring to the application papers, amendments may only be made in the manner provided by §§1.121 and 1.123 through 1.125.

(d) An application may be filed in a language other than English. A verified English translation of the non-English language application and the fee set forth in § 1.17(k) are required to be filed with the application or within such time as may be set by the Office.

[Para. (c) amended, Jan. 17, 1992, 57 FR 2021, effective Mar. 16, 1992]

37 CFR 1.58 Chemical and mathematical formulas and tables.

(a) The specification, including the claims, may contain chemical and mathematical formulas, but shall not contain drawings or flow diagrams. The description portion of the specification may contain tables; claims may contain tables only if necessary to conform to 35 U.S.C. 112 or if otherwise found to be desirable.

(b) All tables and chemical and mathematical formulas in the specification, including claims, and amendments thereto, must be on paper which is flexible, strong, white, smooth, nonshiny, and durable, in order to permit use as camera copy when printing any patent which may issue. A good grade of bond paper is acceptable; watermarks should not be prominent. India ink or its equivalent, or solid black typewriter should be used to secure perfectly black solid lines.

(c) To facilitate camera copying when printing, the width of formulas and tables as presented should be limited normally to 5 inches (12.7 cm.) so that it may appear as a single column in the printed patent. If it is not possible to limit the width of a formula or table to 5 inches (12.7 cm.), it is permissible to present the formula or table with a maximum width of 10 3/4 inches (27.3 cm.) and to place it sideways on the sheet. Typewritten characters used in such formulas and tables must be from a block (nonscript) type font or lettering style having capital letters which are at least 0.08 inch (2.1 mm.) high (elite type). Hand lettering must be neat, clean, and have a minimum character

FIGURE 7.1 (continued)

height of 0.08 inch (2.1 mm.). A space at least 1/4 inch (6.4 mm.) high should be provided between complex formulas and tables and the text. Tables should have the lines and columns of data closely spaced to conserve space, consistent with high degree of legibility.

In order that specifications may be expeditiously handled by the Office, page numbers should be placed at the center of the top or bottom of each page. It is a common practice and a commendable one, to consecutively number all the lines or every fifth line of each page. A top margin of at least 3/4 inch should be reserved on each page to prevent possible mutilation of text when the papers are punched for insertion in a file wrapper.

Applicants should make every effort to file patent applications in a form that is clear and reproducible. The Office may accept for filing date purposes papers of reduced quality but will require that acceptable copies be supplied for further processing. Typed, mimeographed, xeroprinted, multigraphed or non-smearing carbon copy forms of reproduction are acceptable.

Legibility includes ability to be photocopied and photomicrographed so that suitable reprints can be made. This requires a high contrast, with black lines and a white background. Gray lines and/or a gray background sharply reduce photo reproduction quality. Legibility of some application papers may become impaired due to abrasion or aging of the printed material during examination and ordinary handling of the file. It may be necessary to require that legible and permanent copies be furnished at later stages after filing, particularly when preparing for issue.

Some of the patent application papers received by the Patent and Trademark Office are copies of the original, ribbon copy. These are acceptable if, in the opinion of the Office, they are legible and permanent.

The paper used must have a surface such that amendments may be written thereon in ink. So-called "Easily Erasable" paper having a special coating so that erasures can be made more easily may not provide a "permanent" copy. 37 CFR 1.52(a). If a light pressure of an ordinary (pencil) eraser removes the imprint, the examiner should, as soon as this becomes evident, notify applicant by use of Form Paragraph 6.32 that it will be necessary for applicant to order a copy of the specification and claims to be made by the Patent and Trademark Office at the applicant's expense for incorporation in the file. It is not necessary to return this copy to applicant for signature.

¶ 6.32 Application on easily erasable paper
The application papers are objected to because they are not a permanent copy as required by 37 CFR 1.52(a). Reference is made to [1].

Applicant is required either (1) to submit permanent copies of the identified parts or (2) to order a photocopy of the above identified parts to be made by the Patent and Trademark Office at applicant's expense for incorporation in the file. See MPEP 608.01.

Examiner Note:
In the "bracket" identify, 1) all of the specification; 2) pages of the specification; 3) claims; 4) oath, declaration; 5) etc.

See In re Benson, 1959 C.D. 5; 744 O.G. 353. Reproductions

prepared by heat-sensitive, hectographic or spirit duplication processes are also not satisfactory.

The specification is sometimes in such faulty English that a new specification is necessary, but new specifications encumber the record and require additional reading, and hence should not be required or accepted unless it is clear to the examiner that acceptance of a substitute specification would facilitate processing of the application. See 37 CFR 1.125.

Form Paragraph 7.29 may be used where the disclosure contains informalities.

¶ 7.29 Disclosure Objected to, Minor Informalities
The disclosure is objected to because of the following informalities: [1] Appropriate correction is required.

Examiner Note:
Use this paragraph to point out minor informalities such as spelling errors, inconsistent terminology, numbering of elements, etc., which should be corrected. See paragraphs 6.28 to 6.32 for specific informalities.

The specification does not require a date.

If a newly filed application obviously fails to disclose an invention with the clarity required by 35 U.S.C. 112, revision of the application should be required. See MPEP § 702.01.

As the specification is never returned to applicant under any circumstances, the applicant should retain a line for line copy thereof, each line, preferably, having been consecutively numbered on each page. In amending, the attorney or the applicant requests insertions, cancellations, or alterations, giving the page and the line.

37 CFR 1.52(c) relating to interlineations and other alterations is strictly enforced. See In re Swanberg, 129 USPQ 364.

Form Paragraphs 6.29-6.31 should be used where appropriate.

¶ 6.29 Specification, Spacing of Lines
The spacing of the lines of the specification is such as to make reading and entry of amendments difficult. New application papers with lines double spaced on good quality paper are required.

¶ 6.30 Numerous Grammatical Errors
The specification is replete with grammatical and idiomatic errors too numerous to mention specifically. The specification should be revised carefully. Examples of such errors are: [1].

¶ 6.31 Lengthy Specification, Jumbo Case
The lengthy specification has not been checked to the extent necessary to determine the presence of all possible minor errors. Applicant's cooperation is requested in correcting any errors of which applicant may become aware in the specification.

Examiner Note:
This paragraph is applicable in so-called "Jumbo cases".

USE OF METRIC SYSTEM OF MEASUREMENTS IN PATENT APPLICATIONS

In order to minimize the necessity in the future for converting dimensions given in the English system of measurements to

Rev. 14, Nov. 1992

107

FIGURE 7.1 (continued)

the metric system of measurements when using printed patents as research and prior art search documents, all patent applicants are strongly encouraged to use *either* (1) only metric (S.I.) units, or (2) English units together with their metric system equivalents* when describing their inventions in the specifications of patent applications. This practice, however, is not being made mandatory at this time.

The initials S.I. stand for "Systeme International d'Unites", the French name for the International System of Units, a modernized metric system adopted in 1960 by the International General Conference of Weights and Measures based on precise unit measurements made possible by modern technology.

FILING OF NON-ENGLISH LANGUAGE APPLICATIONS

37 CFR 1.52 Language, Paper, Writing, Margins.
*****

(d) An application may be filed in a language other than English. A verified English translation of the non-English language application and the fee set forth in § 1.17(k) are required to be filed with the application or within such time as may be set by the Office.

The Patent and Trademark Office will accord a filing date to an application meeting the requirements of 35 U.S.C. 111 even though some or all of the application papers, including the written description and the claims, is in a language other than English and hence does not comply with 37 CFR 1.52.

A verified English translation of the non-English language papers, the filing fee, the oath or declaration and fee set forth in 37 CFR 1.17(k) should either accompany the application papers or be filed in the Office within the time set by the Office.

A subsequently filed verified English translation must contain the complete identifying data for the application in order to permit prompt association with the papers initially filed. Accordingly, it is strongly recommended that the original application papers be accompanied by a cover letter and a self-addressed return post card, each containing the following identifying data in English: (a) applicant's name(s); (b) title of invention; (c) number of pages of specification, claims, and sheets of drawings; (d) whether oath or declaration was filed and (e) amount and manner of paying the filing fee.

The translation must be a literal translation verified as such by the translator, and must be accompanied by a signed request from the applicant, his or her attorney or agent, asking that the verified English translation be used as the copy for examination purposes in the Office. If the verified English translation does not conform to idiomatic English and United States practice it should be accompanied by a preliminary amendment making the necessary changes without the introduction of new matter prohibited by 35 U.S.C. 132. In the event the verified literal translation is not timely filed in the Office>,< the application will be regarded as abandoned.

It should be recognized that this practice is intended for emergency situations to prevent loss of valuable rights and should not be routinely used for filing applications. There are at least two reasons why this should not be used on a routine basis. First, there are obvious dangers to applicant and the public if he >or she< fails to obtain a correct literal translation. Second, the filing of a large number of applications under the procedure will create significant administrative burdens on the Office.

ILLUSTRATIONS IN THE SPECIFICATION

Graphical illustrations, diagrammatic views, flow charts and diagrams in the descriptive portion of the specification do not come within the purview of 37 CFR 1.58(a), which permits tables and chemical formulas in the specification in lieu of formal drawings. The examiner should object to such descriptive illustrations in the specification and request formal drawings in accordance with 37 CFR 1.81 when an application contains graphs in the specification.

Since the December 7, 1976 issue of patents, all tables and mathematical equations and chemical formulas, or portions thereof, have been reproduced for printing by a computer process developed by the Data Base Contractor. Those portions of chemical formulas which cannot be reproduced by the process, such as dotted, curved, broken and *>wedge-shaped< lines, must be drawn by hand on the photocomposed page. There are, however, some chemical structures which cannot be reproduced because they are either too complex or involve too many lines which cannot be generated by the computer process. The camera copy process, which is used to insert these types of structures onto the printed patent page, is both time consuming and costly to the Office. Because of the reduction factor and failure to comply with the guidelines set forth in 37 CFR 1.58 (a) and (b), the reproduction of these structures is often poor.

Therefore, the specification, including the claims, may contain chemical formulas and mathematical equations, but should not contain drawings or flow diagrams or diagrammatic views of chemical structures. The description portion of the specification may contain tables; claims may contain tables only if necessary to conform to 35 U.S.C. 112.

APPLICATION FILED WITHOUT ALL PAGES OF SPECIFICATION

Applications filed without all pages of the specification are not given a filing date since they are "prima facie" incomplete. The filing date is the date on which the omitted pages are filed. If the oath or declaration for the application was filed prior to the submission of all pages of specification, the submission of any omitted pages must be accompanied by a supplemental oath or declaration referring to the specification originally deposited, as amended to include the pages originally omitted. If the oath or declaration for the application was not filed prior to the submission of the omitted pages, the oath or declaration, when filed>,< must include a specific reference to the pages originally omitted. If any applicant believes that the omitted pages of the application are not necessary for an understanding of the subject matter sought to be patented, applicant may petition to have the application accepted without the omitted pages. Any petition must be accompanied by the petition fee (37 CFR 1.17(h)) and an amendment canceling from the specification all incomplete sentences and any claims which depend upon the omitted pages

FIGURE 7.1 *(continued)*

for disclosure and support and renumbering the pages present in consecutive order. Also, if the oath or declaration for the application was filed prior to the date of the amendment and petition, the amendment must be accompanied by a supplemental declaration by the applicant stating that the invention is adequately disclosed in, and a desire to rely on, the application as thus amended for purposes of an original disclosure and filing date. If the oath or declaration for the application was not filed prior to the date of the petition and amendment, the oath or declaration>,< when filed, must include a specific reference to the amendment cancelling from the specification all incomplete sentences and any claims which depend upon the omitted pages for disclosure and support. The petition requesting that the application be accepted without the omitted pages should be directed to the Office of the Assistant Commissioner for Patents and request relief under 37 CFR 1.182.

APPLICATION FILED WITHOUT AT LEAST ONE CLAIM

35 U.S.C. 111 requires that an application for patent should include, inter alia, "a specification as prescribed by section 112 of this title". Section 112 states that "The specification shall contain a written description...and...shall conclude with one or more claims..." Also, the CAFC stated in *Litton Systems, Inc. v. Whirlpool*, 221 USPQ 97, 105 (Fed. Cir. 1984) that:

"Both statute, 35 U.S.C. §111, and federal regulations, 37 CFR § 1.51, make clear the requirement that an application for a patent must include (1) a specification and claims,..." (emphasis original)

Therefore, a claim is clearly a statutory requirement for according a filing date to an application. 35 U.S.C. 171 makes 35 U.S.C. 112 applicable to design applications. Also, 35 U.S.C. 162 requires the specification in a plant patent application to contain a claim. Thus, any application filed without at least one claim is incomplete and not entitled to a filing date. If the application does not contain at least one claim, a "Notice of Incomplete Application" (form PTO-1123) will be mailed to the applicant(s) indicating that no filing date has been granted and setting a period for submitting a claim. The filing date will be the date of receipt of at least one claim. See *In re Mattson*, 208 USPQ 168 (Comm'r Pats 1980).

608.01(a) Arrangement of Application [R-14]

37 CFR 1.77 Arrangement of application elements.

The elements of the application should appear in the following order:

(a) Title of the invention; or an introductory portion stating the name, citizenship, and residence of the applicant, and the title of the invention may be used.

(b) (Reserved).

(c) (1) Cross-reference to related applications, if any.

(2) Reference to a "microfiche appendix" if any. (See § 1.96(b)). The total number of microfiche and total number of frames should be specified.

(d) Brief summary of the invention.

(e) Brief description of the several views of the drawing, if there are drawings.

(f) Detailed description.

(g) Claim or claims.

(h) Abstract of the disclosure.

(i) Signed oath or declaration.

(j) Drawings.

NOTE

Design patent specification, MPEP § 1503.01.

Plant patent specification, MPEP § 1605.

Reissue patent specification, MPEP § 1411.

The following order of arrangement is preferable in framing the specification and, except for the title of the invention, each of the lettered items should be preceded by the headings indicated.

(a) Title of the Invention.

(b) Cross-References to Related Applications (if any).

(c) Background of the Invention.

1. Field of the Invention.

2. Description of the related art including information disclosed under 37 CFR 1.97**>and 1.98<.

(d) Summary of the Invention.

(e) Brief Description of the Drawing.

(f) Description of the Preferred Embodiment(s).

(g) Claim(s).

(h) Abstract of the Disclosure.

Applicant (typically a pro se) may be advised of the proper arrangement by using Form Paragraph 6.01 or 6.02.

¶ 6.01 *Arrangement of Specification*

The following guidelines illustrate the preferred layout and content for patent applications. These guidelines are suggested for the applicant's use.

Arrangement of the Specification

The following order or arrangement is preferred in framing the specification and, except for the title of the invention, each of the lettered items should be preceded by the headings indicated below.

(a) Title of the Invention.

(b) Cross-References to Related Applications (if any).

(c) Statement as to rights to inventions made under Federally-sponsored research and development (if any).

(d) Background of the Invention.

1. Field of the Invention.

2. Description of related art including information disclosed under 37 CFR §§ 1.97**> and 1.98<.

(e) Summary of the Invention.

(f) Brief Description of the Drawing.

(g) Description of the Preferred Embodiment(s).

(h) Claim(s).

(i) Abstract of the Disclosure.

Examiner Note:

In this paragraph an introductory sentence will be necessary.

This paragraph intended primarily for use in Pro Se applications.

¶ 6.02 *Content of Specification*

Content of Specification

(a) Title of the Invention. (See 37 CFR § 1.72(a)). The title of the invention should be placed at the top of the first page of the specifica-

FIGURE 7.1 (*continued*)

tion. It should be brief but technically accurate and descriptive, preferably from two to seven words.

(b) Cross-References to Related Applications: See 37 CFR 1.78 and § 201.11 MPEP.

(c) Statement as to rights to inventions made under Federally sponsored research and development (if any): see § 310 MPEP.

(d) Background of the Invention: The specification should set forth the Background of the Invention in two parts:

(1) Field of the Invention: A statement of the field of art to which the invention pertains. This statement may include a paraphrasing of the applicable U.S. patent classification definitions or the subject matter of the claimed invention. This item may also be titled "Technical Field".

(2) Description of the Related Art: A description of the related art known to the applicant and including, if applicable, references to specific art related and problems involved in the prior art which are solved by the applicant's invention. This item may also be titled "Background Art".

(e) Summary: A brief summary or general statement of the invention as set forth in 37 CFR § 1.73. The summary is separate and distinct from the abstract and is directed toward the invention rather than the disclosure as a whole. The summary may point out the advantages of the invention or how it solves problems previously existent in the prior art (and preferably indicated in the Background of the Invention). In chemical cases it should point out in general terms the utility of the invention. If possible, the nature and gist of the invention or the inventive concept should be set forth. Objects of the invention should be treated briefly and only to the extent that they contribute to an understanding of the invention.

(f) Brief Description of the Drawing(s): A reference to and brief description of the drawings(s) as set forth in 37 CFR § 1.74.

(g) Description of the Preferred Embodiment(s): A description of the preferred embodiment(s) of the invention as required in 37 CFR § 1.71. The description should be as short and specific as is necessary to describe the invention adequately and accurately.

This item may also be titled "Best Mode for Carrying Out the Invention". Where elements or groups of elements, compounds, and processes, which are conventional and generally widely known in the field of the invention described and their exact nature or type is not necessary for an understanding and use of the invention by a person skilled in the art, they should not be described in detail. However, where particularly complicated subject matter is involved or where the elements, compounds, or processes may not be commonly or widely known in the field, the speculation should refer to another patent or readily available publication which adequately describes the subject matter.

(h) Claim(s) (See 37 CFR 1.75) A claim may be typed with the various elements subdivided in paragraph form. There may be plural indentations to further segregate subcombinations or related steps.

(i) Abstract: A brief narrative of the disclosure as a whole in a single paragraph of 250 words or less.

Examiner Note:

In this paragraph an introductory sentence will be necessary.

This paragraph is intended primarily for use in Pro Se applications. See also "pro se" from paragraphs in Chapter 1700 of the Manual of Patent Examining Form Paragraphs.

608.01(b)   Abstract of the Disclosure [R-14]

37 CFR 1.72. Title and abstract.*

*****

(b) A brief abstract of the technical disclosure in the specification must be set forth on a separate sheet, preferably following the claims under the heading "Abstract of the Disclosure". The purpose of the abstract is to enable the Patent and Trademark Office and the public generally to determine quickly from a cursory inspection the nature and gist of the technical disclosure. The abstract shall not be used for interpreting the scope of the claims.

In all cases which lack an abstract, the examiner in the first Office action should require the submission of an abstract directed to the technical disclosure in the specification. See Form Paragraph 6.12 (below). Applicants may use either "Abstract" or "Abstract of the Disclosure" as a heading.

If the abstract contained in the application does not comply with the guidelines, the examiner should point out the defect to the applicant in the first Office action, or at the earliest point in the prosecution that the defect is noted, and require compliance with the guidelines. Since the abstract of the disclosure has been interpreted to be a part of the specification for the purpose of compliance with paragraph 1 of 35 U.S.C. 112 (*In re Armbruster*, 512 F2d 676, 185 USPQ 152 (CCPA, 1975)), it would ordinarily be preferable that the applicant make the necessary changes to the abstract to bring it into compliance with the guidelines. See Form Paragraphs 6.13-6.16 (below).

Responses to such actions requiring either a new abstract or amendment to bring the abstract into compliance with the guidelines should be treated under 37 CFR 1.111(b) practice like any other formal matter. Any submission of a new abstract or amendment to an existing abstract should be carefully reviewed for introduction of new matter, 35 U.S.C. 132, MPEP § 608.04.

Upon passing the case to issue, the examiner should see that the abstract is an adequate and clear statement of the contents of the disclosure and generally in line with the guidelines. The abstract shall be changed by the examiner's amendment in those instances where deemed necessary. This authority and responsibility of the examiner shall not be abridged by the desirability of having the applicant make the necessary corrections. For example, if the application is otherwise in condition for allowance except that the abstract does not comply with the guidelines, the examiner generally should make any necessary revisions by examiner's amendment rather than issuing an *Ex parte Quayle* action requiring applicant to make the necessary revisions.

Under current practice, in all instances where the application contains an abstract when sent to issue, the abstract will be printed on the patent.

GUIDELINES FOR THE PREPARATION OF PATENT ABSTRACTS

Background

The Rules of Practice in Patent Cases require that each application for patent include an abstract of the disclosure, 37 CFR 1.72(b).

The content of a patent abstract should be such as to enable the reader thereof, regardless of his degree of familiarity with patent documents, to ascertain quickly the character of the

FIGURE 7.1 (continued)

subject matter covered by the technical disclosure and should include that which is new in the art to which the invention pertains.

The abstract is not intended nor designated for use in interpreting the scope or meaning of the claims, 37 CFR 1.72(b).

Content

A patent abstract is a concise statement of the technical disclosure of the patent and should include that which is new in the art to which the invention pertains.

If the patent is of a basic nature, the entire technical disclosure may be new in the art, and the abstract should be directed to the entire disclosure.

If the patent is in the nature of an improvement in old apparatus, process, product, or composition, the abstract should include the technical disclosure of the improvement.

In certain patents, particularly those for compounds and compositions, wherein the process for making and/or the use thereof are not obvious, the abstract should set forth a process for making and/or a use thereof.

If the new technical disclosure involves modifications or alternatives, the abstract should mention by way of example the preferred modification or alternative.

The abstract should not refer to purported merits or speculative applications of the invention and should not compare the invention with the prior art.

Where applicable, the abstract should include the following: (1) if a machine or apparatus, its organization and operation; (2) if an article, its method of making; (3) if a chemical compound, its identity and use; (4) if a mixture, its ingredients: (5) if a process, the steps. Extensive mechanical and design details of apparatus should not be given.

With regard particularly to chemical patents, for compounds or compositions, the general nature of the compound or composition should be given as well as the use thereof, e.g., "The compounds are of the class of alkyl benzene sulfonyl ureas, useful as oral anti-diabetics." Exemplification of a species could be illustrative of members of the class. For processes, the type reaction, reagents and process conditions should be stated, generally illustrated by a single example unless variations are necessary.

Language and Format

The abstract should be in narrative form and generally limited to a single paragraph within the range of 50 to 250 words. **>The< abstract >should<not exceed >25 lines of text. Abstracts exceeding 25 lines of text should be checked to see that it does not exceed< 250 words in length since the space provided for the abstract on the computer tape by the printer is limited. If the abstract cannot be placed on the computer tape because of its excessive length, the application will be returned to the examiner for preparation of a shorter abstract. The form and legal phraseology often used in patent claims, such as "means" and "said," should be avoided. The abstract should sufficiently describe the disclosure to assist readers in deciding whether

there is a need for consulting the full patent text for details.

The language should be clear and concise and should not repeat information given in the title. It should avoid using phrases which can be implied, such as, "This disclosure concerns," "The disclosure defined by this invention," "This disclosure describes," etc.

Responsibility

Preparation of the abstract is the responsibility of the applicant. Background knowledge of the art and an appreciation of the applicant's contribution to the art are most important in the preparation of the abstract. The review of the abstract, for compliance with these guidelines, with any necessary editing and revision on allowance of the application is the responsibility of the examiner.

Sample Abstracts

(1) A heart valve which has an annular valve body defining an orifice and a plurality of struts forming a pair of cages on opposite sides of the orifice. A spherical closure member is captively held within the cages and is moved by blood flow between open and closed positions in check valve fashion. A slight leak or backflow is provided in the closed position by making the orifice slightly larger than the closure member. Blood flow is maximized in the open position of the valve by providing an inwardly convex contour on the orifice-defining surfaces of the body. An annular rib is formed in a channel around the periphery of the valve body to anchor a suture ring used to secure the valve within a heart.

(2) A method for sealing whereby heat is applied to seal, overlapping closure panels of a folding box made from paperboard having an extremely thin coating of moisture-proofing thermoplastic material on opposite surfaces. Heated air is directed at the surfaces to be bonded, the temperature of the air at the point of impact on the surfaces being above the char point of the board. The duration of application of heat is made so brief, by a corresponding high rate of advance of the boxes through the air stream, that the coating on the reverse side of the panels remains substantially non-tacky. The bond is formed immediately after heating within a period of time for any one surface point less than the total time of exposure to heated air of that point. Under such conditions the heat applied to soften the thermoplastic coating is dissipated after completion of the bond by absorption into the board acting as a heat sink without the need for cooling devices.

(3) Amides are produced by reacting an ester of a carboxylic acid with an amine, using as catalyst an alkoxide of an alkali metal. The ester is first heated to at least 75° C. under a pressure of no more than 500 mm. of mercury to remove moisture and acid gases which would prevent the reaction, and then converted to an amide without heating to initiate the reaction.

¶ 6.12 Abstract Missing (Background)

This application does not contain an Abstract of the Disclosure as required by 37 CFR 1.72(b). An abstract on a separate sheet is required.

Examiner Note:

For Pro Se applicant consider form paragraphs 6.14 - 6.16.

FIGURE 7.1 (continued)

¶ 6.13 Abstract Objected to: Minor Informalities

The Abstract of the Disclosure is objected to because [1]. Correction is required. See MPEP 608.01(b).

Examiner Note:

In bracket 1, indicate the informalities that should be corrected. Use this paragraph for minor informalities such as the inclusion of legal phraseology, undue length, etc.

¶ 6.14 Abstract of the Disclosure: Content

Applicant is reminded of the proper content of an Abstract of the Disclosure.

A patent abstract is a concise statement of the technical disclosure of the patent and should include that which is new in the art to which the invention pertains.

If the patent is of a basic nature, the entire technical disclosure may be new in the art, and the abstract should be directed to the entire disclosure.

If the patent is in the nature of an improvement in an old apparatus, process, product or composition, the abstract should include the technical disclosure of the improvement.

In certain patents, particularly those for compounds and compositions, wherein the process for making and/or the use thereof are not obvious, the abstract should set forth a process for making and/or use thereof.

If the new technical disclosure involves modifications or alternatives, the abstract should mention by way of example the preferred modification or alternative.

The abstract should not refer to purported merits or speculative applications of the invention and should not compare the invention with the prior art.

Where applicable, the abstract should include the following: (1) if a machine or apparatus, its organization and operation; (2) if an article, its method of making; (3) if a chemical compound, its identity and use; (4) if a mixture, its ingredients; (5) if a process, the steps. Extensive mechanical and design details of apparatus should not be given.

Examiner Note:

See paragraph 6.16.

¶ 6.15 Abstract of the Disclosure, Chemical Cases

Applicant is reminded of the proper content of an Abstract of the Disclosure.

In chemical patent abstracts, compounds or compositions, the general nature of the compound or composition should be given as well as its use, e.g., "The compounds are of the class of alkyl benzene sulfonyl ureas, useful as oral anti-diabetics." Exemplification of a species could be illustrative of members of the class. For processes, the type reaction, reagents and process conditions should be stated, generally illustrated by a single example unless variations are necessary. Complete revision of the content of the abstract is required on a separate sheet.

¶ 6.16 Abstract of the Disclosure, Language

Applicant is reminded of the proper language and format of an Abstract of the Disclosure.

The abstract should be in narrative form and generally limited to a single paragraph on a separate sheet within the range of 50 to 250 words. It is important that the abstract not exceed 250 words in length since the space provided for the abstract on the computer tape used by the printer is limited. The form and legal phraseology often used in patent claims, such as "means" and "said", should be avoided. The abstract should describe the disclosure sufficiently to assist readers in

deciding whether there is a need for consulting the full patent text for details.

The language should be clear and concise and should not repeat information given in the title. It should avoid using phrases which can be implied, such as, "The disclosure concerns," "The disclosure defined by this invention," "The disclosure describes," etc.

Examiner Note:

See also paragraph 6.14.

608.01(c) Background of the Invention [R-14]

The Background of the Invention ordinarily comprises two parts:

(1) Field of the Invention: A statement of the field of art to which the invention pertains. This statement may include a paraphrasing of the applicable U.S. patent classification definitions. The statement should be directed to the subject matter of the claimed invention.

(2) Description of the related art including information disclosed under 37 CFR 1.97 **>and 1.98<: A paragraph(s) describing to the extent practical the state of the prior art or other information disclosed known to the applicant, including references to specific prior art or other information where appropriate. Where applicable, the problems involved in the prior art or other information disclosed which are solved by the applicant's invention should be indicated. See also MPEP §§ 608.01(a), 608.01(p) and 707.05(b).

608.01(d) Brief Summary of Invention [R-8]

37 CFR 1.73 Summary of the invention.

A brief summary of the invention indicating its nature and substance, which may include a statement of the object of the invention, should precede the detailed description. Such summary should, when set forth, be commensurate with the invention as claimed and any object recited should be that of the invention as claimed.

Since the purpose of the brief summary of invention is to apprise the public, and more especially those interested in the particular art to which the invention relates, of the nature of the invention, the summary should be directed to the specific invention being claimed, in contradistinction to mere generalities which would be equally applicable to numerous preceding patents. That is, the subject matter of the invention should be described in one or more clear, concise sentences or paragraphs. Stereotyped general statements that would fit one case as well as another serve no useful purpose and may well be required to be canceled as surplusage, and, in the absence of any illuminating statement, replaced by statements that are directly in point as applicable exclusively to the case in hand.

The brief summary, if properly written to set out the exact nature, operation and purpose of the invention, will be of material assistance in aiding ready understanding of the patent in future searches. See >MPEP< § 905.04. The brief summary should be more than a mere statement of the objects of the

FIGURE 7.1 (*continued*)

PARTS, FORM AND CONTENT OF APPLICATION   608.01(g)

invention, which statement is also permissible under 37 CFR 1.73.

The brief summary of invention should be consistent with the subject matter of the claims. Note final review of application and preparation for issue, >MPEP< § 1302.

608.01(e) Reservation Clauses Not Permitted

37 CFR 1.79 Reservation clauses not permitted.

A reservation for a future application of subject matter disclosed but not claimed in a pending application will not be permitted in the pending application, but an application disclosing unclaimed subject matter may contain a reference to a later filed application of the same applicant or owned by a common assignee disclosing and claiming that subject matter.

608.01(f) Brief Description of Drawings [R-14]

37 CFR 1.74 Reference to drawings.

When there are drawings, there shall be a brief description of the several views of the drawings and the detailed description of the invention shall refer to the different views by specifying the numbers of the figures, and to the different parts by use of reference letters or numerals (preferably the latter).

Application Branch will review the specification, including the brief description>,< prior to assigning a filing date to the application to *>ensure< that all figures of drawings described in the specification are present. If the specification describes a figure which is not present in the drawings, Application Branch will mail a "Notice of Incomplete Application" >(<form PTO-1123), MPEP § 601.01, stating that the filing date of the application will be the date of receipt of the omitted figures. Therefore, it is important that all figures of drawings be correctly labelled and described in the brief description and elsewhere in the specification. See also, MPEP § 608.02.

The examiner should see to it that the figures are correctly described in the brief description of the drawing, that all section lines used are referred to, and that all needed section lines are used.

608.01(g) Detailed Description of Invention [R-14]

A detailed description of the invention and drawings follows the general statement of invention and brief description of the drawings. This detailed description, required by 37 CFR 1.71, MPEP § 608.01, must be in such particularity as to enable any person skilled in the pertinent art or science to make and use the invention without involving extensive experimentation. An applicant is ordinarily permitted to use his or her own terminology, as long as it can be understood. Necessary grammatical corrections, however, should be required by the examiner, but it must be remembered that an examination is not made for the purpose of securing grammatical perfection.

The reference characters must be properly applied, no single reference character being used for two different parts or for a given part and a modification of such part. In the latter case, the reference character, applied to the "given part," with a prime affixed may advantageously be applied to the modification. Every feature specified in the claims must be illustrated, but there should be no superfluous illustrations.

The description is a dictionary for the claims and should provide clear support or antecedent basis for all terms used in the claims. See 37 CFR 1.75, MPEP *§ 608.01(i), >§< 608.01(o), and >§< 1302.01.

NOTE. — Completeness, MPEP § 608.01(p).

USE OF SYMBOL "Phi" IN PATENT APPLICATION

The Greek letter Phi has long been used as a symbol in equations in all technical disciplines. It further has special uses which include the indication of an electrical phase or clocking signal as well as an angular measurement. The recognized symbols for the upper and lower case Greek Phi characters, however, do not appear* on most typewriters. This apparently has led to the use of a symbol composed by first striking a zero key and then backspacing and striking the "cancel" or "slash" key to result in Ø>,< an approximation of accepted symbols for the Greek character Phi. In other instances the symbol is composed using the upper or lower case letter "O" with the "cancel" or "slash" superimposed thereon by backspacing or is simply handwritten in a variety of styles. These expedients result in confusion because of the variety of type sizes and styles available on modern typewriters.

In recent years, the growth of data processing has seen the increasing use of this symbol ("O") as the standard representation of zero. The "slashed" or "cancelled zero" is used to indicate zero and avoid confusion with the upper case letter "O" in both text and drawings.

Thus, when the symbol "Ø" in one of its many variations, as discussed above, appears in patent applications being prepared for printing, confusion as to the intended meaning of the symbol arises. Those (such as examiners, attorneys, and applicants) working in the art can usually determine the intended meaning of this symbol because of their knowledge of the subject matter involved, but editors preparing these applications for printing have no such specialized knowledge and confusion arises as to which symbol to print. The result, at the very least, is delay until the intended meaning of the symbol can be ascertained.

Since the Office does not have the resources to conduct a technical editorial review of each application before printing, and in order to eliminate the problem of printing delays associated with the usage of these symbols, any question about the intended symbol will be resolved by the editorial staff of the Office of Publications by printing the symbol "ø" whenever that symbol is used by the applicant. Any Certificate of Correction necessitated by the above practice will be at the patentee's expense (37 CFR 1.323) because the intended symbol was not accurately presented by the Greek upper or lower case Phi letters (Ø, ø) in the patent application.

FIGURE 7.1 *(continued)*

608.01(h)   Mode of Operation of Invention [R-8]

The best mode contemplated by the inventor of carrying out his >or her< invention must be set forth in the description. >see 35 U.S.C. 112. There is no statutory requirement for the disclosure of a specific example. A patent specification is not intended nor required to be a production specification. *In re Gay*, 309 F2d 768, 135 USPQ 311 (CCPA 1962). The absence of a specific working example is not necessarily evidence that the best mode has not been disclosed, nor is the presence of one evidence that it has. *In re Honn*, 364 F2d 454, 150 USPQ 652 (CCPA 1966). In determining the adequacy of a best mode disclosure, only evidence of concealment (accidental or intentional) is to be considered. That evidence must tend to show that the quality of an applicant's best mode disclosure is so poor as to effectively result in concealment. *In re Sherwood*, 204 USPQ 537 (CCPA 1980).<**

The question of whether an inventor has or has not disclosed what he or she feels is his or her best mode is a question separate and distinct from the question of sufficiency of the disclosure, *In re Gay*, 135 USPQ 311 (CCPA 1962); *In re Glass*, 181 USPQ 31 (CCPA 1974). See 35 U.S.C. 112 and 37 CFR 1.71(b). *Sylgab Steel & Wire Corp. v. Imoco-Gateway Corp.*, 357 F. Supp. 657, 178 USPQ 22 (N.D. Ill. 1973); *H. K. Porter Co., Inc. v. Gates Rubber Co.*, 187 USPQ 692, 708, (D. Colo. 1975).**

>If the best mode contemplated by the inventor at the time of filing the application is not disclosed, such defect cannot be cured by submitting an amendment seeking to put into the specification something required to be there when the application was originally filed. *In re Hay*, 534 F2d 917, 189 USPQ 790 (CCPA 1976). Any proposed amendment of this type should be treated as new matter.<

Patents have been held invalid in cases where the patentee did not disclose the best mode known to him. See *Flick-Reedy Corp. v. Hydro-Line Manufacturing Co.*, 351 F.2d 546, 146 USPQ 694 (CA 7 1965), cert. denied, 383 U.S. 958, 148 USPQ 771 (1966); *Indiana General Corp. v. Krystinel Corp.*. 297 F. Supp. 427. 161 USPQ 82 (S.D.N.Y. 1969), affirmed, 421 F.2d 1033, 164 USPQ 321 (CA 2 1970); *Dale Electronics, Inc. v. R.C.L. Electronics, Inc.*, 488 F.2d 382, 180 USPQ 235 (CA 1 1973); *Union Carbide Corp. v. Borg-Warner Corp.*, 550 F.2d 355, 193 USPQ 1 (CA 6 1977); *Reynolds Metals Co. v. Acorn Building Components Inc.*, 548 F.2d 155, 163, 192 USPQ 737 (CA 6 1977).

NOTE. — Completeness, >MPEP< § 608.01(p).

608.01(i)   Claims [R-8]

37 CFR 1.75 Claim(s).

(a) The specification must conclude with a claim particularly pointing out and distinctly claiming the subject matter which the applicant regards as his invention or discovery.

(b) More than one claim may be presented provided they differ substantially from each other and are not unduly multiplied.

(c) One or more claims may be presented in dependent form, referring back to and further limiting another claim or claims in the same application. Any dependent claim which refers to more than one other claim ("multiple dependent claim") shall refer to such other claims in the alternative only. A multiple dependent claim shall not serve as a basis for any other multiple dependent claim. For fee calculation purposes under § 1.16, a multiple dependent claim will be considered to be that number of claims to which direct reference is made therein. For fee calculation purposes, also, any claim depending from a multiple dependent claim will be considered to be that number of claims to which direct reference is made in that multiple dependent claim. In addition to the other filing fees, any original application which is filed with, or is amended to include, multiple dependent claims must have paid therein the fee set forth in § 1.16(d). Claims in dependent form shall be construed to include all the limitations of the claim incorporated by reference into the dependent claim. A multiple dependent claim shall be construed to incorporate by reference all the limitations of each of the particular claims in relation to which it is being considered.

(d)(1) The claim or claims must conform to the invention as set forth in the remainder of the specification and the terms and phrases used in the claims must find clear support or antecedent basis in the description so that the meaning of the terms in the claims may be ascertainable by reference to the description. (See § 1.58(a).)

(2) See §§ 1.141 to 1.146 as to claiming different inventions in one application.

(e) Where the nature of the case admits, as in the case of an improvement, any independent claim should contain in the following order, (1) a preamble comprising a general description of all the elements or steps of the claimed combination which are conventional or known, (2) a phrase such as "wherein the improvement comprises," and (3) those elements, steps and/or relationships which constitute that portion of the claimed combination which the applicant considers as the new or improved portion.

(f) If there are several claims, they shall be numbered consecutively in Arabic numerals.

(g) All dependent claims should be grouped together with the claim or claims to which they refer to the extent possible.

NOTE

Numbering of Claims, >MPEP< § 608.01(j).
Form of Claims, >MPEP< § 608.01(m).
Dependent claims, >MPEP< § 608.01(n).
Examination of claims, >MPEP< § 706.
Claims in excess of fee, >MPEP< § 714.10.

608.01(j)   Numbering of Claims

37 CFR 1.126 Numbering of claims.

The original numbering of the claims must be preserved throughout the prosecution. When claims are canceled, the remaining claims must not be renumbered. When claims are added, except when presented in accordance with § 1.121(b), they must be numbered by the applicant consecutively beginning with the number next following the highest numbered claim previously presented (whether entered or not). When the application is ready for allowance, the examiner, if necessary, will renumber the claims consecutively in the order in which they appear or in such order as may have been requested by applicant.

In a single claim case, the claim is not numbered. Form Paragraph 6.17 may be used to notify applicant.

FIGURE 7.1 *(continued)*

¶ 6.17 Numbering of Claims, 37 CFR 1.126

The numbering of claims is not in accordance with 37 CFR 1.126. The original numbering of the claims must be preserved throughout the prosecution. When claims are canceled, the remaining claims must not be renumbered. When claims are added, except when presented in accordance with 37 CFR § 1.121(b), they must be numbered consecutively beginning with the number next following the highest numbered claims previously presented (whether entered or not).

Misnumbered claims [1] have been renumbered [2], respectively.

608.01(k) Statutory Requirement of Claims

35 U.S.C. 112 requires that the applicant shall particularly point out and distinctly claim the subject matter which he or she regards as his or her invention. The portion of the application in which he or she does this forms the claim or claims. This is an important part of the application, as it is the definition of that for which protection is granted.

608.01(l) Original Claims

In establishing a disclosure, applicant may rely not only on the description and drawing as filed but also on the original claims if their content justifies it.

Where subject matter not shown in the drawing or described in the description is claimed in the case as filed, and such original claim itself constitutes a clear disclosure of this subject matter, then the claim should be treated on its merits, and requirement made to amend the drawing and description to show this subject matter. The claim should not be attacked either by objection or rejection because this subject matter is lacking in the drawing and description. It is the drawing and description that are defective; not the claim.

It is of course to be understood that this disclosure in the claim must be sufficiently specific and detailed to support the necessary amendment of the drawing and description.

608.01(m) Form of Claims [R-8]

While there is no set statutory form for claims, the present Office practice is to insist that each claim must be the object of a sentence starting with "I (or we) claim", "The invention claimed is" (or the equivalent). If, at the time of allowance, the quoted terminology is not present, it is inserted by the clerk. Each claim begins with a capital letter and ends with a period. Periods may not be used elsewhere in the claims except for abbreviations. A claim may be typed with the various elements subdivided in paragraph form.

There may be plural indentations to further segregate subcombinations or related steps. In general, the printed patent copies will follow the format used but printing difficulties or expense may prevent the duplication of unduly complex claim formats.

Reference characters corresponding to elements recited in the detailed description and the drawings may be used in conjunction with the recitation of the same element or group of elements in the claims. The reference characters, however, should be enclosed within parentheses so as to avoid confusion with other numbers or characters which may appear in the claims. The use of reference characters is to be considered as having no effect on the scope of the claims.

Many of the difficulties encountered in the prosecution of patent applications after final rejection may be alleviated if each applicant includes, at the time of filing or no later than the first response, claims varying from the broadest to which he or she believes he or she is entitled to the most detailed that he or she is willing to accept.

Claims should preferably be arranged in order of scope so that the first claim presented is the broadest. Where separate species are claimed, the claims of like species should be grouped together where possible and physically separated by drawing a line between claims or groups of claims. (Both of these provisions may not be practical or possible where several species claims depend from the same generic claim.) Similarly, product and process claims should be separately grouped. Such arrangements are for the purpose of facilitating classification and examination.

The form of claim required in 37 CFR 1.75(e) is particularly adapted for the description of improvement type inventions. It is to be considered a combination claim. The preamble of this form of claim is considered to positively and clearly include all the elements or steps recited therein as a part of the claimed combination.

For rejections not based on prior art see >MPEP< § 706.03.

608.01(n) Dependent Claims [R-8]

37 CFR 1.75(c) reads as follows for applications filed prior to January 24, 1978:

(c) When more than one claim is presented, they may be placed in dependent form in which a claim may refer back to and further restrict a single preceding claim. Claims in dependent form shall be construed to include all the limitations of the claim incorporated by reference into the dependent claim.

MULTIPLE DEPENDENT CLAIMS

37 CFR 1.75(c) reads as follows for applications filed on and after January 24, 1978.

37 CFR 1.75 Claim(s).

* * * * *

(c) one or more claims may be presented in dependent form, referring back to and further limiting another claim or claims in the same application. Any dependent claim which refers to more than one other claim ("multiple dependent claim") shall refer, to such other claims in the alternative only. A multiple dependent claim shall not serve as a basis for any other multiple dependent claim. For fee calculation purposes under § 1.16, a multiple dependent claim will be considered to be that number of claims to which direct reference is made therein. For fee calculation purposes, also, any claim depending from a multiple dependent claim will be considered to be that number of claims to which direct reference is made in that multiple dependent claim. In addition to the other filing fees, any original application which is filed with, or is amended to include, multiple dependent claims must have paid therein the fee set forth in § 1.16(d). Claims in dependent

FIGURE 7.1 (continued)

form shall be construed to include all the limitations of the claim incorporated by reference into the dependent claim. A multiple dependent claim shall be construed to incorporate by reference all the limitations of each of the particular claims in relation to which it is being considered.

* * * * *

Generally, a multiple dependent claim is a dependent claim which refers back in the alternative to more than one preceding independent or dependent claim.

The second paragraph of 35 U.S.C. * 112 has been revised in view of the multiple dependent claim practice introduced by the Patent Cooperation Treaty. Thus, >35 U.S.C.<* 112 authorizes multiple dependent claims in applications filed on and after January 24, 1978, as long as they are in the alternative form (e.g., "A machine according to claims 3 *or* 4, further comprising ---"). Cumulative claiming (e.g.,"A machine according to claims 3 *and* 4, further comprising --- ") is *not* permitted. A multiple dependent claim may refer in the alternative to only one set of claims. A claim such as "A device as in claims 1, 2, 3, or 4, made by a process of claims 5, 6, 7, or 8" is improper. Section 112 allows reference to only a particular claim. Furthermore, a multiple dependent claim may *not* serve as a basis for any other multiple dependent claim, either directly or indirectly. These limitations help to avoid undue confusion in determining how many prior claims are actually referred to in a multiple dependent claim.

A multiple dependent claim which depends from another multiple dependent claim should be objected to by using Form Paragraph 7.45.

¶ 7.45 *Improper Multiple Dependent Claims*
Claim [1] objected to under 37 CFR 1.75(c) as being in improper form because a multiple dependent claim [2]. See MPEP 608.01(n). Accordingly, [3] has not been further treated on the merits.

Examiner's Note:
1. In bracket 2, insert " should refer to other claims in the alternative only", and/or, "cannot depend from any other multiple dependent claim".
2. Use this paragraph rather than 35 U.S.C. 112, fifth paragraph.
3. In bracket 3, insert "the claim has" or "these claims have".

Assume each claim example given below is from a different application.

ACCEPTABLE MULTIPLE DEPENDENT CLAIM WORDING

Claim 5. A gadget according to claims 3 or 4, further comprising---
Claim 5. A gadget as in any one of the preceding claims, in which ---
Claim 3. A gadget as in either claim 1 or claim 2, further comprising ---
Claim 4. A gadget as in claim 2 or 3, further comprising -
Claim 16. A gadget as in claims 1, 7, 12 or 15, further comprising ---
Claim 5. A gadget as in any of the preceding claims, in which ---

Claim 8. A gadget as in one of claims 4-7, in which ---
Claim 5. A gadget as in any preceding claim, in which ---
Claim 10. A gadget as in any of claims 1-3 or 7-9, in which ---

Claim 11. A gadget as in any one of claims 1, 2 or 7-10 inclusive, in which ---

UNACCEPTABLE MULTIPLE DEPENDENT CLAIM WORDING

A. Claim does not refer back in the alternative only
Claim 5. A gadget according to claim 3 and 4, further comprising ---
Claim 9. A gadget according to claims 1-3, in which ---
Claim 9. A gadget as in claims 1 or 2 and 7 or 8, which ---
Claim 6. A gadget as in the preceding claims in which ---
Claim 6. A gadget as in claims 1, 2, 3, 4 and/or 5, in which ---
Claim 10. A gadget as in claims 1-3 or 7-9, in which ---

B. Claim does not refer to a preceding claim
Claim 3. A gadget as in any of the following claims, in which ---
Claim 5. A gadget as in either claim 6 or claim 8, in which ---

C. Reference to two sets of claims to different features
Claim 9. A gadget as in claim 1 or 4 made by the process of claims 5, 6, 7, or 8, in which ---

D. (Reference back to another multiple dependent claim)
Claim 8. A gadget as in claim 5 (claim 5 is a multiple dependent claim) or claim 7, in which ---

>35 U.S.C.<* 112 indicates that the limitations or elements of each claim incorporated by reference into a multiple dependent claim must be considered separately. Thus, a multiple dependent claim, as such, does not contain all the limitations of all the alternative claims to which it refers, but rather contains in any one embodiment only those limitations of the particular claim referred to for the embodiment under consideration. Hence, a multiple dependent claim must be considered in the same manner as a plurality of single dependent claims.

Restriction Practice

For restriction purposes, each embodiment of a multiple dependent claim >is considered< in the same manner as a single dependent claim. Therefore, restriction may be required between the embodiments of a multiple dependent claim. Also, some embodiments of a multiple dependent claim may be held withdrawn while other embodiments are considered on their merits.

Handling of Multiple Dependent Claims by the Application *>Branch<

The Application Division is responsible for verifying whether multiple dependent claims filed with the application are in

FIGURE 7.1 (continued)

Notice of Allowance has been mailed will be permitted only if the criteria of 37 CFR 1.312 have been satisfied.

The inclusion of a copyright or mask work notice in a design or utility patent application, and thereby any patent issuing therefrom, under the conditions set forth above will serve to protect the rights of the author/inventor, as well as the public, and will serve to promote the mission and goals of the Patent and Trademark Office. Therefore, the inclusion of a copyright or mask work notice which complies with these conditions will be permitted. However, any departure from these conditions may result in a refusal to permit the desired inclusion. If the authorization required under condition (3) above does not include the specific language "(t)he [copyright or mask work] owner has no objection to the facsimile reproduction by anyone of the patent document or the patent disclosure, as it appears in the Patent and Trademark Office patent files or records,..." the notice will be objected to as improper by the examiner of the application. If the examiner maintains the objection upon reconsideration, a petition may be filed in accordance with 37 CFR 1.181.<

608.02 Drawing [R-14]

35 U.S.C. 113 Drawings.

The applicant shall furnish a drawing where necessary for the understanding of the subject matter to be patented. When the nature of such subject matter admits of illustration by a drawing and the applicant has not furnished such a drawing, the Commissioner may require its submission within a time period of not less than two months from the sending of a notice thereof. Drawings submitted after the filing date of the application may not be used (i) to overcome any insufficiency of the specification due to lack of an enabling disclosure or otherwise inadequate disclosure therein, or (ii) to supplement the original disclosure thereof for the purpose of interpretation of the scope of any claim.

37 CFR 1.81 Drawings required >in patent application<.

(a) The applicant for a patent is required to furnish a drawing of his >or her< invention where necessary for the understanding of the subject matter sought to be patented; this drawing >, or a high quality copy thereof,< must be filed with the application. >Since corrections are the responsibility of the applicant, the original drawing(s) should be retained by the applicant for any necessary future correction.<

(b) Drawings may include illustrations which facilitate an understanding of the invention (for example, flow sheets in cases of processes, and diagrammatic views).

(c) Whenever the nature of the subject matter sought to be patented admits of illustration by a drawing without its being necessary for the understanding of the subject matter and the applicant has not furnished such a drawing, the examiner will require its submission within a time period of not less than two months from the date of the sending of a notice thereof.

(d) Drawings submitted after the filing date of the application may not be used to overcome any insufficiency of the specification due to lack of an enabling disclosure or otherwise inadequate disclosure therein, or to supplement the original disclosure thereof for the purpose of interpretation of the scope of any claim.

[Para. (a) amended, 53 FR 47809, Nov. 28, 1988, effective Jan. 1, 1989]

37 CFR 1.84 Standards for drawings.

(a) *Paper and ink.* Drawings >or high quality copies thereof which are submitted to the Office< must be made upon paper which is flexible, strong, white, smooth, non-shiny and durable. **India ink, or its

equivalent in quality, is preferred for pen drawings to secure perfectly black solid lines. The use of white pigment to cover lines is not normally acceptable. >See paragraph (p) of this section for use of color drawings in utility patent applications.<

(b) *Size of sheet and margins.* The size of the sheets on which drawings are made may be exactly 8 1/2 by 14 inches (21.6 by 35.6 cm.) >, exactly 8 1/2 by 13 inches (21.6 by 33.1 cm.), < or exactly 21.0 by 29.7 cm. (DIN size A4). All drawing sheets in a particular application must be the same size. One of the shorter sides of the sheet is regarded as its top.

(1) On 8 1/2 by 14 inch drawing sheets, the drawing must include a top margin of 2 inches (5.1 cm.) and bottom and side margins of 1/4 inch (6.4 mm.) from the edges, thereby leaving a "sight" precisely 8 by 11 3/4 inches (20.3 by 29.8 cm.). Margin border lines are not permitted. All work must be included within the "sight". The sheets may be provided with two 1/4 inch (6.4 mm.) diameter holes having their centerlines spaced 11/16 inch (17.5 mm.) below the top edge and 2 3/4 inches (7.0 cm.) apart, said holes being equally spaced from the respective side edges.

(2) >On 8 1/2 by 13 inch drawing sheets, the drawing must include a top margin of 1 inch (2.5 cm.) and bottom and side margins of 1/4 inch (6.4 mm.) from the edges, thereby leaving a "sight" precisely 8 by 11 3/4 inches (20.3 by 29.8 cm.). Margin border lines are not permitted. All work must be included within the "sight." The sheets may be provided with two 1/4 inch (6.4 mm.) diameter holes having their centerlines spaced 11/16 inch (17.5 mm.) below the top edge and 2 3/4 inches (7.0 cm.) apart, said holes being equally spaced from the respective side edges.

(3)< On 21.0 by 29.7 cm. drawing sheets, the drawing must include a top margin of at least 2.5 cm., a left side margin of 2.5 cm., a right side margin of 1.5 cm., and a bottom margin of 1.0 cm. Margin border lines are not permitted. All work must be contained within a sight size not to exceed 17 by 26.2 cm.

(c) *Character of lines.* All drawings must be made with drafting instruments or by a process which will give them satisfactory reproduction characteristics. Every line and letter must be durable, black, sufficiently dense and dark, uniformly thick and well defined; the weight of all lines and letters must be heavy enough to permit adequate reproduction. This direction applies to all lines however fine, to shading, and to lines representing cut surfaces in sectional views. All lines must be clean, sharp, and solid. Fine or crowded lines should be avoided. Solid black should not be used for sectional or surface shading. Freehand work should be avoided wherever it is possible to do so.

(d) *Hatching and shading.* (1) Hatching should be made by oblique parallel lines spaced sufficiently apart to enable the lines to be distinguished without difficulty.

(2) Heavy lines on the shade side of objects should preferably be used except where they tend to thicken the work and obscure reference characters. The light should come from the upper left-hand corner at an angle of 45°. Surface delineations should preferably be shown by proper shading, which should be open.

(e) *Scale.* The scale to which a drawing is made ought to be large enough to show the mechanism without crowding when the drawing is reduced in size to two-thirds in reproduction, and views of portions of the mechanism on a larger scale should be used when necessary to show details clearly; two or more sheets should be used if one does not give sufficient room to accomplish this end, but the number of sheets should not be more than is necessary.

(f) *Reference characters.* The different views should be consecutively numbered figures. Reference numerals (and letters, but numerals are preferred) must be plain, legible and carefully formed, and not be encircled. They should, if possible, measure at least one-eighth of an inch (3.2 mm.) in height so that they may bear reduction to one twenty-

Rev. 14, Nov. 1992

117

FIGURE 7.1 *(continued)*

fourth of an inch (1.1 mm.); and they may be slightly larger when there is sufficient room. They should not be so placed in the close and complex parts of the drawing as to interfere with a thorough comprehension of the same, and therefore should rarely cross or mingle with the lines. When necessarily grouped around a certain part, they should be placed at a little distance, at the closest point where there is available space, and connected by lines with the parts to which they refer. They should not be placed upon hatched or shaded surfaces but when necessary, a blank space may be left in the hatching or shading where the character occurs so that it shall appear perfectly distinct and separate from the work. The same part of an invention appearing in more than one view of the drawing must always be designated by the same character, and the same character must never be used to designate different parts. Reference signs not mentioned in the description shall not appear in the drawing and vice versa.

(g) *Symbols, legends.* Graphical drawing symbols and other labeled representations may be used for conventional elements when appropriate, subject to approval by the Office. The elements for which such symbols and labeled representations are used must be adequately identified in the specification. While descriptive matter on drawings is not permitted, suitable legends may be used, or may be required, in proper cases, as in diagrammatic views and flowsheets or to show materials or where labeled representations are employed to illustrate conventional elements. Arrows may be required, in proper cases, to show direction of movement. The lettering should be as large as, or larger than, the reference characters.

(h) [Reserved]

(i) *Views.* The drawing must contain as many figures as may be necessary to show the invention; the figures should be consecutively numbered if possible in the order in which they appear. The figures may be *>plan<*, elevation, section, or perspective views, and detail views of portions of elements, on a larger scale if necessary, may also be used. Exploded views, with the separated parts of the same figure embraced by a bracket, to show the relationship or order of assembly of various parts are permissible. >When an exploded view is shown in a figure which is on the same sheet as another figure, the exploded view should be placed in brackets.< When necessary, a view of a large machine or device in its entirety may be broken and extended over several sheets if there is no loss in facility of understanding the view. Where figures on two or more sheets form in effect a single complete figure, the figures on the several sheets should be so arranged that the complete figure can be understood by laying the drawing sheets adjacent to one another. >The figures, even though on separate sheets, should be labeled as separate figures, for example as Fig. 1a, Fig. 1b, etc., so that it would be apparent that the views actually comprise one figure.< The arrangement should be such that no part of any of the figures appearing on the various sheets is concealed and that the complete figure can be understood even though spaces will occur in the complete figure because of the margins on the drawing sheets. The plane upon which a sectional view is taken should be indicated on the general view by a broken line, the ends of which should be designated by numerals corresponding to the figure number of the sectional view and have arrows applied to indicate the direction in which the view is taken. A moved position may be shown by a broken line superimposed upon a suitable figure if this can be done without crowding, otherwise a separate figure must be used for this purpose. Modified forms of construction can only be shown in separate figures. Views should not be connected by projection lines nor should centerlines be used.>When a portion of a figure is enlarged for magnification purposes, the figure and the enlarged figure must be labeled as a separate figures.<

(j)*Arrangement of views.* All views on the same sheet should stand in the same direction and, if possible, stand so that they can be read with the sheet held in an upright position. If views longer than the width of

the sheet are necessary for the clearest illustration of the invention, the sheet may be turned on its side so that the top of the sheet with the appropriate top margin >to be used as the heading space< is on the right-hand side. One figure must not be placed upon another or within the outline of another.

(k) *Figure for Official Gazette.* The drawing should, as far as possible, be so planned that one of the views will be suitable for publication in the *Official Gazette* as the illustration of the invention.

(l) **>*Identification of drawings.*< Identifying indicia (such as the >application number, group art unit, title of the invention,< attorney's docket number, inventor's name, number of sheets, etc.) not to exceed 2 3/4 inches (7.0 cm.) in width may be placed in a centered location between the side edges within three-fourths inch (19.1 mm.) of the top edge. >Either this marking technique on the front of the drawing or the placement, although not preferred, of this information and the title of the invention on the back of the drawings is acceptable.< Authorized security markings may be placed on the drawings provided they *>are< outside the illustrations and are removed when the material is declassified. Other extraneous matter will not be permitted upon the face of a drawing.

(m) *Transmission of drawings.* Drawings transmitted to the Office should be sent flat, protected by a sheet of heavy binder's board, or may be rolled for transmission in a suitable mailing tube; but must never be folded. If received creased or mutilated, new drawings will be required.

>(n) *Numbering of drawing sheets.* The drawing sheets may be numbered in consecutive arabic numbers at the top of the sheets, in the middle, but not in the margin. Such numbering will be deleted for printing purposes since page numbers are added at the time of printing the patent by the Office.

(o) *Copyright or Mask Work Notice.* A copyright or mask work notice may appear in the drawing but must be placed within the "sight" of the drawing immediately below the figure representing the copyright or mask work material and be limited to letters having a print size of 1/ 8 to 1/4 inches (3.2 to 6.4 mm.) high. The content of the notice must be limited to only those elements required by law. For example, "©1983 John Doe"(17 U.S.C. 401) and "*M* John Doe" (17 U.S.C. 909) would be properly limited and, under current statutes, legally sufficient notices of copyright and mask work, respectively. Inclusion of a copyright or mask work notice will be permitted only if the authorization language set forth in § 1.71(e) is included at the beginning (preferably as the first paragraph) of the specification.

(p) *Limited use of color drawings in utility patent applications.* Paragraph (a) of this section requires that drawings in utility patent applications must be in black on white paper. However, on rare occasion, color drawings may be necessary as the only practical medium by which to disclose the subject matter sought to be patented in a utility patent application. The Patent and Trademark Office will accept color drawings in utility patent applications only after granting of a petition by the applicant under § 1.183 of this part which requests waiver of the requirements of paragraph (a) of this section. Any such petition should be directed to the Office of the Deputy Assistant Commissioner for Patents and must include the following:

(1) The appropriate fee set forth in § 1.17(h).

(2) Five (5) sets of color drawings on DIN size A4 (21.0 by 29.7 cm.) sheets.

(3) A proposed amendment to insert in the specification the following language as the first paragraph in the portion of the specification relating to the brief description of the drawing:

"The file of this patent contains at least one drawing executed in color. Copies of this patent with color drawing(s) will be provided by the Patent and Trademark Office upon request and payment of the necessary fee."<

(See § 1.152 for design drawings, § 1.165 for plant drawings, and

FIGURE 7.1 (continued)

§ 1.174 for reissue drawings.)

[Paras. (a), (b), (i), (j), & (l) amended, paras. (n), (o), & (p) added, 53 FR 47809, Nov. 28, 1988, effective Jan. 1, 1989]

Drawings on paper are acceptable although bristol board is preferred. **>Corrections< thereto **must be made in the form of replacement sheets since **>the Office does not release drawings for correction. See 37 CFR 1.85<.

Good quality copies made on office copiers are acceptable if the lines are uniformly thick, black, and solid.

Drawings are currently accepted in *>three< different formats. It is however required that all drawings in a particular application be the same size for ease of handling and reproduction.

Design patent drawings, 37 CFR 1.152, MPEP § 1503.02.

Plant patent drawings, 37 CFR 1.165, MPEP § 1606.

Reissue application drawings, MPEP §§ 608.02(k) and 1413.

Correction of drawings, MPEP § 608.02(p). Prints, preparation and distribution, MPEP §§ 508 and 608.02(m). Prints, return of drawings, MPEP § 608.02(y).

For pencil notations of classification and name or initials of assistant examiner to be placed on drawings see MPEP § 717.03.

The filing of a divisional or continuation case under the provisions of 37 CFR 1.60 (unexecuted case), does not obviate the need for formal drawings. See MPEP § 608.02(b).

DEFINITIONS

A number of different terms are used when referring to drawings in patent applications. The following definitions are used in this Manual.

Original drawings: The drawing submitted with the application when filed. It may be either a formal or an informal drawing.

Substitute drawing: A drawing filed later than the filing date of an application. Usually submitted to replace an original informal drawing.

Formal drawing: A drawing in a form that complies with 37 CFR 1.84. Formal drawings are stamped "approved" by the Draftsman. **

Informal drawing: A drawing which does not comply with the form requirements of 37 CFR 1.84. Drawings may be informal because they are not on the proper size sheets, the quality of the lines is poor, or for other reasons such as the size of reference elements. Such objections are made by the Draftsman on form PTO-948.

Drawing print: This term is used for the white paper print prepared by the Micrographics Branch of the Office Services Divisions of all original drawings. The drawing prints contain the notation "Print of Drawing as originally filed" near the top. Drawing prints should be placed on the top on the right hand flap of the application file wrapper.

Interference print: This term is used to designate the copy prepared of the original drawings** filed in file cabinets separate from the file wrappers and are used to make interference searches.

The following Form Paragraphs should be used when notifying applicants of drawing corrections.

¶ 6.38 Acknowledgment of Proposed Drawing Correction

The proposed drawing correction and/or the proposed substitute sheets of drawings, filed on [1] have been [2].

Examiner Note:

1. In bracket 2, insert either approved or disapproved.

2. If approved, either form paragraph 6.39 and 6.40 or 6.41 or 6.44 must follow.

3. If disapproved, an explanation must be provided.

¶ 6.39 PTO No Longer Makes Drawing Changes

The Patent and Trademark Office no longer makes drawing changes. 1017 OG 4. It is applicant's responsibility to ensure that the drawings are corrected. Corrections must be made in accordance with the instructions below.

Examiner Note:

This paragraph is to be used whenever the applicant has filed a request for the Office to make drawing changes. Form paragraph 6.40 must follow.

¶ 6.40 Information on How To Effect Drawing Changes

Information on How To Effect Drawing Changes

1. **Correction of Informalities** (Draftsman's objections on PTO-948). In order to correct any informalities in the drawings, applicant MUST **file new drawings with the changes incorporated herein. The art unit number, serial number and number of drawing sheets should be written on the reverse side of the drawings. Applicant may delay filing of the new drawings until receipt of the "Notice of Allowability" (PTOL-37). If delayed, the new drawings MUST be filed within the THREE MONTH shortened statutory period set for response in the "Notice of Allowability" (PTOL-37). Extensions of time may be obtained under the provisions of 37 CFR 1.136(a). The drawings should be filed as a separate paper with a transmittal letter addressed to the Official Draftsman.
**

2. **Corrections other than Informalities Noted by the Draftsman on the PTO-948.**

All changes to the drawings, other than informalities noted by the draftsman, MUST be made in the same manner as above except that, normally, a red ink sketch of the changes to be incorporated into the new drawings MUST be approved by the examiner before the application will be allowed. No changes will be permitted to be made, other than correction of informalities, unless the examiner has approved the proposed changes.

3. **Timing of Corrections**

Applicant is encouraged to correct drawings upon an indication of allowable subject matter. However, applicant is required to submit acceptable corrected drawings within the three month shortened statutory period set in the "Notice of Allowability" PTOL-37). Within that three month period, two weeks should be allowed for review by the Office of the correction. If a correction is determined to be unacceptable by the Office, applicant must arrange to have an acceptable correction re-submitted within the original three month period to avoid the necessity of obtaining an extension of time and of paying the extension fee. Therefore, applicant should file corrected drawings as soon as possible.

FIGURE 7.1 *(continued)*

¶ *6.41 Reminder That PTO No Longer Makes Drawing Changes*

Applicant is reminded that the Patent and Trademark Office no longer makes drawing changes and that it is applicant's responsibility to ensure that the drawings are corrected in accordance with the instructions set forth in paper no. [1], mailed on [2].

Examiner Note:

This paragraph is to be used when the applicant has been previously provided with information on how to effect drawing changes (i.e., either by way of form paragraph 6.40 or a PTO-1474 has been previously sent).

¶ *6.42 Reminder That Applicant Must Make Drawing Changes*

Applicant is reminded that in order to avoid an abandonment of this application, the drawings must be corrected in accordance with the instructions set forth in paper no. [1] mailed on [2].

Examiner Note:

This paragraph is to be used when allowing the application and when applicant has previously been provided with information on how to effect drawing changes (i.e., by way of form paragraph 6.40 or a PTO-1474 has been previously sent).

¶ *6.43 Drawings Contain Informalities, Application Allowed*

The drawings filed on [1] are acceptable subject to correction of the informalities indicated on the attached Notice re Drawings, PTO-948. In order to avoid abandonment of this application, correction is required.

Examiner Note:

Use this paragraph when allowing the case, particularly at time of first action issue. Form paragraph 6.40 or 6.41 must follow.

¶ *6.44 Drawing Informalities Previously Indicated*

In order to avoid abandonment, the drawing informalities noted in paper no. [1], mailed on [2], must now be corrected. Correction can only be effected in the manner set forth in the above noted paper.

Examiner Note:

Use this paragraph when allowing the case and applicant has previously been informed of informalities in the the drawings.

¶ *6.47 Examiner's Amendment Involving Drawing Changes*

The following changes to the drawings have been approved by the Examiner and agreed upon by applicant: [1]. In order to avoid abandonment of the application, applicant must make the above agreed upon drawing changes.

Examiner Note:

1. In bracket 1, Insert the agreed upon drawing changes.
2. Form paragraphs 6.39 and 6.40 must follow.

DRAWING SYMBOLS

37 CFR 1.84(g) indicates that graphic drawing symbols and other labeled representations may be used for conventional elements where appropriate, subject to approval by the Office. Also, suitable legends may be used, or may be required, in proper cases.

The publications listed below have been reviewed by the Office and the symbols therein are considered to be generally acceptable in patent drawings. Although the Office will not "approve" all of the listed symbols as a group because their use and clarity must be decided on a case-by-case basis, these publications may be used as guides when selecting graphic symbols. Overly specific symbols should be avoided. Symbols with unclear meanings should be labeled for clarification.

These publications are available from the American National Standards Institute Inc., 1430 Broadway, New York, New York 10018.

The publications reviewed are the following:

Y32.2-1970 Graphic Symbols for Electrical & Electronics Diagrams

Y32.10-1967 Graphic Symbols for Fluid Power Diagrams

Y32.11-1961 Graphic Symbols for Process Flow Diagrams in the Petroleum & Chemical Industries

Y32.14-1962 Graphic Symbols for Logic Diagrams

Z32.2.3-1949 (R1953) Graphic Symbols for Pipe Fittings, Valves and Piping

Z32.2.4-1949 (R1953) Graphic Symbols for Heating, Ventilating & Air Conditioning

Z32.2.6-1950 Graphic Symbols for Heat-Power Apparatus

FIGURE 7.1 (continued)

The following symbols should be used to indicate various materials where the material is an important feature of the invention. The use of conventional features is very helpful in making prior art searches.

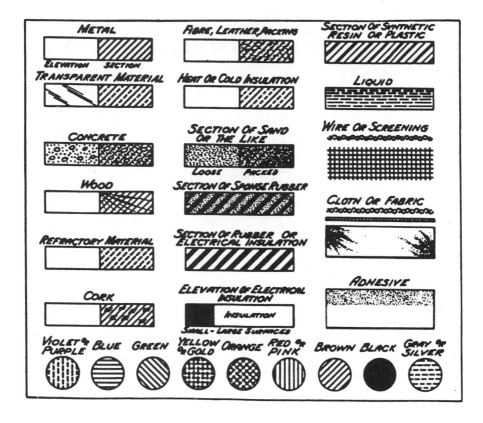

FIGURE 7.2   Selected Approved Forms for Formal Papers

Patent and Trademark
Forms Booklet

UNITED STATES DEPARTMENT OF COMMERCE
Patent and Trademark Office

FIGURE 7.2 *(continued)*

DECLARATION FOR PATENT APPLICATION

Docket Number (Optional)

As a below named inventor, I hereby declare that:

My residence, post office address and citizenship are as stated below next to my name.

I believe I am the original, first and sole inventor (if only one name is listed below) or an original, first and joint inventor (if plural names are listed below) of the subject matter which is claimed and for which a patent is sought on the invention entitled
_____, the specification of which

is attached hereto unless the following box is checked:

☐ was filed on _____ as United States Application Number or PCT International Application
Number _____ and was amended on _____ (if applicable).

I hereby state that I have reviewed and understand the contents of the above identified specification, including the claims, as amended by any amendment referred to above.

I acknowledge the duty to disclose information which is material to the examination of this application in accordance with Title 37, Code of Federal Regulations, § 1.56(a).

I hereby claim foreign priority benefits under Title 35, United States Code, § 119 of any foreign application(s) for patent or inventor's certificate listed below and have also identified below any foreign application for patent or inventor's certificate having a filing date before that of the application on which priority is claimed.

Prior Foreign Application(s)

Priority Claimed

(Number)	(Country)	(Day/Month/Year Filed)	☐ Yes ☐ No
(Number)	(Country)	(Day/Month/Year Filed)	☐ Yes ☐ No
(Number)	(Country)	(Day/Month/Year Filed)	☐ Yes ☐ No

I hereby claim the benefit under Title 35, United States Code, § 120 of any United States application(s) listed below and, insofar as the subject matter of each of the claims of this application is not disclosed in the prior United States application in the manner provided by the first paragraph of Title 35, United States Code, § 112, I acknowledge the duty to disclose material information as defined in Title 37, Code of Federal Regulations, § 1.56(a) which occurred between the filing date of the prior application and the national or PCT international filing date of this application.

(Application Number)	(Filing Date)	(Status – patented, pending, abandoned)
(Application Number)	(Filing Date)	(Status – patented, pending, abandoned)

I hereby appoint the following attorney(s) and/or agent(s) to prosecute this application and to transact all business in the Patent and Trademark Office connected therewith:

Address all telephone calls to _____ at telephone number _____
Address all correspondence to _____

I hereby declare that all statements made herein of my own knowledge are true and that all statements made on information and belief are believed to be true; and further that these statements were made with the knowledge that willful false statements and the like so made are punishable by fine or imprisonment, or both, under Section 1001 of Title 18 of the United States Code and that such willful false statements may jeopardize the validity of the application or any patent issued thereon.

Full name of sole or first inventor (given name, family name) _____
Inventor's signature _____ Date _____
Residence _____ Citizenship _____
Post Office Address _____

Full name of second joint inventor, if any (given name, family name) _____
Second Inventor's signature _____ Date _____
Residence _____ Citizenship _____
Post Office Address _____

☐ Additional inventors are being named on a separate sheet attached hereto.

FIGURE 7.2 (continued)

VERIFIED STATEMENT CLAIMING SMALL ENTITY STATUS (37 CFR 1.9(f) & 1.27(b))--INDEPENDENT INVENTOR	Docket Number (Optional)

Applicant or Patentee: _____

Serial or Patent No.: _____

Filed or Issued: _____

Title: _____

As a below named inventor, I hereby declare that I qualify as an independent inventor as defined in 37 CFR 1.9(c) for purposes of paying reduced fees to the Patent and Trademark Office described in:

☐ the specification filed herewith with title as listed above.

☐ the application identified above.

☐ the patent identified above.

I have not assigned, granted, conveyed or licensed and am under no obligation under contract or law to assign, grant, convey or license, any rights in the invention to any person who would not qualify as an independent inventor under 37 CFR 1.9(c) if that person had made the invention, or to any concern which would not qualify as a small business concern under 37 CFR 1.9(d) or a nonprofit organization under 37 CFR 1.9(e).

Each person, concern or organization to which I have assigned, granted, conveyed, or licensed or am under an obligation under contract or law to assign, grant, convey, or license any rights in the invention is listed below:

☐ No such person, concern, or organization exists.

☐ Each such person, concern or organization is listed below.

Separate verified statements are required from each named person, concern or organization having rights to the invention averring to their status as small entities. (37 CFR 1.27)

I acknowledge the duty to file, in this application or patent, notification of any change in status resulting in loss of entitlement to small entity status prior to paying, or at the time of paying, the earliest of the issue fee or any maintenance fee due after the date on which status as a small entity is no longer appropriate. (37 CFR 1.28(b))

I hereby declare that all statements made herein of my own knowledge are true and that all statements made on information and belief are believed to be true; and further that these statements were made with the knowledge that willful false statements and the like so made are punishable by fine or imprisonment, or both, under section 1001 of Title 18 of the United States Code, and that such willful false statements may jeopardize the validity of the application, any patent issuing thereon, or any patent to which this verified statement is directed.

NAME OF INVENTOR	NAME OF INVENTOR	NAME OF INVENTOR
Signature of inventor	Signature of inventor	Signature of inventor
Date	Date	Date

PTO/SB/09 (11-90)   Patent and Trademark Office; U.S. DEPARTMENT OF COMMERCE

FIGURE 7.2 *(continued)*

VERIFIED STATEMENT CLAIMING SMALL ENTITY STATUS (37 CFR 1.9(f) & 1.27(c))--SMALL BUSINESS CONCERN	Docket Number (Optional)

Applicant or Patentee: _____

Serial or Patent No.: _____

Filed or Issued: _____

Title: _____

I hereby declare that I am

☐ the owner of the small business concern identified below:

☐ an official of the small business concern empowered to act on behalf of the concern identified below:

NAME OF SMALL BUSINESS CONCERN _____

ADDRESS OF SMALL BUSINESS CONCERN _____
_____

    I hereby declare that the above identified small business concern qualifies as a small business concern as defined in 13 CFR 121.12, and reproduced in 37 CFR 1.9(d), for purposes of paying reduced fees to the United States Patent and Trademark Office, in that the number of employees of the concern, including those of its affiliates, does not exceed 500 persons. For purposes of this statement, (1) the number of employees of the business concern is the average over the previous fiscal year of the concern of the persons employed on a full-time, part-time or temporary basis during each of the pay periods of the fiscal year, and (2) concerns are affiliates of each other when either, directly or indirectly, one concern controls or has the power to control the other, or a third party or parties controls or has the power to control both.

    I hereby declare that rights under contract or law have been conveyed to and remain with the small business concern identified above with regard to the invention described in:

☐ the specification filed herewith with title as listed above.

☐ the application identified above.

☐ the patent identified above.

    If the rights held by the above identified small business concern are not exclusive, each individual, concern or organization having rights in the invention must file separate verified statements averring to their status as small entities, and no rights to the invention are held by any person, other than the inventor, who would not qualify as an independent inventor under 37 CFR 1.9(c) if that person made the invention, or by any concern which would not qualify as a small business concern under 37 CFR 1.9(d), or a nonprofit organization under 37 CFR 1.9(e).

    Each person, concern or organization having any rights in the invention is listed below:

☐ no such person, concern, or organization exists.

☐ each such person, concern or organization is listed below.

    Separate verified statements are required from each named person, concern or organization having rights to the invention averring to their status as small entities. (37 CFR 1.27)

    I acknowledge the duty to file, in this application or patent, notification of any change in status resulting in loss of entitlement to small entity status prior to paying, or at the time of paying, the earliest of the issue fee or any maintenance fee due after the date on which status as a small entity is no longer appropriate. (37 CFR 1.28(b))

    I hereby declare that all statements made herein of my own knowledge are true and that all statements made on information and belief are believed to be true; and further that these statements were made with the knowledge that willful false statements and the like so made are punishable by fine or imprisonment, or both, under section 1001 of Title 18 of the United States Code, and that such willful false statements may jeopardize the validity of the application, any patent issuing thereon, or any patent to which this verified statement is directed.

NAME OF PERSON SIGNING _____

TITLE OF PERSON IF OTHER THAN OWNER _____

ADDRESS OF PERSON SIGNING _____

SIGNATURE _____ DATE _____

PTO/SB/ 10 (11-90)   Patent and Trademark Office; U.S. DEPARTMENT OF COMMERCE

FIGURE 7.2 (continued)

VERIFIED STATEMENT CLAIMING SMALL ENTITY STATUS (37 CFR 1.9(f) & 1.27(d))--NONPROFIT ORGANIZATION	Docket Number (Optional)

Applicant or Patentee: _____

Serial or Patent No. : _____

Filed or Issued: _____

Title: _____

I hereby declare that I am an official empowered to act on behalf of the nonprofit organization identified below:

NAME OF NONPROFIT ORGANIZATION _____

ADDRESS OF NONPROFIT ORGANIZATION _____

_____

TYPE OF NONPROFIT ORGANIZATION:

☐ UNIVERSITY OR OTHER INSTITUTION OF HIGHER EDUCATION

☐ TAX EXEMPT UNDER INTERNAL REVENUE SERVICE CODE (26 U.S.C. 501(a) and 501(c)(3))

☐ NONPROFIT SCIENTIFIC OR EDUCATIONAL UNDER STATUTE OF STATE OF THE UNITED STATES OF AMERICA
(NAME OF STATE _____)
(CITATION OF STATUTE _____)

☐ WOULD QUALIFY AS TAX EXEMPT UNDER INTERNAL REVENUE SERVICE CODE (26 U.S.C. 501(a) and 501(c)(3)) IF LOCATED IN THE UNITED STATES OF AMERICA

☐ WOULD QUALIFY AS NONPROFIT SCIENTIFIC OR EDUCATIONAL UNDER STATUTE OF STATE OF THE UNITED STATES OF AMERICA IF LOCATED IN THE UNITED STATES OF AMERICA
(NAME OF STATE _____)
(CITATION OF STATUTE _____)

I hereby declare that the nonprofit organization identified above qualifies as a nonprofit organization as defined in 37 CFR 1.9(e) for purposes of paying reduced fees to the United States Patent and Trademark Office regarding the invention described in:

☐ the specification filed herewith with title as listed above.

☐ the application identified above.

☐ the patent identified above.

I hereby declare that rights under contract or law have been conveyed to and remain with the nonprofit organization regarding the above identified invention.

Each person, concern or organization having any rights in the invention is listed below:

☐ no such person, concern, or organization exists.

☐ each such person, concern or organization is listed below.

If the rights held by the nonprofit organization are not exclusive, each individual, concern or organization having rights in the invention must file separate verified statements averring to their status as small entities and that no rights to the invention are held by any person, other than the inventor, who would not qualify as an independent inventor under 37 CFR 1.9(c) if that person made the invention, or by any concern which would not qualify as a small business concern under 37 CFR 1.9(d) or a nonprofit organization under 37 CFR 1.9(e).

I acknowledge the duty to file, in this application or patent, notification of any change in status resulting in loss of entitlement to small entity status prior to paying, or at the time of paying, the earliest of the issue fee or any maintenance fee due after the date on which status as a small entity is no longer appropriate. (37 CFR 1.28(b))

I hereby declare that all statements made herein of my own knowledge are true and that all statements made on information and belief are believed to be true; and further that these statements were made with the knowledge that willful false statements and the like so made are punishable by fine or imprisonment, or both, under section 1001 of Title 18 of the United States Code, and that such willful false statements may jeopardize the validity of the application, any patent issuing thereon, or any patent to which this verified statement is directed.

NAME OF PERSON SIGNING _____

TITLE IN ORGANIZATION OF PERSON SIGNING _____

ADDRESS OF PERSON SIGNING _____

SIGNATURE _____ DATE _____

PTO/SB/ 11 (11-90)   Patent and Trademark Office; U.S. DEPARTMENT OF COMMERCE

FIGURE 7.2 *(continued)*

VERIFIED STATEMENT BY A NON-INVENTOR SUPPORTING A CLAIM BY ANOTHER FOR SMALL ENTITY STATUS	Docket Number (Optional)

Applicant or Patentee: _____

Serial or Patent No.: _____

Filed or Issued: _____

Title: _____

I hereby declare that I am making this verified statement to support a claim by _____ for small entity status for purposes of paying reduced fees to the United States Patent and Trademark Office, regarding the invention described in:

☐ the specification filed herewith with title as listed above.

☐ the application identified above.

☐ the patent identified above

I hereby declare that I would qualify as an independent inventor as defined in 37 CFR 1.9(c) for purposes of paying fees to the United States Patent and Trademark Office, if I had made the above identified invention.

I have not assigned, granted, conveyed or licensed and am under no obligation under contract or law to assign, grant, convey or license, any rights in the invention to any person who would not qualify as an independent inventor under 37 CFR 1.9(c) if that person had made the invention, or to any concern which would not qualify as a small business concern under 37 CFR 1.9(d) or a nonprofit organization under 37 CFR 1.9(e). Note: Separate verified statements are required from each person, concern or organization having rights to the invention averring to their status as small entities. (37 CFR 1.27)

Each person, concern or organization to which I have assigned, granted, conveyed, or licensed or am under an obligation under contract or law to assign, grant, convey, or license any rights in the invention is listed below:

☐ no such person, concern, or organization exists.

☐ each such person, concern or organization is listed below.

I acknowledge the duty to file, in this application or patent, notification of any change in status resulting in loss of entitlement to small entity status prior to paying, or at the time of paying, the earliest of the issue fee or any maintenance fee due after the date on which status as a small entity is no longer appropriate. (37 CFR 1.28(b))

I hereby declare that all statements made herein of my own knowledge are true and that all statements made on information and belief are believed to be true; and further that these statements were made with the knowledge that willful false statements and the like so made are punishable by fine or imprisonment, or both, under section 1001 of Title 18 of the United States Code, and that such willful false statements may jeopardize the validity of the application, any patent issuing thereon, or any patent to which this verified statement is directed.

_____

NAME OF PERSON SIGNING

_____

ADDRESS OF PERSON SIGNING

_____

SIGNATURE

_____

DATE

PTO/SB/12 (11-90)   Patent and Trademark Office; U.S. DEPARTMENT OF COMMERCE

FIGURE 7.3   Schedule of Patent Office Fees

UNITED STATES DEPARTMENT OF COMMERCE
Patent and Trademark Office
ASSISTANT SECRETARY AND COMMISSIONER
OF PATENTS AND TRADEMARKS
Washington, D.C. 20231

NOTICE OF FINAL RULEMAKING
PATENT AND TRADEMARK FEE REVISIONS

The Patent and Trademark Office is amending its rules of practice in patent and trademark cases, Parts 1 and 2 of Title 37, Code of Federal Regulations, to adjust patent and trademark fee amounts. The adjustments are in accordance with the applicable provisions of title 35, United States Code, section 31 of the Trademark (Lanham) Act of 1946, and section 10101 of the Omnibus Budget Reconciliation Act of 1990 (Public Law 101-508), all as amended by the Patent and Trademark Office Authorization Act of 1991 (Public Law 102-204).

A notice was published in the *Federal Register* on Friday, August 21, 1992 at 57 FR Part VI, and in the *Offical Gazette of the United States Patent and Trademark Office* on Tuesday, August 25, 1992 in Volume 1141, Number 4, pages 68 through 84. The effective date for the new fee amounts is Thursday, October 1, 1992.

Any fee amount that is paid on or after October 1, 1992 is subject to the new fee schedule.

Your attention is drawn to the following changes in the fee schedule:

- Patent statutory fees established by rule on December 10, 1991 are being adjusted by 3.3 percent, which reflects the Administration's projected Consumer Price Index-U (CPI) for the 12-month period beginning October 1, 1991.

- Patent non-statutory fees and Patent Cooperation Treaty fees are adjusted to recover planned costs in fiscal year 1993.

- Trademark fees are adjusted, in the aggregate, by changes in the CPI of 3.3 percent.

- PTO is establishing two new fees: (1) a fee for accessing APS-Text at a Patent and Trademark Depository Library (PTDL) and (2) a fee for dividing a trademark application.

The Commissioner is immediately suspending collection of the fee for using APS-Text in a PTDL to provide additional time to solicit input from the private sector on alternative collection methods, and other options for accessing patent search and retrieval in the Libraries. The Office will provide written notice thirty days before starting to collect the fee.

If you have any questions or comments, or would like to have a copy of the *Federal Register* notice, please contact the Office of Long-Range Planning and Evaluation by phone at 703-305-8510 or by fax at 703-305-8436.

Bradford R. Huther
Assistant Commissioner
   for Finance and Planning

FIGURE 7.3 *(continued)*

U. S. PATENT AND TRADEMARK OFFICE
Effective October 1, 1992

The U. S. Patent and Trademark Office has amended its rules of practice in patent and trademark cases, Parts 1 and 2 of Title 37, Code of Federal Regulations to adjust patent and trademark fee amounts.

Any fee payment due and paid on or after October 1, 1992, must be paid in the revised amount. The date of mailing indicated on a proper Certificate of Mailing under either 37 CFR 1.8 or 37 CFR 1.10 will be considered to be the date of receipt and payment in the Office.

As this fee sheet is a summary and the content of rules also may be changing, you should refer to the notice published in the Federal Register on August 21, 1992 at 57 FR Part VI. See also the Official Gazette of the United States Patent and Trademark Office of August 25, 1992.

The fees which are subject to reduction for small entities who have established status (37 CFR 1.27) are shown in a separate column.

Fee Code	37 CFR	Description	Fee	Small Entity Fee If applicable
		PATENT FEES		
Filing Fees				
101 / 201	1.16(a)	Basic filing fee - utility	710.00	355.00
102 / 202	1.16(b)	Independent claims in excess of three	74.00	37.00
103 / 203	1.16(c)	Claims in excess of twenty	22.00	11.00
104 / 204	1.16(d)	Multiple dependent claim	230.00	115.00
105 / 205	1.16(e)	Surcharge- Late filing fee or oath or declaration.	130.00	65.00
106 / 206	1.16(f)	Design filing fee	290.00	145.00
107 / 207	1.16(g)	Plant filing fee	480.00	240.00
108 / 208	1.16(h)	Reissue filing fee	710.00	355.00
109 / 209	1.16(i)	Reissue independent claims over original patent	74.00	37.00
110 / 210	1.16(j)	Reissue claims in excess of 20 and over original patent	22.00	11.00
139	1.17(k)	Non-English specification	130.00	
Extension Fees				
115 / 215	1.17(a)	Extension for response within first month	110.00	55.00
116 / 216	1.17(b)	Extension for response within second month	360.00	180.00
117 / 217	1.17(c)	Extension for response within third month	840.00	420.00
118 / 218	1.17(d)	Extension for response within fourth month	1,320.00	660.00
Appeals/Interference Fees				
119 / 219	1.17(e)	Notice of appeal	270.00	135.00
120 / 220	1.17(f)	Filing a brief in support of an appeal	270.00	135.00
121 / 221	1.17(g)	Request for oral hearing	230.00	115.00
Issue Fees				
142 / 242	1.18(a)	Utility issue fee	1,170.00	585.00
143 / 243	1.18(b)	Design issue fee	410.00	205.00
144 / 244	1.18(c)	Plant issue fee	590.00	295.00
Miscellaneous Fees				
111	1.20(j)	Extension of term of patent	1000.00	
112	1.17(n)	Requesting publication of SIR - Prior to examiner's action	820.00*	
113	1.17(o)	Requesting publication of SIR - After examiner's action	1,640.00*	
145	1.20(a)	Certificate of correction	100.00	
147	1.20(c)	For filing a request for reexamination	2,250.00	
148 / 248	1.20(d)	Statutory Disclaimer	110.00	55.00

Reduced by Basic Filing Fee Paid

FIGURE 7.3 (continued)

Fee Code	37 CFR	Description	Fee	Small Entity Fee if applicable
Patent Petition Fees				
122		Petitions to the Commissioner, unless otherwise specified	130.00	
126	1.17(p)	Submission of an Information Disclosure Statement (§1.97(c))	200.00	
138	1.17(j)	Petition to institute a public use proceeding	1,350.00	
140 / 240	1.17(l)	Petition to revive unavoidably abandoned application	110.00 /	55.00
141 / 241	1.17(m)	Petition to revive unintentionally abandoned application	1,170.00 /	585.00
Maintenance Fees :	**Applications Filed on or after December 12, 1980**			
183 / 283	1.20(e)	Due at 3.5 years	930.00 /	465.00
184 / 284	1.20(f)	Due at 7.5 years	1,870.00 /	935.00
185 / 285	1.20(g)	Due at 11.5 years	2,820.00 /	1,410.00
186 / 286	1.20(h)	Surcharge - Late payment within 6 months.	130.00 /	65.00
187	1.20(i)	Surcharge after expiration	620.00	
PCT Fees - National Stage				
154 / 254	1.492(e)	Surcharge - Late filing fee or oath or declaration	130.00 /	65.00
156	1.492(f)	English translation - after twenty months	130.00	
956 / 957	1.492(a)(1)	IPEA - U.S.	640.00 /	320.00
958 / 959	1.492(a)(2)	ISA - U.S.	710.00 /	355.00
960 / 961	1.492(a)(3)	PTO not ISA or IPEA	950.00 /	475.00
962 / 963	1.492(a)(4)	Claims meet PCT Article 33(1)-(4) - IPEA - U.S.	90.00 /	45.00
964 / 965	1.492(b)	Claims - extra independent (over three)	74.00 /	37.00
966 / 967	1.492(c)	Claims - extra total (over twenty)	22.00 /	11.00
968 / 969	1.492(d)	Claims - multiple dependent	230.00 /	115.00
970 / 971	1.492(a)(5)	For filing with EPO or JPO search report	830.00 /	415.00
PCT Fees - International Stage				
150	1.445(a)(1)	Transmittal fee	200.00	
151	1.445(a)(2)	PCT search fee - no U.S. application	620.00	
152	1.445 (a)(3)	Supplemental search per additional invention	170.00	
153	1.445(a)(2)	PCT search- prior U.S. application	410.00	
190	1.482(a)(1)	Preliminary examination fee - ISA was the U.S.	450.00	
191	1.482(a)(1)	Preliminary examination fee - ISA not the U.S.	670.00	
192	1.482(a)(2)	Additional invention - ISA was the U.S.	140.00	
193	1.482(a)(2)	Additional invention - ISA not the U.S.	230.00	
PCT Fees to WIPO				
800		Basic fee (first thirty pages)	525.00*	
801		Basic supplemental fee (for each page over thirty)	10.00*	
803		Handling fee	161.00*	
805 - 898		Designation fee per country	127.00*	
PCT Fee to EPO				
802		International search	1,635.00*	

*WIPO and EPO fees subject to periodic change due to fluctuations in exchange rate. Refer to Patent Official Gazette for current amounts.

FIGURE 7.3 *(continued)*

Fee Code	37 CFR	Description	Fee
Patent Service Fees			
561	1.19(a)(1)(i)	Printed copy of patent w/o color, regular service	3.00
562	1.19(a)(1)(ii)	Printed copy of patent w/o color, expedited local service	6.00
563	1.19(a)(1)(iii)	Printed copy of patent w/o color, ordered via EOS, expedited service	25.00
564	1.19(a)(2)	Printed copy of plant patent, in color	12.00
565	1.19(a)(3)	Copy of utility patent or SIR, with color drawings	24.00
566	1.19(b)(1)(i)	Certified or uncertified copy of patent application as filed, regular service	12.00
567	1.19(b)(1)(ii)	Certified or uncertified copy of patent application, expedited local service	24.00
568	1.19(b)(2)	Certified or uncertified copy of patent-related file wrapper and contents	150.00
569	1.19(b)(3)	Certified or uncertified copy of document, unless otherwise provided	25.00
570	1.19(b)(4)	For assignment records, abstract of title and certification, per patent	25.00
571	1.19(c)	Library Service	50.00
572	1.19(d)	List of U.S. patents and SIRs in subclass	3.00
573	1.19(e)	Uncertified statement re status of maintenance fee payments	10.00
574	1.19(f)	Copy of non-U.S. document	25.00
575	1.19(g)	Comparing and Certifying Copies, Per Document, Per Copy	25.00
576	1.19(h)	Additional filing receipt, duplicate or corrected due to applicant error	25.00
577	1.21(c)	Filing a Disclosure Document	10.00
578	1.21(d)	Local delivery box rental, per annum	50.00
579	1.21(e)	International type search report	40.00
580	1.21(g)	Self-service copy charge, per page	0.25
581	1.21(h)	Recording each patent assignment, agreement or other paper, per property	40.00
583	1.21(i)	Publication in Official Gazette	25.00
584	1.21(j)	Labor charges for services, per hour or fraction thereof	30.00
585	1.21(k)	Unspecified other services	AT COST
586	1.21(l)	Retaining abandoned application	130.00
587	1.21(n)	Handling fee for incomplete or improper application	130.00
588	1.21(o)	Automated Patent System (APS- Text) terminal session time, per hr.	40.00
590	1.24	Patent coupons	3.00
591	1.21(p)	APS-Text terminal session time, per hr., at the PTDLs	70.00*
589	1.296	Handling fee for withdrawal of SIR	130.00
Patent Enrollment Fees			
609	1.21(a)(1)	Admission to examination	300.00
610	1.21(a)(2)	Registration to practice	100.00
611	1.21(a)(3)	Reinstatement to practice	15.00
612	1.21(a)(4)	Copy of certificate of good standing	10.00
613	1.21(a)(4)	Certificate of good standing - suitable for framing	20.00
615	1.21(a)(5)	Review of decision of Director, Office of Enrollment and Discipline	130.00
616	1.21(a)(6)	Regrading of Examination	130.00

* Collection of the fee for APS-Text access at the PTDLs has been suspended until further notice.

FIGURE 7.3 (continued)

Fee Code	37 CFR	Description	Fee
		TRADEMARK FEES	

Trademark Processing Fees

Fee Code	37 CFR	Description	Fee
361	2.6(a)(1)	Application for registration, per class	210.00
362	2.6(a)(2)	Filing an Amendment to Allege Use under § 1(c), per class	100.00
363	2.6(a)(3)	Filing a Statement of Use under § 1(d)(1), per class	100.00
364	2.6(a)(4)	Filing a Request for a Six-month Extension of Time for Filing a Statement of Use under § 1(d)(1), per class	100.00
365	2.6(a)(5)	Application for renewal, per class	300.00
366	2.6(a)(6)	Additional fee for late renewal, per class	100.00
367	2.6(a)(7)	Publication of mark under §12(c), per class	100.00
368	2.6(a)(8)	Issuing new certificate of registration	100.00
369	2.6(a)(9)	Certificate of Correction, registrant's error	100.00
370	2.6(a)(10)	Filing disclaimer to registration	100.00
371	2.6(a)(11)	Filing amendment to registration	100.00
372	2.6(a)(12)	Filing § 8 affidavit, per class	100.00
373	2.6(a)(13)	Filing § 15 affidavit, per class	100.00
374	2.6(a)(14)	Filing combined §§ 8 & 15 affidavit, per class	200.00
375	2.6(a)(15)	Petition to the Commissioner	100.00
376	2.6(a)(16)	Petition for cancellation, per class	200.00
377	2.6(a)(17)	Notice of opposition, per class	200.00
378	2.6(a)(18)	Ex parte appeal, per class	100.00
379	2.6(a)(19)	Dividing an application, per new application (file wrapper) created	100.00

Trademark Service Fees

Fee Code	37 CFR	Description	Fee
461	2.6(b)(1)(i)	Printed copy of each registered mark, regular service	3.00
462	2.6(b)(1)(ii)	Printed copy of each registered mark, expedited local service	6.00
463	2.6(b)(1)(iii)	Printed copy of each registered mark ordered via EOS, expedited service	25.00
464	2.6(b)(4)(i)	Certified copy of registered mark, with title and/or status, regular service	10.00
465	2.6(b)(4)(ii)	Certified copy of registered mark, with title and/or status, expedited local service	20.00
466	2.6(b)(2)(i)	Certified or uncertified copy of trademark application as filed, regular service	12.00
467	2.6(b)(2)(ii)	Certified or uncertified copy of trademark application as filed, expedited local service	24.00
468	2.6(b)(3)	Certified or uncertified copy of trademark-related file wrapper and contents	50.00
469	2.6(b)(5)	Certified or uncertified copy of trademark document, unless otherwise provided	25.00
470	2.6(b)(7)	For assignment records, abstracts of title and certification per registration	25.00
475	1.19(g)	Comparing and certifying copies, per document, per copy	25.00
480	2.6(b)(9)	Self-service copy charge, per page	0.25
481	2.6(b)(6)	Recording trademark assignment, agreement or other paper, first mark per document	40.00
482		For second and subsequent marks in the same document	25.00
484	2.6(b)(10)	Labor charges for services, per hour or fraction thereof	30.00
485	2.6(b)(11)	Unspecified other services	AT COST
488	2.6(b)(8)	Each hour of T-SEARCH terminal session time	40.00
490	1.24	Trademark coupons	3.00

GENERAL FEES

Finance Service Fees

Fee Code	37 CFR	Description	Fee
607	1.21(b-1)	Establish deposit account	10.00
608	1.21(b)(2)	Service charge for below minimum balance	25.00
608	1.21(b)(3)	Service charge for below minimum balance restricted subscription deposit account	25.00
617	1.21(m)	Processing returned checks	50.00

Computer Service Fees

Fee Code	37 CFR	Description	Fee
618		Computer records	AT COST

PATENT LICENSING

8

A patent grants to an inventor the right to exclude others from copying the invention. If the inventor wishes to go into business, he or she may wish to retain the patent. In the event an infringer appears, the inventor can use it to stop the infringement.

On the other hand, an inventor may not wish to go into business, may not have the expertise to do so, or may not have the capital investment required. In that event, the inventor may wish to sell all of his or her patent rights to someone else and get something in return, such as a lump sum cash payment or perhaps royalties based upon the sales by a new owner. With a sale of the patent by an assignment, the inventor relinquishes essentially all rights and a new owner then stands in place of the inventor with the ability to stop infringers.

There is, however, yet another alternative between retaining the patent rights and selling the patent to someone else. That alternative is licensing. Licensing affords the opportunity to divide between two or more people or companies the rights, obligations, and risks associated with a patent and with being in business. The division of those rights, obligations, and risks can vary over a broad range. License provisions come in many variations. The purpose of a license is to define the rights, obligations, and risks of two or more parties and to provide solutions to disputes, if they should arise. Licenses can become as lengthy and complicated as is appropriate to the particular situation and as is desired by the parties. While this book cannot begin to discuss licenses in thorough detail, some of the more important aspects of typical licenses may be considered. "Licensors" and "Licensees" have a broad range of opportunity to negotiate terms that meet their business goals.

EXCLUSIVITY

The license may be exclusive or nonexclusive. With a nonexclusive license, the patent owner may later license other additional parties. All licensees may make and sell the invention and will be required to pay a royalty to the patent owner.

However, the parties may prefer that one licensee have all the rights. With such an exclusive license, the licensee is able to stop all others from infringing the patent, including the patent owner. Often a licensee prefers an exclusive license, since he or she may not want the patent owner to be licensing competitors. Because the exclusive license is more desirable to the licensee and prevents the patent owner from licensing others, an exclusive license generally requires a greater royalty.

In the event that an exclusive license is granted, it is advisable to also provide for some minimum performance by the licensee. The licensor does not want to be put in a position where the licensee can sit on its hands, sell no products, and pay no royalties and yet continue to hold onto the exclusive license. This would prevent the patent owner from licensing someone else or from going into the business himself. A typical minimum performance provision requires that a certain number of units be sold or at least that a certain minimum royalty be paid to keep the license. That minimum royalty may change from year to year in accordance with an agreed-upon schedule.

FIELD AND TERRITORIAL RESTRICTIONS

The parties may want the license to be limited to a particular product or commercial field. For example, a new lubrication system might be exclusively licensed to one car manufacturer for the field of motor vehicles. With such a limitation, the licensor would still be free to license others—for example, for manufacturing industrial machinery.

The parties may also negotiate a license that is territorially restricted. For example, one licensee might be licensed to make and sell the invention east of the Mississippi, while another is licensed to sell the invention west of the Mississippi. With both territorial and field of use restrictions in a license, the parties must be careful not to violate anti-trust laws.

ROYALTIES AND ROYALTY BASIS

Patent attorneys are often asked what is a "usual" patent royalty. There is none. Royalties can vary from a fraction of 1 percent of sales price to as high as 30 percent of sales price, although both extremes are rare. The amount of royalty is determined by negotiation as a result of the negotiating strength of the parties and the economic forces affecting the business. A relatively high royalty might be reasonable for a low volume, new item with a high profit margin. A relatively low royalty would be appropriate for a high volume, low profit product in a highly competitive market. While a royalty of 3 percent to 8 percent might be common, market forces play such an important role that a "usual" guideline is of little value. The parties negotiating a royalty should recognize that the royalty must provide both a reasonable incentive to both parties, as well as a significant return to each in proportion to the individual contribution to the commercial success of the product.

Royalties are not always based upon a percentage of sales price. A royalty may be so many dollars or cents per unit sold and may also change according to a schedule. For example, the royalty may decrease as sales volume increases or change with inflation.

TERM AND TERMINATION

The license may last until the patent expires after its 17-year life, or it may continue for a shorter term. Sometimes a license may be canceled at any time by either party and sometimes it is automatically renewed annually unless terminated by a party. A license may be issued for five years with the requirement that a new license then be negotiated.

It is important that a license spell out what happens if the license is terminated at the desire of one or both parties, or if it is terminated because one party did not live up to its obligations. For example, if the license is terminated, will the licensee be permitted to sell remaining articles in stock?

OTHER TERMS

The license may provide that the licensee is permitted to grant sublicenses to others for a royalty that is shared by the licensor. Alternatively, such sublicensing may be prohibited. The cost of any litigation might be divided equally between the licensee and licensor, or the entire cost placed upon one of them. An obligation to enforce the patent by suing any infringer might be placed upon the licensor.

In a nonexclusive license, the licensee might be entitled to a "most favored nations" clause under which the licensee gets the benefit of the most favorable license terms the licensor may later grant to someone else. The license may provide that later improvements made by the licensor will also be included in the license or that improvements made by the licensee will be assigned to the licensor. Finally, in the event that a dispute arises between the licensor and licensee, the license might require that it be settled in an arbitration proceeding, rather than in a court of law.

The above represents only a few of the options and possibilities available in licensing. While licensing opens doors of opportunity for parties to tailor an agreement to their business expectations, it also opens the door to uncertainties and complications. A longer and more detailed license makes a more extensive attempt to foresee and solve potential future problems.

FOREIGN PATENTS

9

With few exceptions, patents are issued by countries and provided protection only within the territorial limits of the issuing country. Therefore, if important markets exist for an invention in other countries, the owner of an invention may wish to seek patent protection in those countries. Most countries, and particularly most industrialized countries, have patent systems quite similar to that of the United States. The same kind of subject matter is patentable in most countries, although some exclude pharmaceuticals, foodstuffs, and a few other things from patent protection. The courts of some countries tend to favor local citizens, so investment in patent protection there may not be valuable. In Eastern European and former Soviet republics, the form of the patent system is unclear and will probably continue to be while they address more pressing problems. Consult your patent attorney about specific countries.

While a few countries merely register inventions, most countries examine the applications to determine whether the invention is different enough from prior technology that it is entitled to be patented under their law. Most countries require something quite similar to nonobviousness, although it might be called by a different name, such as "inventive step" as in Europe. Also, in most countries the procedure for obtaining a patent is similar to the procedure in the United States. A patent examiner reviews your patent application, states in writing whether he or she believes you are entitled to a patent. If the examiner does not, you have an opportunity to convince him or her a patent should be allowed.

Therefore, in general the owner of an invention who wishes to seek a patent in one or more foreign countries must file a patent application in each country in which a patent is sought.

There are some helpful exceptions, such as the European Patent Convention.

Not only is it necessary to file a foreign patent application for each country or region in which a patent will be sought, but all such patent applications must be filed within critical time limits. The reason the time limits are so important is that in nearly all countries of the world, a patent application for an invention must be filed before the invention is made public, such as by publishing or selling the invention. The one-year grace period that the U.S. law provides, giving an inventor a year from the time the invention is publicly disclosed until a patent application must be filed, is a very rare exception in world patent law. As a result, if the only applicable law were the national laws of each country, an inventor or owner of an invention would be faced with an impossible burden of filing patent applications throughout the world before the invention was made public anywhere.

INTERNATIONAL TREATIES

Over a century ago, in 1883, a group of countries signed a treaty to prevent this burden and also to ensure that the signing countries would not pass laws discriminating against citizens of other countries. This treaty provided that foreigners would be treated like citizens, and it greatly reduced the time deadline problem described above.

This treaty, known as the Paris Convention, was modified several times thereafter. It allows an inventor who has filed a patent application in his or her home country to file patent applications in foreign countries and get special priority treatment. This priority applies only if the inventor files in the foreign countries within one year of the date the home country patent was filed. The special priority is that the filing date for a patent application in his home country will also be the legal, effective filing date under the law of a foreign country if the foreign patent application is filed within one year of the date on which the home country patent application was filed. Therefore, you can file your foreign patent applications anytime within the one year following the date you filed in your home country. If you do so, in each foreign country the filing date will become retroactive to the filing date in your home country.

As a result, a U.S. inventor can file his or her patent application in the United States Patent and Trademark Office and the next day, or any time thereafter, make the invention as public as he or she wishes—the inventor will still retain the right to obtain a patent in foreign countries. This means that, if you file your U.S. patent application before the invention is made public, it doesn't matter how public you make the invention after filing your U.S. application, so long as you file foreign applications within one year of filing in the United States. However, owners of inventions must remember that, in the event that the invention is made public *before* filing the U.S. patent application, the right to obtain a patent in most foreign countries is destroyed. Therefore, it is very important that the invention not be made public before your home country application is filed if foreign patent protection is desired.

While there are several other treaties, two have been signed within the past two decades that are of particular value to most U.S. applicants. They are the European Patent Convention and the Patent Cooperation Treaty.

EUROPEAN PATENT OFFICE

Fourteen European countries, approximating, but not identical to, the common market countries, signed a treaty in 1973 forming the European Patent Office (EPO), located in Munich, Germany. This Treaty provides an alternative to filing individual national patent applications in one or more of those 14 European countries. The treaty allows you to file one patent application in the European Patent Office, designate as many of the fourteen countries as you wish, and pay a fee based in part on the number of countries designated. The patent application may be in English, German, or French, and communications with the patent examiner will be held in the language of the application.

Filing a patent application in this manner is considerably less expensive than filing individually in all 14 countries, though it is considerably more expensive than filing in one country. For cost effectiveness, a general rule of thumb is that if you wish to seek patent protection in four or more of these European countries, you should use the European Patent Office. Otherwise you should file directly in the particular countries.

Another advantage of the European Patent Office is that you deal with only one patent examiner for all the countries that you have designated. Therefore, you are not attempting to communicate with many different European patent examiners, trying to convince each of them that your patent should be granted. If the European patent examiner agrees that you are entitled to a patent, his or her decision applies to all the designated European countries. The examiner's approval is communicated to the patent office for each country that you have designated. Then you pay issue fees to each country and file translations, and each country then issues its own national patent for your invention.

At the time that this book was written, there was no single European or common market patent, although negotiations have been conducted toward that goal for several years.

PATENT COOPERATION TREATY

The European Patent Convention offers an *alternative* to filing in individual European countries in order to reduce costs and avoid duplication of effort. Another treaty, the Patent Cooperation Treaty (PCT), offers an intermediate step. (You can interpose the step following the filing of your first patent application in your home country and before the filing of national applications in individual foreign countries or in the European Patent Office.) The PCT allows you to postpone the filing of national applications if, instead, within one year of filing your U.S. patent application, you file a single patent application under the Patent Cooperation Treaty. In a PCT application you designate those countries and/or the European Patent Office in which you will, in the future, file a patent application. Most industrialized nations are members of the Patent Cooperation Treaty and may be designated. Thus, the Patent Cooperation Treaty offers a considerably less expensive alternative to national filing within the one year period of the Treaty of Paris. However, it only postpones the national filing and its substantial costs—the PCT does not eliminate them.

The Patent Cooperation Treaty allows an applicant to file a single patent application in a single, strictly controlled international format in one of the designated receiving offices for the PCT. Since the U.S. Patent and Trademark Office is a designated receiving office, this means that a U.S. patent applicant may file this international PCT application in the U.S. Patent and Trademark Office. The PCT application preserves the special priority benefit of having the U.S. patent application date be the legal international filing date in later filed national patent applications. Therefore, the PCT application is like a link in a chain, connecting the date of filing of the U.S. patent application through the PCT to the national patent applications in the EPO and/or the various countries that are designated.

Under the PCT, an international patent search is performed, and a nonbinding, preliminary examination by a U.S. patent examiner may be obtained. If it is, then the filing of those national patent applications, including an EPO application, may be postponed until 30 months after the filing of the original U.S. patent application. Although there are other advantages to the PCT, one of its principal advantages is that it enables an inventor to postpone the very significant cost of filing foreign patent applications in specific countries and/or the European Patent Office, thereby allowing time for the invention to be sold and become more profitable. The nonbinding preliminary examination gives an examiner's opinion on whether you are entitled to a patent, but that opinion is not binding on other examiners. You do get an opportunity to amend your patent claims in view of the examiner's opinion, if you wish.

PRACTICAL ASPECTS

Usually patent applications in each foreign country are filed by patent agents who are residents of the country. Consequently, the filing of foreign patent applications usually begins with your patent attorney sending a copy of the U.S. patent application documents to a foreign patent agent. Since PCT patent applications can be filed in the U.S. Patent and Trademark Office, a U.S. patent attorney can prepare and file the PCT patent application. However, after the time has elapsed under the Patent Cooperation Treaty and it becomes necessary to file in each national country, or if you do not file a PCT application, typically your patent attorney will send the U.S. patent application papers to the foreign agents. In non–English-speaking countries, the patent agent must obtain a translation, but if you can have it translated here, you may do so to save money. The Patent Office in each country corresponds with the local agent, who then corresponds with your U.S. patent attorney with respect to communications with the foreign patent examiner and issuance of the patent.

The filing and maintenance of foreign patent applications and the maintenance of foreign patents can be very expensive. Most countries seem to view patent application as a substantial revenue source. Additionally, unlike the United States, in most foreign countries patent agents are permitted to get together and set agreed-upon fixed fees, thereby eliminating competitive forces among them. Most countries require the appointment of a patent agent having an office within its territory.

The result is that, even though the foreign agents do not do any original writing to describe and claim the invention, the filing of foreign patent applications can sometimes exceed the cost of preparing and filing an application in the United States. Translation costs can range from $1,000–$3,000. As a general rule of thumb, you can expect the cost of filing a typical patent application in an English-speaking country to range from $1,000–$2,000 and in a non–English-speaking country to range from $2,000–$3,000. In some countries, such as Japan, the cost may be $3,000–$5,000. The cost of filing a patent application in the European Patent Office might typically be on the order of $10,000 and the cost of issuing such a patent in all European countries can easily be on the order of $20,000. In essentially all foreign countries, periodic, usually annual, taxes must be paid to avoid cancellation of the patent. Each country has its own cost schedule and the amounts vary greatly. All these costs are dependent upon currency exchange rates.

The cost of a patent application filed under the Patent Cooperation Treaty might typically be on the order of $2,000–$4,000, with the cost of requesting (technically, "demanding") the nonbinding preliminary examination on the order of $1,000.

It should be remembered that all of these cost estimates are subject to a substantial number of variabilities for particular cases and localities and consequently may not be accurate for your particular set of circumstances. These cost estimates are only intended as rough guidelines. However, foreign patent agents are willing to provide specific cost estimates upon submission to them of copies of the U.S. patent application documents. In general, these estimates are reliable.

It is important to emphasize that timing is of critical importance in the filing of foreign patent applications. Be sure to allow sufficient time for the filing to be accomplished—the procedure should be initiated well in advance of the deadline. Preferably, documents should be sent to the foreign patent agents at least one month before the filing deadline to allow time for unexpected delays. However, in some circumstances the applications can be filed on short notice, and generally, the foreign patent agents are quite cooperative. But an applicant is well advised to avoid the risk of unexpected delays that could destroy the effectiveness of a foreign patent application.

COPYRIGHTS

III

WHAT IS A COPYRIGHT?

10

Like patent law, copyright is a form of legal protection provided by statutes of the U.S. government and is granted to authors of "original works of authorship," including literary, dramatic, musical, artistic, and certain other intellectual works. In addition to published works, unpublished works are also subject to protection, regardless of the nationality or domicile of the author. This protection exists from the time the work is created in fixed form—that is, in any tangible medium of expression, now known or later developed, from which the work can be perceived, reproduced, or otherwise communicated, either directly or with the aid of a machine or device. A copyright in a work of authorship ordinarily immediately becomes the property of the author who created it, and only he or she or those deriving their rights through him or her can rightfully claim copyright. However, this is not true for an employee who was hired to create the work.

Copyright law provides individuals and companies with the right to demand payment from others for the use of said copyrighted materials. Naturally, the actual monetary value of these rights hinges on the demand for granting permission to use a work protected by copyright law. The movie *Star Wars*, for instance, generated sales of related products and characters in excess of $1.5 billion. And the copyrighted products of Charles Schulz's *Peanuts* characters have become a big business. The cost to obtain the image of Snoopy and Charlie Brown, for example, could very well cost an arm and a leg. Then too, among Walt Disney Company's most valuable assets are its copyrighted characters. Obviously, business has good reason to protect its copyrighted goods.

All copyright matters arising after its effective date of January 1, 1978, fall under the jurisdiction of The Copyright Revision Act of 1976. Previously, copyright law was governed by the Copyright Act of 1909 and common law. Now, with the new act, Congress by statute preempts all common law of copyright. Correspondence on this subject should be addressed to the Copyright Office, Library of Congress, Washington, D.C. 20559.

COPYRIGHTABLE WORKS

Works of authorship that can be copyrighted are in the following categories:

1. Literary works.
2. Musical works, including any accompanying words.
3. Dramatic works, including any accompanying music.
4. Pantomimes and choreographic works.
5. Pictorial, graphic, and sculptural works.
6. Motion pictures and other audiovisual works.
7. Sound recordings.

This list is a broad classification and is not inclusive. For example, computer programs are clearly copyrightable, although for a while there was some uncertainty when the statute was written. Advertising copy can even be copyrighted, including graphics and text material, and so can maps, architectural blueprints, and greeting cards. Copyright is being extended to computer displays.

WHAT CANNOT BE COPYRIGHTED

The copyright statute states, "In no case does copyright protection for an original work of authorship extend to any idea, procedure, process, system, method of operation, concept, principle, or discovery, regardless of the form in which it is described, explained, illustrated, or embodied in such work." Thus, only an author's expression of an idea is protected, not the idea itself.

To be more specific, those categories of work generally not copyrightable include:

1. Works that have not been fixed in a tangible form of expression. Examples might be something that is improvisational, such as a speech, a song, or a performance that has not been written or recorded.

2. Names, short phrases, slogans, titles; symbols or designs; mere variations of typographic ornamentation, lettering, or coloring; mere listings of ingredients or contents. Contrary to public opinion, the titles of books and movies are not copyrightable.

3. Works that consist entirely of information that is common property and contains no original authorship. This would include calendars, height and weight charts, and lists or tables taken from public documents or other common sources. A selection and arrangement of such information is copyrightable if some nontrivial amount of creative effort was required. However, even an extensive arrangement, say, the names, addresses, and phone numbers in a telephone book, may not constitute a copyrightable work if not much choice and creative effort was exercised, despite the amount of work required.

4. A functional part of a useful object. An example of this might be a hubcap with an ornamental or aesthetic design. Such a product could be considered for a design patent. In a famous case that questioned the copyrightability of a sculpture that served as a lamp base, a favorable ruling was given. The lamp had a figure of a woman from whose head a pipe and lightbulb socket extended. The court ruled that, although the statue supported the light, its sculptural shape and features by themselves were not functional and therefore were copyrightable. This means that the more functional something is, the less probable it is that it can be copyrighted, while the more the artistic features are separate and distinct, the better its chances are. For example, the picture on the side of a box is clearly copyrightable.

5. Works of the U.S. government. The statute disallows practically all works that are produced and distributed by the U.S. Printing Office. The principle behind this statute is that the taxpayers pay for the federal government, so they should be able to copy the work created by the government. Included would be any work created by anyone em-

ployed by the government to create the work. The federal government can own a copyrighted work, however. It can receive and hold copyrights transferred to it by assignment, bequest, or otherwise. For instance, the government could purchase a copyrighted work from an individual with a contract specifying that the copyright must be maintained.

6. Works that fall into the public domain. For example, works that were published without a copyright notice when such a notice was required are not protected and therefore become public domain. Likewise, so does a work when its copyright expires.

We have listed what can and cannot be copyrighted, but there are always some things that do not fall clearly into the above categories and thereby become subjects of debate in the courtroom. From time to time these gray areas come up, and the court must decide if the item in dispute is copyrightable. The lamp base case mentioned is a good example. For a long time, there was a question of whether a computer program could be copyrighted before an affirmative decision was made. For years, the issue of obscene material has been debated. Although the courts have expressed the opinion that what is obscene and undesirable is not a basis to deny copyright, in practice some courts do strain the law and rule against such material.

Interestingly, the courts have decided that certain parts of a game cannot be copyrighted, including its rules, concept, and name. However, such things as the board graphics, cards, and the text explaining the rules are copyrightable. This means that someone could reproduce a game such as Monopoly, for example, by offering a different board, cards, and explanation of the rules, although, in essence, it would be the same game. Keep in mind, however, that a game could be patented and its name could have a trademark. In the case of Monopoly, its inventor, Charles B. Darrow, did get a patent and received millions in royalties from Parker Brothers, which later bought him out. Seventeen years later, the monopoly of the patent expired, but the trademark and copyrighted parts remained protected. (In fact, a board game called "Anti-Monopoly" had similar rules with the obvious exception that its object was to break the monopoly.)

Prior to 1990, the creations of an architect could only be protected in the form of the drawings. Thus, while the drawings could not be copied, others were free to examine the drawings or the building itself and copy it directly. The building was not an infringing copy of the drawings. While buildings are somewhat like sculpture, they were considered more like useful mechanical objects and were not protected by copyright. In 1990, however, Congress changed the law to extend copyright portection to architectural works. However, while the overall form and arrangement of spaces and elements in the design can now be protected, standard features or features copied from others are not.

ORIGINALITY

As you recall, a prerequisite of patent law is that an invention must be new, useful, and nonobvious. Specifically, new is the requirement of novelty—something different than what has been done before. In order to determine if an invention has not previously existed, a patent search is in order. While an author must also create something new in order to receive a copyright, the question arises: "How new must it be?" The answer is: "It doesn't have to be very new."

The hurdle that must be overcome to reach a level and degree of newness is to merely create something more than a trivial change or modification. This translates into having the author create something that is recognizably original. Originality does not require aptness, brightness, or an artistic breakthrough. The work must simply have some minimal, unique, artistic qualities and, of course, it cannot be copied from the copyrighted work of another person. The work does not have to be new thoughts. For instance, many authors can write about the same subject, such as a historical event or a famous person (note how many books have been authored about subjects such as the Civil War, Abraham Lincoln, and Winston Churchill). Similarly, many artists have painted the same subject (a rose, a specific beach on the ocean, etc.). A new manner of expression is what counts. In the case of text, it is the words; with an oil painting, it is such things as color, texture, and shape. With this in mind, the courts ascertain that only a distinguishable variation or something more than trivial is required. While there is still vagueness on what constitutes originality, this is the test that is applied.

Most of us do not have a great deal of original thought. Since the standard is originality, there is no need to do a copyright search like one that is conducted for a patent. Besides, such a search could take a lifetime or more and would be expensive.

Then, too, unlike two inventors who apply for a patent on an identical invention, if two writers happen to independently create an identical work, both works are copyrightable. As Judge Learned Hand wrote, "Borrowed the work must indeed not be, for a plagiarist is not himself pro tanto an 'author'; but if by some magic a man who had never known it were to compose anew Keats's "Ode on a Grecian Urn," he would be an 'author,' and, if he copyrighted it, others might not copy that poem, though they might of course copy Keats's." Theoretically, the question about who created the work first is not a significant issue.

A point of interest regarding copyright law is how the courts apply what seems to be a different standard when legal documents are the topic. Technically speaking, there is no reason why these writings should be less copyrightable than other documents, but court rulings have indicated that judges react differently to cases involving these matters. Perhaps it is the typical judge's familiarity with the subject that tends to make him or her require more originality in order to rule the differences as being more than trivial.

RIGHTS FOR A COPYRIGHT OWNER

The Copyright Revision Act of 1976 provides certain exclusive rights that an author has and can authorize others to use, and it includes any of the following:

1. Reproducing the copyrighted work in copies or phonorecords.

2. Preparing derivative works (such as arrangements, translations, or dramatizations) based on the copyrighted work.

3. Distributing copies or phonorecords of the copyrighted work to the public by sale or other transfer of ownership, or by rental, lease, or lending.

4. In the case of literary, musical, dramatic, and choreographic works, pantomimes, and motion pictures and other audiovisual works, performing the copyrighted work publicly.

5. In the case of literary, musical, dramatic, and choreographic works, pantomimes, and pictorial, graphic, or

sculptural works, including the individual images of a motion picture or other audiovisual work, displaying the copyrighted work publicly.

Anyone who violates any of these rights provided to the owner of copyright is committing an illegal act.

Frequently, a collective work exists, such as a periodical issue, anthology, or encyclopedia, in which a number of contributions, constituting separate and independent works in themselves, are assembled into a collective whole. In these instances, copyright in each separate contribution is distinct from copyright in the collective work as a whole, and exists initially in the author's individual contribution. Unless there is a specific contract that has transferred the copyright to the owner of the collective work, it is presumed that nothing other than what appears in the collective work and any later collective work in the same series remains the property of the author of the collective work.

For example, a freelance writer can submit an article to a magazine and receive payment on it, while the magazine carries a copyright notice showing that all of its contents are copyrighted. Even so, the author remains the owner of the copyright of the article unless there is an agreement otherwise. The magazine has only purchased "first rights." Sometimes, an author may request that a copyright notice appear on the first or last page of the article. But even without this notice, unless otherwise agreed by contract, the author still is the copyright owner of the work. Interestingly, a person may purchase an original work of an artist, such as an oil painting or woodcarving, and while he or she owns the actual art, it does not mean he or she can sell photographs of his or her possession to a publisher. This is true because the original copyright rights remain with the artist, even though the piece of art itself has transferred ownership.

Derivative works, which are distinguishable variations that have been substantially copied from earlier works, can also have copyright protection. For example, a writer who owns a copyright can make additions to a previously copyrighted work and copyright the new work. Likewise, anyone can add new elements to a work that is in the public domain, and though one cannot copyright the old work, the new creation can be copyrighted. For instance, a writer can put his or her own creativity into a work by Shakespeare, Balzac, or Emerson, and as a consequence, obtain a copyright. Furthermore, such derivative works as compilations, abridgments, adaptations, dramatizations, and translations all require original effort and are copyrightable in their own right. Keep in mind, however, that if a derivative work is based on copyrighted material, it is necessary to obtain the copyright owner's consent for the derivative work to be copyrightable and publishable. This means that a writer must obtain permission to alter the copyrighted work of another writer, such as Stephen King or James Michener; without such permission, he or she is a copyright infringer.

A person can divide up and transfer rights to a work in any way he or she chooses. Some rights may be sold, and subsequently, other rights in the same work may be sold to another party. An author may sell audio, video, and foreign rights, to name a few. The ownership of a copyright may be transferred in whole or in part by any written means of conveyance or by operation by law, and may be bequeathed by will or pass as personal property by the applicable laws regulating the transfer of the property of a deceased person.

FAIR USE

Although a copyright owner has certain exclusive rights, there are some limitations that Congress has imposed that are referred to as "fair use." For years, the courts have discussed whether certain kinds of copying of copyrighted works should be permitted. Under some circumstances, copying is believed to be socially desirable and yet not unfair to the copyright owner. This is true because the benefits to society as a whole outweigh the relatively small amount of potential harm to the copyright owner. The revised act now provides guidelines for what kinds of uses are considered fair. This means that there is room for flexibility in every case to determine the effect a particular use may have on the rights of a copyright owner. Of course, whenever a question of fairness arises, everyone may have a different idea of what actually constitutes being fair, but the following criteria are what the court looks at to make a decision:

1. The purpose and character of the use, including whether such use has a commercial nature or is for nonprofit educational purposes. The court will allow more leeway when somebody is not using the work for economic gain.

2. The nature of the copyrighted work. There is less chance to use a work with only entertainment value versus some-

thing with social benefit. If the nature of the work is educational or intellectual, such as a political debate or a learned treatise, it is more likely to be considered fair use.

3. The amount and substantiality of the portion used in relation to the copyrighted work as a whole. It may be permissible to take some parts of the other person's work, but not too much. Obviously, the larger the excerpt used, the greater the risk of copyright infringement.

4. The effect of the use on the potential market for, or value of, the copyrighted work. Here the question is, "How much damage in lost business will the copyright owner suffer as a consequence of somebody using the work to distract from sales?" Of course, sometimes, it actually helps the sale when the work has been quoted in another publication and/or different media. With this in mind, the courts might be more lenient when something is taken from an out-of-print book.

When fair use is being evaluated, the above four factors should always be considered. A finding with respect to each factor is taken into consideration and weighed against the findings for the others, keeping in mind the particular right being exercised. Still, the fact that one unfavorable finding exists does not automatically rule out fair use; in each case, it is the net effect of all the findings that controls the decision, since the Act does not require any one factor be given more weight than the others.

In determining fair use, it is important to view the purpose and character of the copyrighted work. For example, when weighing the use of a work, the commercial or nonprofit educational character of a use must be considered. Note, however, that this is not to suggest that fair use will be found only for nonprofit purposes or that fair use will be found in every case when there are nonprofit purposes.

When discussing fair use of a copyrighted work, the subject of reproduction is also an important issue. For instance, it is not an infringement of copyright for a library or archives, or any of its employees acting within the scope of their employment, to reproduce no more than one copy or phonorecord of a work, or to distribute such copy or phonorecord if the following conditions are met: (1) there is no commercial advantage, (2) the collections of the library or archives are open to the public, and (3) the reproduction of the work includes a notice of copyright. For more information regarding what a library and archives may and may not do, we recommend reviewing Section 108 of the Revised Copyright Act of 1976.

Just what is permissible for reproduction for individual use by a copying machine, tape recorder, and video recorder is a highly complicated subject. A court case, for example, ruled that it is not a copyright infringement to copy a television program for private use for the purpose of time translation. In other words, if, for convenience purposes, an individual recorded a television program so that it could be viewed at another time, this would not constitute a copyright infringement. The court, however, did not address the question of whether a copy could be used to build an individual's private collection.

We realize that there might be many unanswered questions not covered in this text concerning the copying of works of jukeboxes, cable television, and so on. If you are in a field that concerns such works, we suggest you consult with knowledgeable people within your industry and an attorney.

DURATION OF COPYRIGHT

In general, copyright in a work created on or after January 1, 1978, subsists from its creation and endures for a term consisting of the life of the author and 50 years after the author's death. In the case of a joint work prepared by two or more authors who did not work for hire, the copyright would continue for 50 years following the last surviving author's death. In the case of anonymous works, pseudonymous works, and works made for hire, the copyright endures for a term of 75 years of its first publication, or a term of 100 years from its creation, whichever expires first. The term of such copyright runs to the end of the calendar year in which it would otherwise expire.

Prior to January 1, 1978, the duration of a copyright for a published work was 28 years, starting with its first publication date. It could also be renewed for another 28-year term. Since the Revised Copyright Act of 1976, there have been certain formulas pertaining to previous works that modify the rights in works created before January 1, 1978. Since this book is focused on people who want information pertaining to new work, we will not delve into the complicated laws that apply to copyrighted law before the present act. Prior to the 1976 Act, while Congress was considering the new statute, it extended the old copyrights, year by year, that were due to expire, and created a great deal of complication. Though we will not cover copyright law regarding these works, if you have an interest in knowing what still remains copyrighted for the purpose of avoiding copyright infringement, we suggest that you consult an attorney on the specific work in question. Interestingly, the present statute that extended copyright protection to the life of the owner(s) plus 50 years is consistent with other countries and existing copyright treaties entered into by the United States.

COPYRIGHT INFRINGEMENT

Earlier in this chapter, we explained that the originality of a work does not have to be very substantial in order to be copyrighted. There is a thin line between what constitutes the public domain and private property in copyright law. Anyone can generally copy such stock elements as plot, theme, and setting—it is the specific form or language by which the work is presented that provides original treatment. As previously stated, nobody can have a monopoly on a subject for a book or a painting. It is the manner of expression that is at issue when copyright infringement is discussed.

The manner of the infringement is also at issue. For example, dramatic works cannot be performed in public without the copyright owner's consent, yet there is more leeway for musical compositions, since if the rule for dramatic works were applied, it would prohibit whistling a tune in public. Musical works must not be performed "for profit" without the copyright owner's consent. Under the Copyright Act, "for profit" would include music played in café orchestras or piped into a hotel elevator. As pointed out under the "Fair Use" section of this chapter, infringement also depends on how much and how the copyrighted work is used, and who uses it. Renting software or phonorecords may also be an infringement. In many situations, there is no absolute test to determine if infringement exists. If you think somebody is infringing on your work, it is up to you to stop the person. As in the case of patents, there is no regulatory agency to do it for you.

The Copyright Act offers certain remedies when the rights of a registered copyright are infringed. First, the court may grant temporary and final injunctions anywhere in the United States on such terms that it deems reasonable to prevent or restrain infringement of a copyright. The court may also order an impounding or destruction of all copies or phonorecords claimed to have been made or used in violation of the copyright owner's exclusive rights, including all plates, molds, matrices, masters, tapes, film negatives, or other articles used to reproduce the work.

Additionally, the infringer of copyright can be liable for the copyright owner's actual damages and any additional profits of the infringer as well as certain statutory damages. Furthermore, at its discretion, the court may allow the recovery of full costs by or against any party other than the United States or an officer thereof, including a reasonable attorney's fee to the prevailing party as part of the costs. If infringement is deemed to be criminal, a fine up to the amount of $25,000 and imprisonment for not more than one year or both may be evoked; for any subsequent offense, the fine can be as high as $50,000 and up to two years imprisonment or both.

If you think somebody has infringed on your copyrighted work, the first thing you must do is establish that you own the copyright for the work. You can accomplish this rather easily by using direct evidence. Since the 1976 Act, your certificate of registration provides that it shall constitute prima facie evidence of the validity of the facts stated in it and the originality of the registered work. A recorded ownership transfer document can be used to show ownership in cases where the person bringing the action acquired rights from somebody else. Next, as the owner of an infringed work, you must clearly establish evidence that there has been an unauthorized copying of your copyrighted work.

You must remember that the copyright office does not enforce rights. If an infringement of rights occurs and the owner is not aware of it or does not elect to take action, the U.S. Copyright Office will not assert a claim for or on behalf of the owner. With the exception of an application for registration of a claim of rights, the copyright office has no authority under the Act to initiate an infringement action, and furthermore, the office will not become a party to it.

As you can see, infringement of a copyright can be a serious offense, so we advise consulting an attorney if you suspect that you are involved in copyright infringement.

BEING A COPYRIGHT OWNER—THINGS TO DO

11

As stated in the previous chapter, there is immediate protection under copyright law from the instant your work is created in fixed form. With this in mind, there is not nearly as much to do to get your work copyrighted as there is to get an invention patented. No searches are necessary. There are no complicated applications that require specifications or claims to be made. In short, it is much easier and less expensive to obtain a copyright than a patent—and it is something that *you* can do. It does not require an attorney, once you know how to do it, although it is preferable if you have not been properly instructed.

Note, however, that copyright law does not offer the same broad protection that patent law does. For starters, there is not a 17-year monopoly on your work. For example, although one writer may be the first to get the "scoop" on a certain news-worthy event, there is no protection under the copyright law to prevent another person from writing about the same thing. All subjects are open season for all writers. Furthermore, a writer could be hired to submit an article to a magazine publisher, have it rejected, and another writer could then be assigned to do the story, and it would not constitute copyright infringement (depending on a prior agreement, however, either written or implied, it is possible that the publisher could be guilty of breach of contract).

In comparing patents and copyrights, there are three basic differences. First, the subject matter differs because patents are directed at physical, scientific, and technological things, whereas copyrights are directed more at artistic and intellectual works. In general, copyrightable works are nonfunctional, such as a writing, painting, or piece of sculpture. Additionally, with works that can be copyrighted, each is so different that generally there is no debate on who did what first. Second, patents offer considerably more protection. Third, unlike the patent process, it is a relatively simple matter to obtain a copyright registration, which will be explained in detail in this chapter.

NOTICE OF COPYRIGHT

When a work is published under the copyright law in the United States, a notice of copyright should be placed on all publicly distributed copies. While this is no longer a mandatory requirement because of U.S. adherence to the Berne Treaty, it is still desirable. As a copyright owner, it is your responsibility to use the copyright notice. Note that it is not necessary to have advance permission from or to register the work with the Copyright Office.

There are three elements that should be present in a copyright notice:

1. The symbol © (the letter C in a circle), or the word "Copyright" or the abbreviation "Copr."

2. The year of first publication of the work; in the case of compilations or derivative works incorporating previously published material, the year date of first publication of the compilation or derivative work is sufficient. It is not necessary to include the year date for a pictorial, graphic, or sculptural work that is accompanied by text matter, if any, that is reproduced in or on greeting cards, postcards, stationery, jewelry, dolls, toys, or any useful articles.

3. The name of the owner of copyright in the work, or an abbreviation by which the name can be recognized, or a generally known alternative designation of the owner. Example: ©John Smith 1980.

Although sometimes the word copyright is spelled out, it is not necessary. The symbol © is an internationally recognized symbol. The "C in a circle" notice is required only on "visually perceptible copies" such as works of text. Certain kinds of works, including musical, dramatic, and literary works, may be fixed not in "copies" but by means of sound in an audio recording. Since audio recordings, like audio tapes and phonograph disks, are "phonorecords," the symbol ℗ (the letter P in a circle) is used rather than the symbol ©. The notice of copyright should be affixed to the copies in such a manner and location as to give reasonable notice of the claim of copyright. In the case of a phonorecord, the notice may be placed on the surface of the phonorecord itself or on its label or container. On copyrighted works such as a computer program, video tape, or movie, the notice should appear on the screen and the container in which it is packaged. On a painting or statue, for example, you might place the notice on the back or base of the art. In the case of a separate contribution to a collective work, a single notice applicable to the collective works as a whole is sufficient to protect each individual work.

In the event that a published work does not have a copyright notice, the omission will not invalidate the copyright in the work.

A copyright notice is still desirable in the United States even though the work has not been registered. Until 1977, if you published your work without a notice, you were, in effect, giving your work to the public. By doing so, anyone has the right to copy it. Since all that is required is putting the copyright notice on your work, it is something that we recommend you automatically do. This is good information to businesspeople who produce advertising literature, catalogs, brochures, training manuals, and so on. It is such a simple thing to do and it provides substantial legal protection. Of course, if you have only an original document and have absolutely no intentions of ever publishing it, then naturally, the copyright notice is unnecessary. If you publish without a notice after March 1989, the work may still be protectable, but to be safe and to gain additional rights, the notice should always be used.

Finally, keep in mind that the purpose of a copyright notice is to prevent somebody else from copying your work. However, it is not proof that the work is actually yours. It simply indicates that you have put a notice on it to comply with the statutory requirements in order to prevent your work from going into the public domain.

WHY YOU SHOULD REGISTER YOUR WORK

Although your work receives legal protection when you fix it in a tangible form, it is still desirable to register your work with the Copyright Office. First, registering it serves as something in the public records. Second, once it is registered, you have the right to file suit against an infringer and *collect* statutory damages. In most situations, you cannot collect statutory damages or attorney's fees for infringements that began prior to the registration of your work. Statutory damages are damages that the court may award instead of actual damages based on the direct evidence of damages that you show the court. This gives the court an additional option, to the benefit of the copyright owner. Keep in mind, however, that if somebody does infringe, you may then file your application for registration, and the other party is liable for actual damages that you can prove that you incurred. In addition, the other party may also be liable for realized profits.

For example, let us suppose that you are the author of self-published manuscript. Although you put a copyright notice on your published book, you never took the effort to register it with the Copyright Office. A book publisher then reproduces and sells 5,000 copies of your work. As a copyright owner, you have the right to stop the person from infringing on your work. In order to sue, however, it is necessary for you to first register your work, or at least apply to register. Once you do, if there is still an infringement, you have the right to sue in order to obtain an injunction and collect any damages and profits you can prove.

REGISTERING YOUR WORK

Application forms are available from the Copyright Office, free of charge. The application is simple to complete and only takes 10 to 15 minutes. There are instructions to assist you in answering all questions. Unlike a patent application, no search will be done to see if the work had already existed. Only rarely is a work ever refused. When your work is rejected, it is generally because the application has been incorrectly completed or your work is not copyrightable subject matter, like a title. Then, too, the obvious may be refused—you cannot submit an ordinary brick and declare it as a piece of sculpture. When you submit a book, do not expect it to be read (although it will probably get a passing glance). It takes about four months for approval to be granted and then becomes effective on the date of receipt by the Copyright Office.

Depending on the nature of your work, one of the following forms must be completed in order to register it:

Form TX	For published and unpublished nondramatic literary works
Form PA	For published and unpublished works of the performing arts (musical and dramatic works, pantomimes, and choreographic works, motion pictures, and other audiovisual works).
Form SR	For sound recordings.
Form VA	For visual arts.
Form RE	For claims to renewal copyright in works copyrighted under the old law.
Form CA	For supplementary registration to correct or amplify information given in the Copyright Office record of an earlier registration.
Form GR/CP	An adjunct application to be used for registration of a group of contributions to periodicals in addition to an application Form TX and PA.

The above forms are applicable for the general classification of copyrightable works. In isolated cases, you may find that your work fits into two of the above classifications. If so, choose the one that you think is most applicable. In the event that you register your work under the wrong classification, your rights will not be affected.

In addition to submitting an application, it is also necessary to submit a copy(s) of your work (called a "deposit"). Just how many deposits are necessary is dependent on the following:

- One complete copy if the work is unpublished.

- Two complete copies of the best edition of the work if it had been first published in the United States after January 1, 1978.

- Two complete copies of the work as first published if it was first published in the United States before January 1, 1978.

- One complete copy of the work as first published if it was first published outside the United States, no matter when it was published.

- One complete copy of the best edition of the collective work if the work is a contribution to a collective work, and was published after January 1, 1978.

With a work that is three-dimensional, such as a statue, photographs taken from three different views should be submitted. Furthermore, the copyright office regulations create exceptions and variations and provide complete exemption from the deposit requirements aimed at providing a satisfactory archival record of a work without imposing practical or financial hardships on the depositor, where the individual author is the owner of copyright in a pictorial, graphic, or sculptural work, and (1) less than five copies of the work have been published, (2) the work has been published in a limited edition consisting of numbered copies, the monetary value of which would make the mandatory deposit of two copies of the best edition of the work burdensome, unfair, or unreasonable.

The fee for each registration is $20. The application, deposit, and fee should be mailed in the same package to the Register of Copyrights, Library of Congress, Washington, D.C., 20559.

TRADEMARKS

IV

WHAT IS A TRADEMARK?

12

A trademark is any word, name, symbol, or device, or any combination thereof, used by a business to distinguish its goods or services from those offered by others. A mark may come in many forms, including pictures, figures, and letters. Its purpose is to allow people to recognize the source of a product so that they know the quality to expect as a result of past experiences. Over a period of time, a business develops a reputation as a result of providing a certain quality of goods or services—and trademark laws permit it to protect that reputation, which, depending on public acceptance, can be very valuable. Like a fine artist's or author's signature put on a work, so may a company's brand name identify its product.

A few examples that illustrate how the public recognizes famous brand names by their visual image are: the bearded Smith Brothers of cough drop fame; Prudential's Rock of Gibraltar; Planters' Mr. Peanut; the golden arches of McDonald's; MGM's lion, Leo; and Ralph Lauren's silhouette of a polo player. Figures 12.1–12.3 give examples of some trademarks. Even phrases are widely recognized, such as Coca-Cola's "The Pause That Refreshes" and "Where's the Beef?" from Wendy's. Under certain circumstances, even a color could be protected as a trademark. In a landmark decision, Owens-Corning Fiberglas Corporation, the maker of Fiberglas insulation, established the rights to the color pink when it is used for home insulation. Yet, when Pepto Bismol attempted to trademark pink, the company was unsuccessful because the color served as a functional purpose—it was a soothing color for the product. That was not true with the Owens-Corning case. Pink was deemed to have no natural association to insulation. Even shapes that are nonfunctional can be trademarked—like the shape of a Coca-Cola bottle. Justice Felix Frankfurter referred to the modern function of trademarks as a form of "commercial magnetism," which serves to draw customers to the article or commodity on which the "congenial symbol" appears. In short, people buy a proven brand name because it represents consistency, and businesses are built by making people want to come back.

Trademark law has been established, case by case, over the centuries, to regulate competition between people offering goods and services. Although applications for federal registration are processed by the U.S. Patent and Trademark Office, each of the states also maintains trademark registers. As more business is transacted in interstate commerce controlled by Congress, the role of state trademark registrations has lessened. Trademark law is intended to provide a fairness in the marketplace for both sellers and buyers. In short, it helps prevent people from being misled.

There are three aspects of trademarks that are important to clearly understand because they are the source of confusion about trademark law to many people. First, there are trademarks and service marks. Originally, there were only trademarks and these were only applicable to goods; no protection was provided for services offered by a business. Eventually, however, the courts recognized that enterprises and individuals who rendered services should be included under the same law. Today, trademark law covers both trademarks (marks for goods) and service marks (marks for services). Although there is a distinct difference, the word "trademark" is generically used to cover both marks. With this in mind, the federal regulatory agency could appropriately be named the U.S. Patent, Trademark, and Service Mark Office! For the remainder of this book, we will generically use the term "trademark" for both trade and service marks.

Second, unlike a patent, a trademark is not a government grant. Under patent law, the government grants a 17-year monopoly, and even under copyright law, the government creates a right to exclude others from copying a literary or artistic work. This is true because, as mentioned earlier in this book, patents and copyrights are based on one's creative efforts. A trademark, however, is based on commercial efforts in the marketplace. It is merely a convenient way to identify goods and services. You do not have to obtain the right to use a trademark from the government, nor does the registration of a mark at the U.S. Patent and Trademark Office by itself necessarily create exclusive rights. Your rights to a trademark are acquired by *use* and you must continue to use it in order for your rights to continue. An individual with a patented invention or copyrighted work does not have to do a thing, and the rights remain in full force. The rights of a registered trademark, on the other hand, may be forfeited or lost during the term for which the registration was granted. An important advantage of registering a trademark is that no one can acquire superior rights by beginning to use the mark after your date of registration. Profits or damages can be recovered under the Trademark Act, although you may be able to recover under common law if you do not register. There is a certificate given to a trademark owner when it is registered. Federal registration certificates are shown in Figures 12.1, 12.2, and 12.3.

Third, a trade name is sometimes confused with a trademark. A trade name is the name of a business enterprise. Gen-

---

FIGURE 12.1   Example of Trademark Using Letters

Int. Cl.: 36

Prior U.S. Cl.: 102

United States Patent and Trademark Office   Reg. No. 1,467,615
Registered Dec. 1, 1987

SERVICE MARK
PRINCIPAL REGISTER

ARAG

ARAG ALLGEMEINE RECHTSSCHUTZ VER-
SICHERUNGS A.G. (FED REP GERMANY
CORPORATION)
BREHMSTRASSE 110
DUSSELDORF, FED REP GERMANY

FOR: UNDERWRITING LEGAL EXPENSE
INSURANCE, IN CLASS 36 (U.S. CL. 102).

OWNER OF FED REP GERMANY REG. NO.
990664, DATED 4-2-1979, EXPIRES 3-22-1989.

SER. NO. 612,786, FILED 8-4-1986.

IRA J. GOODSAID, EXAMINING ATTORNEY

FIGURE 12.2   Example of Trademark Using Design

Int. Cl.: 42

Prior U.S. Cl.: 100

Reg. No. 1,310,481

United States Patent and Trademark Office

Registered Dec. 18, 1984

SERVICE MARK
Principal Register

Wendy's International, Inc. (Ohio corporation)
4288 W. Dublin-Granville Rd.
Dublin, Ohio 43017

   For: RESTAURANT AND CARRY OUT RES-
TAURANT SERVICES, in CLASS 42 (U.S. Cl. 100).
   First use Apr. 1981; in commerce Apr. 1981.
   Owner of U.S. Reg. Nos. 911,053, 1,146,642 and others.
   No claim is made to the exclusive right to use

"Quality"; "Recipe", apart from the mark as shown.

   The lining on the drawing is feature of the mark and does not indicate color.

   Ser. No. 408,681, filed Jan. 10, 1983.

MARY E. HANNON, Examining Attorney

FIGURE 12.3   Example of Trademark Using Letters

Int. Cl.: 9

Prior U.S. Cls.: 21 and 26

United States Patent and Trademark Office
Reg. No. 1,453,041
Registered Aug. 18, 1987

TRADEMARK
PRINCIPAL REGISTER

VANNER, INC. (OHIO CORPORATION)
745 HARRISON DRIVE
COLUMBUS, OH 43204

FOR: ELECTRICAL AND ELECTRONIC AP-
PARATUS, NAMELY, INVERTERS, ISOLA-
TORS, HIGH CURRENT REGULATED BAT-
TERY CHARGERS, BATTERY CHARGING
AND GROUND FAULT INTERRUPTING CIR-
CUITS, FLASHERS, CURRENT BOOSTERS,
AUTOMATIC THROTTLES FOR CONTROL-
LING AN ENGINE TO MAINTAIN SUFFI-
CIENT CURRENT GENERATION, AND CON-
VERTERS, IN CLASS 9 (U.S. CLS. 21 AND 26).

FIRST USE 11-3-1986; IN COMMERCE
11-3-1986.
OWNER OF U.S. REG. NOS. 1,169,106 AND
1,200,250.
NO CLAIM IS MADE TO THE EXCLUSIVE
RIGHT TO USE "INC.", APART FROM THE
MARK AS SHOWN.
THE LINING SHOWN IN THE MARK ON
THE DRAWING IS A FEATURE OF THE
MARK AND DOES NOT INDICATE COLOR.

SER. NO. 635,626, FILED 12-16-1986.

DONALD B. AIKEN, EXAMINING ATTORNEY

eral Motors Corporation is a trade name, although there is not
a product called a General Motors automobile. Chevrolet, however, is a trademark. Likewise, Jell-O is a trademark, and its
owner, General Foods, is a trade name. Perhaps the most famous of all is the product Coca-Cola, which is a trademark, and
its company, Coca-Cola Company, which is also a trade name.
There is no provision under the present federal Trademark
Act that allows the registration of trade names used merely
to identify a business entity. There are some notable exceptions, however, where a trade name can also be a trademark,
and thereby be registered at the U.S. Patent and Trademark
Office. For instance, Johnson & Johnson is both a trade name
and trademark, as well as the "Celanese" portion of Celanese
Corporation.

A trade name may also be a service mark, and accordingly can be registered by the U.S. Patent and Trademark Office. For example, Federal Express uses its name to identify both the company and its service. The name represents a particular service to customers who identify the Federal Express name with same day or overnight delivery service.

Then too, trade names can be registered in individual states where they can be protected, and they are also protected by common law. With this in mind, there are certain remedies under state law and common law for trade name infringement, and even under the Trademark Act, it is not permitted to have a false designation of origin. All of this means that words, names, symbols, and devices, or any combination of them, cannot be used on goods or services in a manner to falsely suggest or create an impression that they are goods or services of another enterprise.

BEING FIRST TO REGISTER

A trademark does not have to be registered in order to be valid. If you use your trademark before anyone else so that, presumably, it is recognized by people, the courts will enforce it by common law. Because, as previously stated, a trademark is acquired by being the first to use, not register, and as long as you keep using it, it is yours. However, by not registering it, you may leave yourself open to a hornet's nest if someone else later begins using the same trademark and a conflict arises. In such a case, it is a question of the dates and locations of use.

For example, two businesses, A and B, that use the same trademark could operate independent enterprises for many years in different geographical areas. Say that A decides to expand its base of operation and move into B's marketing area. The courts must now decide what is fair based on the commercial realities, which may be difficult to decide. In general, the first user in a geographic marketing area is the owner of the mark in that specific territory. However, if A registered its trademark with the U.S. Patent and Trademark Office *before* B had actually started in business, then when A later moves into B's geographic marketing area, A will have the rights to the trademark and B is out of luck. Of course, if B had started in business prior to A's registration, then B would have the rights to the trademark in its geographic marketing area, even though A was the first to register for a federal trademark. In all other areas, however, A would have the trademark rights. With this in mind, if your intentions are to expand in the future, it is prudent to register your trademark at the earliest possible date.

Federal trademark law permits an application to be filed based upon a good faith intent to use. This offers important advantages. If a company selects a proposed new mark, and a search determines there probably are no conflicting marks, the company can immediately apply to register it. It is not necessary to wait, perhaps several months, for the first actual use. Such an application prevents someone else from using the mark and acquiring the legal rights to it after the first company's decision to adopt it, but before the first company has a chance to use it. Being the initial user of a mark is a very important fact in determining who owns it. The date of filing an intent to use application can be treated in law as a date of first use. Although the application can be filed before actual use, a registration will not be issued until after proof is submitted that the mark has been used. Nonetheless, when registered, the first use date can be retroactive to the filing date.

For practical purposes, however, while federal registration can be a valuable thing, it is also a relatively big expense for a small startup business. The federal registration cost can range from $1,000 to $2,000, and, typically, a small entrepreneur on a tight budget may have other priorities for the limited capital. Of course, nobody has a crystal ball, and what may cost a couple of thousand dollars in the short run can involve millions of dollars years later as a result of winning or losing a future law suit. Many small businesses will never expand to other geographic marketing areas, and so the cost of federally registering a trademark could be an unnecessary expense at a time when funds are low.

DOING A TRADEMARK SEARCH

We recommend doing a trademark search as early as possible to avoid the expenses that could occur from a conflict with another trademark owner somewhere down the road. Even if you are just starting a small business, you do not want to build your reputation around your trademark only to be forced to change it later on. With this in mind, it is a question of how extensive your search should be.

If you are planning to do business only in a certain small geographical marketing area, then perhaps you might want to confine your search to it. However, you would still have the risk that another enterprise, operating somewhere else, has a federal or even a state registration and may be able to later move into your area and stop your use. You can conduct your own search in your hometown by combing through telephone books from around the state, viewing trade directories of state associations, and contacting the secretary of state (or an equivalent office if you happen to live in a state where another agency registers trademarks, trade names, and corporate names). You can also use directories such as Standard & Poor and the Thomas Register. There are even commercial computer database services that provide the same information that would be available at the U.S. Patent and Trademark Office. Many trademark attorneys are hooked up with such services. Of course, you might want to do a search in the trademark office itself. Obviously, the more you search, the more you will spend, but sometimes it is better to be safe than sorry. That is a business decision that you will have to make. The cost of a trademark search varies and generally falls in the $200 to $1,000 range.

CRITERIA FOR TRADEMARKS

Rather than starting off by telling you what *is* registrable with the U.S. Patent and Trademark Office, perhaps you should first be told what will cause a trademark to be rejected. The following criteria have been taken from the present Trademark Act:

1. A trademark cannot consist or comprise of immoral, deceptive, or scandalous matter. Nor can it disparage or falsely suggest a connection with persons, living or dead, institutions, beliefs, or national symbols, or bring them into contempt or disrepute.

2. A trademark cannot consist of or comprise the flag or coat of arms or other insignia of the United States, or of any state or municipality, or any foreign nation, or any simulation thereof.

3. A trademark cannot consist of or comprise a name, portrait, or signature identifying a particular living individual except by that person's written consent. The same criteria

are applied to a deceased president of the United States during the lifetime of the surviving spouse, except by written consent.

4. A trademark to be federally registered cannot consist of or comprise a mark that so resembles another registered in the U.S. Patent and Trademark Office or a mark or trade name previously used in the United States and not abandoned, as to be likely, when applied to the goods of the applicant, to cause confusion, to cause mistake, or to deceive. The commissioner can determine that concurrent registrations of the same mark by two owners may be issued if confusion, deception, or mistake will not result from simultaneous use by both of them.

5. A trademark cannot consist of a mark that (a) is merely descriptive or deceptively misdescriptive when applied to the goods of the applicant; (b) is primarily geographically descriptive or deceptively misdescriptive when applied to the goods of the applicant, except that indications of regional origin may be registrable as collective or certification marks; or (c) is primarily merely a surname.

There are, however, exceptions to be applied to these, the main one of which is this: Nothing will prevent the registration of a mark that has become distinctive of the applicant's goods or services in commerce. This means a trademark that is not initially allowable for registration under the federal law can otherwise qualify if it becomes widely recognized by the public.

REGISTERING YOUR TRADEMARK WITH THE U.S. PATENT AND TRADEMARK OFFICE

As is the case with patents, there is a backlog of trademarks pending at the U.S. Patent and Trademark Office, so it generally takes anywhere from three months to a year to get a registration. In order to be entitled to a federal registration, your goods or services must be offered in interstate commerce. To apply for federal registration, you must state in your application either the date when you first engaged in interstate commerce or that you intend to use the mark in interstate commerce. If you state only your intent to use, you must actually use it before you will get a registration. There are time limits within which you must actually use it. The standard for use, however, is somewhat low in this regard, so the required extent of your business in interstate commerce is minimal, but it must not be contrived.

The actual step-by-step trademark registration procedure is as follows:

1. You should mail your application to the U.S. Patent and Trademark Office. You must specify the first date that you used your mark, its first use in commerce, or instead state your intent to use, the goods or services for which you will or do use the mark, and the manner in which the mark is used in connection with the goods. You must also verify that you are the owner of the mark, and to the best of your knowledge and belief, no other person, firm, corporation, or association, has the right to use the mark in an identical form or anything with a resemblance that could cause confusion or deception. If you do claim concurrent use, you must state exceptions to your claim of exclusive use by specifying to the extent of your knowledge, any concurrent use by others, the goods in connection with which the mark is used; and the areas in which each concurrent use exists, the periods of each use, and the goods and area for which you desire registration. You must also supply a drawing of your mark and include specimens or facsimiles of the mark as actually used, as required by the commissioner. If you are not domiciled in the United States, you must designate the name and address of a U.S. citizen who is to be served notices or process in proceedings affecting the mark. Naturally, you must also pay the appropriate filing fee.

2. The examining procedure begins when an examining attorney reviews your application and searches to see if there are any conflicting registered marks. The examining attorney also decides whether your work is a registerable kind of mark; that is, is it descriptive, a surname, et cetera. The trademark office will forward a letter to you indicating problems that could prevent your registration. Generally, you will receive this letter approximately three months after filing your application. Trademark examiners are usually attorneys and have authority to either accept or reject a trademark application for registration.

3. If necessary, you may furnish additional proof requested by the trademark office. You may also make some amend-

ments to the application and point out any errors in the reasoning of the examining attorney.

4. If the application is accepted, the trademark office will publish information about your trademark in its weekly *Official Gazette*. This publication is read by those parties interested in trademarks, some of whom are professional people representing clients with valuable trademarks. If nobody challenges your application, a certificate of trademark registration will be issued by the trademark office.

5. In the event that your application is rejected, you can appeal. The appeal procedures are complicated and necessitate the services of an attorney.

Fortunately, the majority of trademarks are acceptable for registration. Registrations for both a single word and marks having graphical features are reproduced at the end of this chapter.

The filing fee payable to the Patent and Trademark Office is $210 per class in which the named goods fall. But remember that all fees of the Office are raised from time to time, usually annually. A registration must be renewed near the end of each term and an affidavit of use must be filed as described at the end of this chapter. So long as the mark continues to be used, the registration can continue to be renewed.

TRADEMARK NOTICE

It is desirable to display a trademark notice before you have a federal registration. It is simply a good way to inform people that it is your trademark and will help you avoid future conflicts. Before registration, you should put a small TM (™) or the word "Trademark" near your mark. When your federal registration is approved, you should use the words "Registered in the U.S. Patent and Trademark Office" or the letter R enclosed within a circle (®). Some trademark owners use "Reg. U.S. Patent Office" which is also acceptable.

If you fail to give notice by the encircled R, no profits or damages can be recovered under the Trademark Act in the event of a suit for infringement unless the infringer had actual notice of your rights. Profits and damages under the act can only be recovered after you display this statutory notice of your registration or give actual notice to the infringer.

TRADEMARK INFRINGEMENT

In many cases, trademarks can be more valuable than patents, and, contrary to what some people may think, there is far more to creating a sound trademark than simply naming a product. It is also difficult and costly for a business to change a trademark once one has been created and become recognized by the public. Acceptance of quality and continuity of repeat business can be worth millions of dollars in terms of good will. All in all, it is very evident that a good trademark is a valuable asset to protect against infringement—and something that a trademark owner must do. If you do nothing, you may destroy your trademark rights.

According to the Trademark Act, a person shall be liable for infringement if he or she will, without the consent of a trademark registrant:

1. Use in commerce any reproduction, counterfeit, copy, or colorable imitation of a registered mark in connection with the sale, offering for sale, distribution, or advertising of any goods or services on or in connection with which such use is likely to cause confusion, to cause mistake, or to deceive.

2. Reproduce, counterfeit, copy, or colorably imitate a registered mark and apply one of these to labels, signs, prints, packages, wrappers, receptacles, or advertisements intended to be used in commerce on or in connection with the sale, offering for sale, distribution, or advertising of goods or services on or in connection with which such use is likely to cause confusion, to cause mistake, or to deceive.

The criteria for what constitutes trademark infringement are applied in each of the following circumstances:

1. At the time of a new application seeking a registration.

2. When an action is brought for cancellation of a registration to remove a junior mark on the ground that it conflicts with a senior one.

3. In an infringement action, when the plaintiff claims that the defendant is an infringer and is wrongly using the mark.

In all of these instances, the question is whether the resemblance of the two marks as used by the two businesses is likely to deceive or confuse purchasers of the goods or services in question. The test to determine infringement is: *Is an ordinary customer who sees the use of one trademark on one company's goods or services, and then sees a second trademark used on another company's goods or services, likely to believe those two sets of goods or services come from the same company or from a company sponsored or approved by the other company?* The question that must be addressed is what may cause people to have confusion. The general impression of the ordinary purchaser serves as the true guide. Furthermore, it is what the mark looks like as a whole, since people do not ordinarily stop to dissect it. The similarities and the differences should be considered—the two marks can be placed side by side and compared. However, other factors, such as differences in the products, how they are sold, and the way they are used by purchaser, are also important. It should be remembered that the ordinary purchaser relies on memory of a mark.

A difficult case arose in 1989 when Toyota decided to adopt the term LEXUS for a luxury car. Mead objected to Toyota's use of that mark because Mead sold computer legal research services under its mark LEXIS. The District Court found that, although LEXIS was strongly associated with the Mead services, there was no likelihood of confusion because of the cumulative effect of several additional factors. The court reasoned that consumers would not be confused as to the origin of these products because the products were so dissimilar: a LEXUS automobile is a consumer product while LEXIS research service is a commercial product; the products will be sold in a different manner; the two users of the marks are not competitors, nor are they likely to be; and the respective marks are likely to appear in totally different contexts.

HOW TO PROTECT
YOUR TRADEMARK

13

A trademark can be one of your most valuable assets; yet, if not properly treated, you can lose your rights to it. As we stated in Chapter 12, the worth of a trademark can be millions of dollars and may even exceed the value of a high-priced patent. Paradoxically, the more successful your trademark is, the less your risk of losing it. As it becomes more valuable, however, your need to protect it increases.

A simple and relatively inexpensive way to get some initial protection for your trademark is to register it with the U.S. Patent and Trademark Office. But simply having, registering, and subsequently renewing a trademark does not guarantee that your rights cannot be later lost. In comparison, it is not necessary to offer to the public an invention covered by a patent, nor does a copyrighted work ever have to be reproduced. However, there are certain responsibilities that you have in order to keep your trademark rights, and as you will observe in this chapter, under certain circumstances, those rights can be lost through neglect. One obvious, assumed responsibility is that you cannot use your mark deceptively or in a fraudulent trade. If so, you may have to forfeit all rights to be protected under trademark law.

USE IT OR LOSE IT

As we explained earlier, you do not have to federally register your trademark in order for it to be valid. Yet even with a registration, your trademark can be considered abandoned if you do not use it, which would then permit somebody else to use it. The thing to remember about trademark law is that the mark's use and consequent value rest on its use by people to distinguish your goods and/or services from others in the marketplace. Mere lapse of time alone does not constitute abandonment—it is possible that a business might not use its trademark due to such events as a scarcity of raw materials, lack of funds or demand, bankruptcy, war, fire, and so on. The court finds abandonment if you (1) stopped using it, and (2) intended to abandon it. In the event that somebody comes along with the same trademark, the particular circumstances surrounding its discontinuance must be explored, addressing questions such as: Did you stop using it? Did you go into another field? Did you have plans to resurrect it at some later time? Do you have any memos or letters supporting your intentions? All in all, what does the totality of all the evidence show? Naturally, if nobody else has an interest in using your trademark, you do not have a problem.

On the other hand, if somebody wants to register a trademark and another party already has the same one registered for related goods or services, the new applicant must prove that the existing registered mark has been abandoned. To accomplish this, the applicant must initiate a cancellation proceeding, which is like a mini lawsuit, in the U.S. Patent and Trademark Office. The proceeding is a relatively inexpensive hearing that requires both parties to present evidence that must be evaluated to determine whether the previously registered trademark has been abandoned. If the trademark is judged to be abandoned, its registration is canceled and the later applicant is entitled to register the trademark as his or her property.

EXCLUSIVELY YOURS

It is not enough to merely mind your own business and routinely use your trademark. You can lose your trademark by neglecting to stop others from using it. Many cases are on record where companies have lost exclusive rights to trademarks because they inadequately protected them. Sometimes even tolerating the use of an identical or similar trademark can result in the forfeiture of an owner's rights. With this in mind, a company must diligently police the marketplace, continually pursuing potential trademark infringers. You must be willing to challenge anyone who infringes your trademark; failure to voice your timely objection may result in allowing the other party to use it with the belief that it was unobjectionable. Once the other party's use gains recognition, the trademark ceases to be distinctive.

Everyone within your organization should be instructed to develop an awareness of any unauthorized usage of your trademark. Included is everyone from top management in the executive suite to the sales representatives in the field. Somebody should be assigned the job to systematically examine magazines, newspapers, trade publications, and radio and television productions making references to your company's trademark(s). Clipping services can be contracted to scout any mentioning of your trademark in editorial as well as advertising content. Somebody within your organization should also be responsible to review the *Official Gazette*, the trademark office's weekly publication listing trademarks that will soon be registered. In the event that you come across a conflicting mark, you should then start an opposition proceeding to protest it. Companies with very valuable trademarks, such as Coca-Cola and McDonald's, have very active legal departments that routinely look for anything bearing even the slightest resemblance to their marks, and you can be sure they will oppose anything they consider to be an infringement.

In addition to being on the lookout for other companies infringing on your trademark rights, you must also be on guard that your trademark is not being editorially altered. Rarely does a writer or editor understand trademark law and, unknowingly, an article or a writing that incorrectly uses your trademark may appear. In such instances, you should write to the author and/or publisher to politely inform the person of the error and give instructions on the proper way to use your trademark for future quotations concerning your company and product. If you choose to ignore such editorial uses, your trademark rights can be put in jeopardy.

The degeneration of a trademark frequently occurs so insidiously that its owner may unknowingly forfeit the rights simply because of failure to respond when necessary. With this in mind, in addition to being on guard to police other companies, you must also examine your company's internal business practices. You should use your trademark in a consistent manner and constantly review how your trademark is presented on all product packaging, letterheads, brochures, sales materials, advertisements, promotional materials, and so on. You should not deviate from your established trademark in even minor details. Uniformity is a prime requisite. Every employee, including designers, copywriters, and artists, should be informed that it is never permissible to alter your accepted typographic treatments, combine the trademark with other devices or words, or change proportions of elements. Everyone should clearly understand that any substantial alteration of your legally registered trademark can significantly endanger the company's rights. Ignorance of the law is no excuse.

You should place your trademark (1) physically on your product, or (2) on the container of the product, or (3) on point-of-sale displays closely associated with the product, or (4) on tags or labels attached to the products. It is also a good idea to place your trademark on two or more of the above—do not be afraid to flaunt it. If you sell services, use it in advertising, at places of business, and on equipment and materials used to perform the services.

THE DANGER OF BECOMING GENERIC

The basic purpose of a trademark is to identify and distinguish your goods or service from somebody else's. Since its function is to specify a product's origin, a term is not functioning as a trademark if it *describes* a product or a characteristic or feature of a product or, worse yet, is the common name for the product. Under the Trademark Act, there can be no trademark rights for a common descriptive name of an object—the generic name of a product. It does not help if the product is patented. The reasoning behind the law is that if a product were identified by a certain word, and that word was a trademark of a particular company, that company would enjoy an unfair advantage over its competition, because if nobody else could use that word, its competitors could not tell people what they sold.

Consequently, it is possible that a company could promote its product so successfully that unless certain precautionary measures were taken, the public would come to use a trademark as the common name for the product. This could cause the company to lose its registered trademark rights. For this reason, a company must be careful not to create a situation where its product's trademark is misconstrued and used as the appropriate word to describe the product regardless of the company that produces it. Once a trademark is ruled to have been transformed into a generic word, all trademark rights are lost. As you can see, a generic word does not fit the definition of a trademark in a U.S. statutory law that reads, "any word, name, symbol, or device, or any combination thereof adopted and used by a manufacturer or merchant to identify his or her goods and distinguish them from those manufactured or sold by others."

Many brand names have become generic words in this country, resulting in the loss of trademark rights by their owners. One notable example of a trademark that became generic is the product manufactured by Bayer called "acetylsalicylic acid" originally marketed with the trademark "Aspirin." Originally, Bayer correctly anticipated that the public would not be able to pronounce or remember *acetylsalicylic acid*, so it shortened the name to a catchy word, *aspirin*. Another famous product originally a registered trademark is Cellophane, a type of wrapping paper, manufactured by du Pont de Nemours and Company. The company constantly and inexplicably used the coined name in describing wrapping paper, sometimes making reference to a class of cellulose products, not as a unique brand that it exclusively produced. When a competitor used the word cellophane to describe its product, du Pont objected and took the company to court. They lost the case, and thereby freed the word to become public domain, forever giving it lower-case ignominy. Today, the word cellophane can be found in the dictionary defined as "a transparent substance made from cellulose, used as a wrapping to keep food, candy, tobacco, etc., fresh and clean." Likewise, King-Seeley Thermos Co. suffered the same fate when its vacuum bottle, Thermos, also went the generic route, losing its trademark status. Literally scores of once-famous trademarks have become part of the English language, including such words as linoleum, mimeograph, shredded wheat, and yo-yo.

There are many things you can do to protect your trademark—and you must make a point to do them or risk jeopardizing it. For instance, you might refer to the trademark as a brand name, like the 3M Company does with its SCOTCH Brand Cellophane Tape. For years, the company has practiced this, always careful not to allow its trademark to become generic. Likewise, Kimberly-Clark Corporation refers to its famous tissue product as Kleenex Brand. The word brand emphasizes the trademark significance of the word.

No reference should ever be made in print using the lower case about your product. Always treat your mark as a proper noun. Likewise, other danger signals are the use of the possessive, "nouning," "verbing," and the appearance of the plural. Xerox Corporation, for example, works hard to remind the public that they do not "xerox" things, they "copy" things. Again, you do not want your trademark to become part of the English language like formerly trademarked products such as milk of magnesia, mineral oil, and zipper. You should constantly protect your trademark rights by correcting anyone who improperly uses the mark.

The public must be taught that there is a difference between your brand and a generic name. Of course, it can be accomplished by what you say in your advertising. Another way is to make up brochures, booklets, audio and video cassettes, and other literature to routinely distribute to interested parties such as customers, trade magazines, distributors—anyone whom you believe is in need of an education. We recommend a friendly but firm approach.

USING NONDESCRIPTIVE WORDS

When an entrepreneur first begins a business, there is a tendency to choose a trademark that best describes the product. There is a logical reason for doing this: one wants people to quickly know something about the product. In the short run, this may be a plus to a small business, but it can come back to haunt the company. Furthermore, as we have indicated in this chapter as well as the preceding chapter, descriptive words are not good candidates to be federally registered as trademarks. A furniture manufacturer, for instance, should not name a product "comfort chair," nor should a hamburger fast-food operator name a product "tasty burger." It is okay, however, to use a word that is descriptive in another context but is not descriptive of your actual products.

Celestial Seasonings, for example, works well for the Boulder, Colorado herbal tea company.

What are the legally strongest words to use as a trademark? *Words that have no meaning.* Words like Xerox, Kodak, and Exxon. It was the Standard Oil Company's (New Jersey) ninetieth year when, in November 1972, it changed its name to Exxon. In an effort to choose what the world's largest oil company believed was a good trademark, nearly 10,000 names were produced from a computer. Later the list was narrowed down to 234, then to 16, and finally to 8. Linguistic studies were made on these final 8 names in more than 100 languages in order to ensure that none of them had an actual meaning or any adverse connotations. Nearly 7,000 people were interviewed, including about 4,000 in 40 different cities throughout the United States, and over 15,000 telephone directories were examined. It took three years for Exxon to choose its name. The company then spent 100 million dollars executing the necessary changes, including: converting all Esso, Enco, and Humble signs for 25,000 U.S. service stations to the red, white, and blue Exxon rectangle. Other signs for each station included the ones on the freeway as well as the signs on the gas pumps. There were also changes for sales receipts, stationery, credit cards, and so on. Emblems on trucks, plaques, and the names on 18,000 buildings, storage tanks, tankers, and other equipment had to be replaced to read Exxon. The company changed the certificates for its 224 million outstanding shares of stock held by 780,000 shareholders. As you can see, the importance of selecting its trademark was the cause of a very expensive venture for Exxon. Consequently, it is certainly in the company's best interest to protect that trademark.

LICENSING—BE PARTICULAR

Once you have a patent or copyright, you do not risk losing your rights if you make a poor choice of a licensee. In the case of a trademark, however, you *do* run that risk. Because the purpose of a trademark is to distinguish your goods from others, you can lose your rights by licensing it to someone whom you do not require to maintain your standard of quality. The key to licensing your trademark to a third party is for you to jealously supervise the conduct of the licensee. Failure on this person's part to maintain the quality of your product and properly represent its origin can cause you to lose your rights. When you lose control of the quality, public deception occurs, as the mark no longer indicates what people expect from the product. To protect a mark, to make it stand up in court, you must not only have some legal basis to demonstrate that you have control, but you must have exercised control by actually checking the licensee's goods.

Ralph Lauren, one of the world's premier fashion designers, carefully guards his licensing operations. According to a top official at Polo/Ralph Lauren, a line of watches priced at $100–$300 each could bring in an estimated $150 million. However, the firm does not license or produce watches because Lauren is not interested in watches priced under $1,000.

Polo/Ralph Lauren opted against a mass-market underwear license in order to produce a more expensive line of underwear on its own. This approach allows Polo/Ralph Lauren greater control over the quality of the products bearing its name. Similarly, the firm has chosen to keep its shoe business relatively small, rather than produce a cheaper line of footwear. By the same token, every trademark owner should share the same concern about a licensee's quality—it is not just prudent business; if you do not, you can lose your trademark rights.

RENEWING A REGISTERED TRADEMARK

In order for your trademark to remain registered by the U.S. Patent and Trademark Office, you must renew it. To do so, you must file an application stating that the mark is still being used in commerce. You must file the renewal application six months before the expiration of the registration with the appropriate fee. If you fail to file during this period, you have another three months, but there is an additional fee that must be paid. You must also submit a specimen or facsimile of the mark as it is currently used. If you are not using the mark, you must indicate the special circumstances that excuse such nonuse and state that it was not due to any intention to abandon the mark. Before November 19, 1989, registrations were issued for 20 years, but applications filed after that date will lead to 10-year registrations.

In addition to renewal, it is also necessary to file an affidavit within the sixth year following the date of registration, attesting to the fact that the mark is either still in use or that its nonuse is excusable because of special circumstances and not because of any intention to abandon the mark. By requiring this, the trademark office is able to remove inactive marks from its register.

HELP IN SELECTING A NEW TRADEMARK $\boxed{14}$

THE PROBLEM AND THE INCENTIVE

Many people involved in advertising and marketing are creative, artistic types. They often conceive brilliantly unique ideas to translate into words and graphics. Their creative efforts seek to attract a consumer's attention and sell a product. Often such people are free spirits, unconfined by conventional thinking and analysis, and are consequently able to come up with clever, new ideas. Unfortunately, the very same unrestrained, unconventional thought processes that enable them to perform their creative responsibilities so well may also cause them to be unaware of, or unconcerned with, the rigid, orderly, and confining rules of trademark law. Some might even see trademark law as an annoying impediment to delivering their communication to potential customers.

In small start-up businesses, the trademark seems like a minor problem compared to such problems as financing, manufacturing, and marketing. Indeed, to many it probably is, and therefore not much thought may be given to selection of a trademark. Most people don't learn much about trademark law in ordinary life experiences in the way one might learn to perform a service, build a product, or maintain financial records and then use that knowledge in the business.

Unfortunately, a failure to take into account the principles of trademark law when first choosing a trademark can often result in a costly problem for the business. Perhaps the result could be litigation or loss of the right to use the mark after building its reputation with an investment of time, work, and high standards of honesty and quality. Perhaps the result will be both. Perhaps others will be permitted to use the mark and get a free piggyback ride on the company's investment and reputation. At a minimum, the business may receive less value from the trademark than it could have.

Usually the problem of a poor choice for a trademark does not become apparent until long after the initial creative work was done. Since the people charged with choosing a trademark are usually of high intelligence and easily capable of understanding the principles of trademark law, it is unfortunate that most of these problems could be avoided if they had begun their creative efforts on the trademark selection project with an understanding of a few basic principles of trademark law.

COMMERCIAL COMMUNICATION

Advertising and marketing people communicate to a segment of the public. The communications take a variety of forms. They may include words and sounds, as well as pictures and other graphics. But communications also serve a variety of different purposes. Some merely seek to catch the attention of one or more members of the public. Others convey information, such as information about the product or its use. Some simply relay an image. Most importantly for trademark law, some communication serves to distinguish one seller of goods or services from another.

Problems begin to arise when the purpose of the component parts of a commercial communication get confused or mixed up. Specifically, the purpose of a trademark is to communicate a distinction between competitors. The purpose of the trademark is *not* to communicate information about the product. A trademark is not intended to be used to tell how one competitor's product differs from others or what the product does. A trademark is supposed to function like the names of people. A person's name tells you absolutely nothing about that person. It merely allows you to distinguish one person from another. Only the reputation, which gets appended to the name along with your own personal observations, gives information about the person.

Big problems arise when a mark is created with a purpose in mind beyond distinguishing competitors. The most common erroneous purpose is to convey information about the product. When a person who is attempting to create a trademark begins by trying to think of words that tell something about the product, two bad results become likely. First, the words are apt to be descriptive and therefore not protectable as trademarks or only entitled to weak protection. That will enable others to use the same mark or a very similar one. The second bad result will probably be that the selected words will be just like those many other competitors or others in related fields have selected, because many of them probably took the same uninformed approach.

Of course, another erroneous purpose for selecting a mark is to create a mark that looks something like a competitor's so the latecomer to the field will look like a well established old hand. Here the purpose is in direct, opposing conflict with the purpose of trademarks and later trouble can be expected.

It is difficult to attract the attention of a consumer and difficult to retain that attention once it is attracted. Therefore, most commercial messages must be short and concise. It is not surprising that there is a temptation to make the trademark do double duty by trying to have it tell about the product. The first principle for creative people to have in mind, however, when they begin a project involving a trademark, is that the sole purpose of the trademark is to distinguish one competitor from another. Don't try to do more. Try to do that well.

THE SPECTRUM AS A GUIDE

Unfortunately, most words and graphics do not easily and clearly fall into either the category of distinctive, in which they solely distinguish one competitor from the other, or the category of information conveying, in which they solely convey information. Instead, all words fall somewhere along a broad, continuous spectrum.

At one end of the spectrum is the entirely newly invented coined word or graphical symbol that has no meaning or significance anywhere in our language or human experience. Examples are the trademarks "KODAK," "XEROX," or "EXXON." An example of such a symbol would be the five-circle Olympic

Symbol. There were no such things before these were created as trademarks. They convey absolutely no information. Consequently, they do the best job of distinguishing one competitor from the other. Because they have no meaning or significance, the public can easily associate the coined words or symbols with only one competitor, and they can readily distinguish that competitor from others. It becomes clear to consumers and easy for them to remember that all products bearing a certain word or graphical feature come from the same competitor. Terms that otherwise have no meaning make the best trademarks, are the easiest to protect, and have the greatest legal strength.

Unfortunately, those terms that make the best trademarks tell members of the consuming public nothing when they are first observed. Only after they are seen several times by the public do they come to have a meaning, and their only meaning is as a symbol of a particular company. Commercial communicators sometimes are reluctant to use such meaningless terms because, in the critical early stages, they communicate very little. When there is such a short time for a commercial communication, it is difficult to devote some of that time to what, in the beginning, conveys no information. It is difficult to be concerned about long-term results.

At the other end of the spectrum from the coined, meaningless term or symbol is the generic term. For example, the words "automobile," "restaurant," or "hammer" all have a very specific meaning when used in association with those particular products. Thus, it is clear that a manufacturer of hand tools for carpentry could never be distinguished from a competitor by means of the word "hammer". Furthermore, all of the competitors who make hammers must be able to tell the public what the product is they are selling. Consequently, generic terms can never be trademarks because they cannot distinguish one competitor from another. They are perceived by ordinary customers solely as communicating information.

Interestingly, the generic character of a word is dependent upon the commercial context in which it is used—specifically, the type of product on which it is used. For example, the term "hammer" could be an excellent trademark for computer software because it communicates no information about any characteristic or feature of the software, unless, of course, it is software for designing hammers. This brings us to the first intermediate location on the spectrum between the extremes. There are many words in a language and all have a meaning.

Some words, like "hammer," have a meaning in one context, such as hand tools, but no meaning in others, such as software. Nouns of that nature may be perceived by a customer as generic if used with the product they represent, but could be perceived as meaningless if used where they have no meaning. If a word has no meaning in connection with the product for which it is used, it is arbitrary. Arbitrary words stand near coined words as strong marks.

Then there are the adjectives. They too can have a meaning, or no meaning, depending upon the product with which they are used. For example, the word "fast" describes a characteristic of an automobile and a computer, but communicates no information about a hat. Thus, the word "fast," when perceived by a member of the public, can distinguish one competitor from the other when used in association with hats, but cannot distinguish competitors when used in association with computers and automobiles. When an adjective has a meaning with respect to the product, it is descriptive. If it has no meaning, it is an arbitrary, good mark. If it is perceived by the public as descriptive, it stands near generic words at the unprotectable end of the spectrum.

Somewhere on the spectrum, between coined words and generic words, are all the other words. Where they sit on the spectrum depends upon what, if any, relationship they have to the product. The weaker the connection between the meaning of the word or symbol and the characteristics of the product, the closer the word or symbol sits to the coined words. At the coined end of the spectrum sit the marks that have the strongest legal protection. The more there is a connection between the product and the word or symbol—that is, the more it is descriptive—the closer it sits to the generic end of the spectrum. The closer a mark sits to the generic end, the more difficult it is to protect, and even if protected, the weaker is the protection.

If a mark is to be selected solely to get the strongest protection in the long term, then one wants a mark as close to the coined end as possible. If one insists on conveying some image or other information, it can be done to some extent, but one needs all the creativity and energy possible. There are terms called "suggestive" by the courts that do not actually describe anything about the product for which they are used, but do generate some kind of desirable image for the product. However, that image or significance is remote and results from substantial activity by the human mind. These are considered protectable. For example, the word "Bravo" does not describe a product, but it does create an image of customers enthusiastically applauding a product. "Downy" doesn't describe a fabric softener, but does create the image of the softness of small feathers.

Finally, it should always be remembered that once a mark is positioned on the spectrum, it can move if the public's perception of it changes. It is the public's perception that principally determines where a word or symbol sits on the spectrum. Thus, if a word used as a mark is descriptive, with sufficient public exposure it may slide enough along the spectrum to become protected as the public grows in an awareness of its association to one particular company. However, sliding can occur in the other direction, too. A mark that starts out as protectable can slide into descriptive or generic if the public use and perception of it changes. Advertising can help push a mark along the spectrum.

PROCEDURES FOR FINDING A MARK

First, don't try to think of characteristics or features of the product in order to select corresponding words. That is where the uninformed usually start. Second, don't think that finding a mark will be easy. It won't. If you want a coined word, you can have your computer put together lists of randomly selected letters and then go through them, eliminating most. You can also try doing it yourself, like playing Scrabble with no rules. Simple misspelling does not make a coined word, especially where the resulting word sounds the same. For example, changing "car" to "Kar" does little.

It may be boring, but go through a dictionary word by word if you want an arbitrary or suggestive word. With each word, ask yourself if it would make a good mark. Perhaps a word appears attractive, but is not enough alone. Write it down to use with another one you will find later. You can also comb through descriptive text as if it were a list of words, without thinking about the meaning of the sentences. Just search for a good word. Perhaps you should confine yourself to text unrelated to your product. Sometimes you can piece together words from parts of other words. Look at words to see if there are useful parts. For example, word parts like "ette" and "onics" carry some image with them. You can find others. A medical treatment for preparing a colon for examination and also providing electrolytes is sold under the trademark "Colyte." That is a new, meaningless word, but has parts that serve as a memory aid. Go through magazines with lots of advertising for products not in your field. Scan for interesting words or graphics ideas that you can change and adapt to you. Ignore the meaning of the communication itself.

An approach that might work is to get some creative people together and have a little party. After you explain that you want suggestions for a trademark, turn them loose. One suggestion will build on another. Many will be silly, but so what? After a short while serve a little wine or other favorite beverage. The ideas will get a little unusual, but a good one might turn up. Be sure to write them down or turn on a recorder so that after the party you will have the fruits of their efforts.

Whatever method you use, as you get ideas, apply the trademark principles you see in these chapters to them. As you go, discard those words or graphical symbols that are likely to cause problems because they will be difficult to protect under the trademark law. Stay away from the generic and information conveying end of the spectrum.

COMPUTER
TECHNOLOGY

PROTECTING COMPUTER TECHNOLOGY

15

Computers have become as much a part of our lives as automobiles and television. Computer technology has spawned a major business boom in its field with many competitors, including some of the world's largest multinational corporations as well as some of the world's smallest companies. Software for those computers has become one of the world's greatest cottage industries, because individuals can write software with only a small investment in one computer. In nearly all aspects of the industry, innovation is a major key to being a successful competitor. It is not surprising that competitors have turned to intellectual property law to help them protect their contributions.

Interestingly, while most innovative creations are protected principally under only either patent or copyright law, computer technology depends on both for protection. Of course, the industry also relies on trademark protection and trade secret protection, as well as licensing and contract law. But that law usually still applies its conventional principles, which are decades or centuries old and merely extended to computer technology in a reasonably foreseeable manner. However, protection with patents and copyrights has been anything but reasonably foreseeable. Congress, state legislatures, and courts, as well as lawyers and businesspeople, have struggled long and hard to determine what can be protected and how.

HISTORICAL DEVELOPMENT

Before the second World War, there was essentially no such thing as a computer—if we ignore the abacus, adding machines, slide rules, and a few obscure other devices. These were mechanical devices in which you could see and describe all the physical parts, and conventional patent law principles applied. In the 1940s and 1950s, the electronic computer left universities and laboratories and went out into the business world in the form of multimillion dollar machines seen, owned, and understood by very few people. For a couple of decades, computer circuits were protected by patents, and software was protected as trade secrets, both in pretty much conventional ways.

Then, in the 1970s and early 1980s, the computer technology explosion began. People began to see how computer technology could be used in many new ways. Hardware became less expensive—in fact, cheap. Thousands of businesspeople began to see opportunities through innovation. With that, trade secret protection began to be impractical, because software became widely circulated and easily copied. Demand was created for hardware and software innovations that could do new things inexpensively. Many tasks were delegated to computers, such as business record keeping and processing, computer assisted design, communication, data collection and distribution, and document creation.

With so many people making innovative contributions, they naturally turned to the law to protect their creations—just as it had protected other creations in science and the arts. Early in the 20th century, the invention of the phonorecord had raised some problems for copyright law, but it had never before been faced with some of the questions presented by this new computer technology. Could software be protected by patents and/or copyrights? Software wasn't quite like any of those earlier technologies.

Patent law had long protected manufacturing methods and processes, so how about methods for operating a computer? Patent law seemed like a natural place to protect software. What about unique mathematical data manipulations and computational methods? Could they be protected, and if so, how? The courts had already said a mathematical formula or laws of nature can't be patented. They also said a mental process can't be patented, because they didn't want anyone to be guilty of patent infringement for what he or she thinks or even for solving a math problem with a pencil and paper.

What about copyright protection for software? Software is a part of a machine used to control the machine's operation. Patent law was the traditional place to protect the applications of science such as machines and their operation. Copyright only applied to the writings of an author, usually creations of an artistic nature. The courts said writings include not only obvious writings like books and plays, but also included paintings and sculptures. But software is not like those things. One doesn't sit and read software, nor does one gaze at it in a museum. While one can read the source code for software, it isn't very pleasant reading. You can't even read software object code, so how could it be protected? Computer software is science, not art. There are no stories, no human-to-human communications, just control of a machine.

Lurking in the background of all these specific questions were the broader issues of social policy. The ultimate goal was to bring useful innovations to the marketplace, where they are available to benefit all citizens. But successful innovation requires two foundations. First, it requires a foundation of knowledge, upon which the innovation is built. This means an innovator must have a wealth of underlying technical information that is extended by the new idea. Therefore, we want earlier technology to be both available to study and free to copy. Second, successful innovation requires incentive both to invest effort in solving a problem and to invest money and take risks to bring the improvement to production and market. Therefore, we want technology to be exclusively owned so the innovator can expect to profit from these investments rather than have others get a free ride on the innovator's effort. But one person's innovation is the next person's underlying technology on which to build a further improvement. So a reasonable balance must be struck between exclusive ownership and free availability.

Throughout the 1970s and 1980s, the courts struggled on a case-by-case basis to try to determine what could be patented, what could be copyrighted, and what couldn't be protected at all. Congress made some revisions to the statutes. The U.S. Supreme Court addressed the issue. By the 1990s we began to have some pretty good principles to apply to help answer these and many other questions, but the case-by-case analysis continues today. The result is that we know a lot more now about what can be protected and how, but some uncertainty still remains.

PROTECTION OF COMPUTER TECHNOLOGY BY COPYRIGHT

It is clear today that computer software can be protected by copyright and computer hardware cannot. Software includes source code and object code, regardless of whether humans can understand it. Writing programs is a new kind of writing. It is similar to traditional writing, which consists of a long sequence of many words. The words themselves are old, but they are arranged in a new way. The software that can be protected includes programs for controlling both the computer and databases, which are compilations of computer readable data accessed by the computer under the control of the program. Mask works and chips can be protected by something similar to copyright, addressed in a later subchapter.

However, saying that these can be protected is not enough, because not everything about them is protected. It must be remembered that in applying copyright law to computer software, the courts had to adapt law made for artistic creation to the protection of something that was essentially a scientific technology used to control a machine. There was plenty of misfit that had to be accommodated.

One fundamental principle of copyright law is that it does not protect an idea, procedure, process, or method of operation. That sounds exactly like what a computer program is, but copyright does protect the *manner of expression* of any of those. Traditionally, an author's unique new teaching method, newly discovered scientific principle, or boy-meets-girl general story line cannot be protected by copyright. They are ideas, and other authors may write about the same subjects. However, the author's manner of expression, the unique order and sequence of words that the author uses to express those ideas, can be protected by copyright. The problem, of course, is to find the dividing line between ideas and manner of expression in software.

One thing to look at is whether the idea can be expressed in more than one manner. In the software context, can a computer be programmed with one or more different sequences of instructions to accomplish the same operation or result? If there is only one sequence of instructions possible, a court is likely to conclude that the sequence is not copyrightable, because to protect it would prevent others from using the underlying idea.

All software has both ideas and manner of expression. Clearly, its broad purpose is an idea. For example, preparing a calendar and scheduling work flow or operating a bulletin board. The broad ideas are not protected because other authors must be able to write their own software that accomplishes the same tasks. Ordinarily, a specific sequence of instructions is an expression just like the specific sequence of words in a book, so it usually can be protected. But we would not want to limit protection to only exact identical copies of every detail. In between the broadest idea and the specific instructions are various intermediate levels of decreasing generality. What about the order in which the program asks for input data? What about the screen displays or a sequence of menus? These are the grey areas that can sometimes be protected. An intermediate level of generality, like the unique plot of a play, is more likely to be protected when the author's contribution is unique and the author created one way of doing it by making his or her own personal choices (but many other ways remain for other authors to use by exerting their own effort).

Like all copyrightable works, software must be original with the author. There will be no protection for what is old and copied from others. However, a work may include parts that are old and the work as a whole can still be protected. Old routines and subroutines may be positioned together in an original order and sequence, much like a compilation of old folk tales. The order and sequence can be protected even though the components themselves are not.

Another aspect of originality is the extent of personal choices that an author makes from among many possible, perhaps infinite, alternatives. Words or musical notes can be combined in many sequences, and so can computer instructions. The more the software is the result of an author making such choices for his personal reasons, the more likely the effort is protectable. The more the author's choices are dictated by a lack of alternatives or by functional purposes such as machine characteristics or market demand, the less the likelihood that the software can be protected.

COPYRIGHT INFRINGEMENT
OF COMPUTER SOFTWARE

Infringement is the unauthorized copying of a protectable portion of a copyrighted work. Copying means the infringer lifted something out of one work and carried it over to include it in another. Thus, anyone who independently creates something cannot be an infringer, regardless of the similarity of his or her work to a copyrighted work.

The copyright statute itself authorizes a form of copying that is unique to software. If you are the owner of a copy of a computer program, you are authorized to make a copy of it. You can do that for archival purposes or as an essential step in using the program. This allows you to protect yourself against accidental destruction or theft of your copy. It also allows you to copy the program onto your hard disk. You must destroy the copy you made if your possession of the original copy is no longer rightful. Obviously, if you began with an unauthorized copy, you are not authorized to make and keep a copy of it. If you borrowed an authorized copy, you are not an owner of a copy, so you can't copy it either.

The most difficult questions arise when only some, but not all, of a copyrighted program is copied. Whether copying only some is infringement is not simply a matter of how much or what proportion is copied. Rather, it depends more upon whether what was copied is protectable. Unfortunately, determining what is protectable is unreliable and uncertain. The courts and the industry are still struggling to find answers. But those in the industry often must copy what they can in order to compete or even survive.

One increasingly used test for determining what is protectable is the abstraction-successive filtering-comparison method. We begin with the copyrighted work and first remove the abstract ideas that are unprotectable. To do this, we start with the most general concept of what the program is intended to accomplish, then work down into the outline, first on a more general level and then with more details. We may get into the flow charts and algorithms. We look at the component modules, routines, and subroutines and how they are arranged and interconnected. At some level the judge must decide where the line has been crossed from abstract idea to manner of expression.

After the ideas have been removed, the judge will then remove any expression of an idea that seems a necessary way to communicate the idea. If there are only a few ways to express the idea—that is, to instruct the computer to operate—then such a necessary manner of expression will also be removed. The judge will be influenced by where she or he feels the proper balance is struck between sufficient unique contribution from the author and sufficient available alternatives for other authors.

Then the judge removes anything that was written as a result of external considerations rather than choices made by the author. For example, instructions written in a particular manner because of the requirements of particular hardware or to comply with industry standards or the end users requirements would be removed. Finally, the court removes what was not the author's creation, such as public domain software that the author copied.

What is left is what is protectable. The court then compares the protectable portion of the copyrighted program to what was copied. If any significant portion beyond a trivial or insignificant portion was copied, there is infringement.

REGISTERING COMPUTER SOFTWARE IN THE COPYRIGHT OFFICE

Don't equate registering with copyrighting. Registration is not necessary to get protection under the copyright statute, but it is desirable. Registering software is much like registering any other work. You complete the form TX from the Register of Copyrights and send in the required copies and the fee.

The required copies that must be submitted to register a computer program are different than for other writings. For software you must submit "identifying portions" of the program in a form that can be read by a human without a machine. The first choice of the Copyright Office is for a printed copy of the first 25 and the last 25 pages of source code or all the code if less than 50 pages.

However, if the work contains trade secret materials, there are some alternatives to help you avoid disclosing those secrets. You can block out trade secret portions, so long as the blocked-out portion is less than the remaining portion. You can send in the first and last 10 pages with nothing blocked out. You can also deposit the source code and meet other requirements.

Along with the "identifying portions," you can also deposit reproductions (such as printouts or photographs) of the computer screens. If you specifically claim the screens as a part of your copyrighted work, then you must include reproductions.

CHIPS AND MASK WORKS

The development of integrated circuits over the past three decades has made the personal computer available at lower prices than were once thought possible. The manufacture of these chips requires the creation of extensive, detailed masks (which are somewhat like photographic negatives) showing the physical layout of the circuits on the silicon substrates. They are used with various photographic and chemical processes to form the actual circuits.

These masks and the circuits they form in the chips were probably not copyrightable when first invented. Congress created a special kind of protection for chips and masks, somewhat resembling copyright but having some characteristics of patents and trade secrets.

A qualifying owner of a mask work fixed in a semiconductor chip product can get the exclusive right to reproduce or license reproduction for a period of 10 years. The work must be registered within two years of the time it is first commercially exploited anywhere in the world or the protection is terminated. Protection, as with copyright, does not extend to ideas, procedures, processes, concepts, or principles. The works must be original and not consist of designs that are standard, commonplace, or familiar in the semiconductor industry. However, the law expressly permits reverse engineering. This allows others to take the chip apart, learn the principles of its operation, and apply those principles in their own designs.

PROTECTION OF COMPUTER TECHNOLOGY BY PATENTS

The readily visible, physical parts of computers are protectable by patents. Their electronic circuits and mechanical devices are protected just like such things were protected long before computers. But what about software? Can you patent software? The answer is both yes and no, because the answer depends upon what you consider to be the patenting of software. It is necessary to investigate what aspects of software you can patent and what aspects you cannot patent.

Software can be viewed on different levels in different ways. On its most detailed level, it is a long series of discrete instructional steps arranged in an order. Each step is represented by combinations of words, letters, numbers, and other symbols. At this level, software is protectable by copyright and not by patent law. But some software includes a unique combination of data manipulation steps that work together to accomplish some useful result. Typically, these steps are a procedure for solving a mathematical problem and together may be called an algorithm. At this level, some patent protection is available in the right circumstances.

You should remember that law is usually extended to new areas, such as new technology, by analogy. Courts are more likely to apply old legal principles to new fact situations when they can be made comfortable by the similarities between the old traditional application of the principles and their extension to the new technology. Traditionally, methods and processes for manipulating physical things were patentable and mathematical formulas and a series of mental thought process steps were not. So essentially, the more the algorithm or other steps of a program could be made to look like a conventional process or method for manipulating something physical, the more likely it became that it could be patented. The more it looked like an attempt to patent a mathematical formula, the less was the likelihood. Further, conventional processes usually consisted of anywhere from 2 to 10 steps. While there is no generally accepted limit on the number of steps, if you can't state the software method or algorithm within somewhere near a dozen or so steps, you can expect difficulty getting a patent. A combination of the dozens, hundreds, or thousands of steps on the level of source code cannot be patented.

The direction the patent law took was driven by important policy considerations that are important to an understanding of which aspects of software can be patented and which can't. The courts wanted some patent protection for this new technology because experience shows that giving protection stimulates the improvement of technology and makes its fruits plentiful in the market. However, the courts don't want to foreclose anyone from using principles of mathematics that are the basic tools of science. They are too fundamental, and allowing patents for them would inhibit other good inventions. That would be like patenting gravity or photosynthesis. The courts only want to permit people to patent the application of scientific principles to machines and other physical things, not the principles themselves.

So, what can be patented? If the steps of the software can be described other than by the direct or indirect statement of a mathematical algorithm, then it can be patented—if it meets the other usual requirements, such as being new and different enough from the prior technology. Typically, however, the unique method of the software is a series of mathematical operations—that is, the manipulation of numbers. These steps might include multiplying, taking square roots, or comparing two numbers and selecting the greater. Most are considerably more complicated, but each is a well known data processing step. It makes no difference whether the invention is described in terms of mathematical notation and symbols or in prose.

If the invention includes such mathematical steps, that fact does not exclude it from patent protection, but we must look further to decide if it could be patented. No patent will be allowed if it would preclude all use of the mathematical algorithm. But the patent will be permitted for an application of the algorithm to something physical. A way to determine whether all uses of the algorithm would be precluded is to take the definition of the invention (that is, the patent claim—see Chapter 7) and remove the algorithm from it. If something physical is left that interacts with the algorithm, then the invention can be patented. For example, the use of an old algorithm, with some additional new mathematical manipulation steps in order to control the opening of a tire mold, can be patented.

Thus, the more the software algorithm is intimately associated with some physical operation or structure, the more likely it is to be granted a patent. If it just manipulates data, it probably cannot be patented. So, if the software does its job with a conventional computer, keyboard, and monitor or other conventional peripherals, it is unlikely that it can be patented. However, if the mathematical manipulations of the algorithm intimately cooperate with a physical device, such as a read only memory, then that can be enough to get the patent.

The court will be on the lookout for attempts to make an algorithm look patentable by attaching some trivial physical object or physical manipulation to the definition of the invention. For example, causing an insignificant alarm or displaying the value derived from an algorithm may not be enough. Confining the invention to a field of use, such as the chemical conversion of hydrocarbons or seismic prospecting, may also not be enough. Mere data-gathering steps to sense values to use in the algorithm may not be enough. What matters is whether the connection to the physical world is an integral part of the invention or just an add-on to get a patent.

There are still many questions to be answered and much uncertainty remains. Close cases will be dependent in part on the skill of the patent attorney who describes the invention in the claims and the judge who makes the decisions. That is the best humans can do when dealing with such a revolutionary new technology as computers.

OTHER INTELLECTUAL PROPERTY

TRADE SECRETS

16

BACKGROUND PRINCIPLES

Lawyers often refer to "common law," and trade secret law is a part of the common law. An understanding of common law assists in understanding trade secret law. The rules of common law are not written in any statute, ordinance, or bill passed by a legislative body. Instead, as each case comes before a judge, the judge draws upon experience and knowledge of the society in which he or she lives to find the rules that are generally understood to govern conduct in the society. The judge then describes those rules and applies them to the case. Judges' descriptions of those rules (for many cases) are preserved in libraries, where they may be researched, and together they define the common law.

Trade secret law has arisen in that same manner over the course of many decades and many cases. Judges determine the guiding principles by balancing competing interests and then do what they believe to be fair and just in the circumstances. That is essentially what judges are still doing in trade secret cases today. Trade secret law does not have a lot of technicalities like patent and copyright law.

In determining what is fair and just in a trade secret case, the judge must balance two important competing interests. One interest is the need to make new knowledge available to all people so that they are free to improve upon it. Consumers' lives can be improved when someone learns from predecessors and then extends the preceding knowledge. One person's new idea is a foundation for the next person's new idea, and the flow of new ideas should be maintained. This would lead to the conclusion that everyone should know and be free to use every new idea so people can advance knowledge and thereby improve society.

The other competing interest recognizes the need to provide incentive to make new ideas available in the marketplace. That incentive usually is in the form of possible profit, fame, recognition, or power. Incentives induce people to exert effort toward making improvements and investing money and time to make improvements available to consumers. The innovator should obtain a reward so others will try. This would suggest that the law prohibit anyone from using someone else's innovation.

Obviously, we cannot both maintain ideas protected in secret and, at the same time, communicate them broadly and make them free for all to use. Consequently, a balance must be struck in each case between the need for citizens to know in order to make improvements, and the need to provide sufficient incentive to innovators to bring improvements to consumers.

We already have patent and copyright systems that attempt to balance those interests. But many valuable innovations and valuable information cannot be patented. For example, most aspects of computer programs; business ideas; business data, such as customer lists; and small, minor scientific improvements are not able to be patented. Some innovations are not important enough to justify the expense of seeking a patent. Other innovations are too important to disclose in a patent, such as the proverbial Coke formula. Trade secret law is essentially common law that has developed to meet these needs in a balanced manner.

OUTLINE OF TRADE SECRET LAW

A judge who is faced with a trade secret case and seeks to determine what is fair and just likes to apply older, well established principles to new situations by analogy. In doing this in trade secret law, the courts have applied four other areas of law. First, they often apply property law, referring sometimes to trade secrets as intangible personal property. They are intangible because they cannot be touched or felt and are personal property because they are not land or attachments to land. Under property law principles, trade secrets can be sold, assigned to others, and licensed. They probably could be taxed if they could be readily identified and described.

Contract law is also often applied. Typically, the owner of a trade secret agrees with someone else to maintain the trade secret information in confidence—that is, in secret. If a person breaks that agreement, he or she may be found to be in breach of the contract. Contracts can be expressed in a written document. They can also arise verbally or can be implied from surrounding circumstances or action in law, perhaps to prevent someone from getting an unjust free ride based upon the effort of another.

Trade secret law also draws upon the principles of "tort" law, the law of wrongdoing, for which the wrongdoer is accountable to the person who is injured by the wrongdoing. Such wrongdoing would include unlawfully taking trade secret property from the owner and converting it to the use and benefit of the person who took it. It would also include fraud and deception to obtain knowledge of a trade secret and the breach of a duty, such as is assumed by an officer of a company or other person who is the recipient of information held for the benefit of another.

Finally, some states have made the taking or the unlawful use of a trade secret a criminal offense.

In applying the general principles from these areas of the law, there are usually three main questions that must be addressed in each trade secret situation. The first question is whether a trade secret exists—that is, is there something protectable? The second question is whether there was some wrongdoing in connection with the trade secret. Not only must a trade secret exist, but there must be some wrongdoing, such as a "tort," breach of a contract, or violation of some other duty. The wrongdoing is in the form of wrongful communication of the secret or wrongful use of the secret. The third question is, what should the court do to correct the injustice that the court finds? These three questions will now be addressed in order.

WHAT IS A TRADE SECRET?

A trade secret is almost anything and everything useful or advantageous in business activity but not generally known or easily ascertainable by others in the trade. The subject matter includes scientific or technical information, designs, patterns, processes, procedures, formulas, business plans, financial information, and listings of names, addresses, or phone numbers. Although the subject matter of a trade secret may be almost anything, two additional requirements are business value and secrecy.

The requirement that a trade secret must have business value is usually relatively easy to determine. The items listed above, as well as computer programs and databases, business plans, supplier's lists, and concealed price codes, all have apparent business value to the owner. On the other hand, something like the name and address of the company president's girlfriend or favorite vacation location would not have business value.

The requirement that the trade secret be a secret does not mean it must be an absolute secret confined to a single person. Clearly, the secret can be known by others in the company who need to know in order to utilize the trade secret. It can also be disclosed to outside consultants. On the other hand, the trade secret cannot be generally known in the trade, or it is not a secret. However, the fact that the information was once known, and indeed even once published in a public document such as a patent, but has now become lost to obscurity, does not necessarily destroy the secrecy. If extensive effort is required to assemble the information, it can be a trade secret even though it has been, at some time, publicly disclosed. But if the information can be readily assembled by a person in the trade, it is not a trade secret.

The courts require not only that it be secret, but that the owner demonstrate that he or she intentionally held it as a trade secret. This intent could be demonstrated by the existence of written contracts with employees or from precautionary security measures, such as the erection of signs as part of the efforts to keep others away from the area of the company in which the trade secret information might be observed. The courts look at all of the surrounding facts to determine whether the trade secret owner has attempted to maintain it as a trade secret. For example, one court said that the erection of a sign restricting access was not, itself, enough. Another court said that the fact that the trade secret owner disclosed it at a conference where competitors were not present did not alone demonstrate a lack of intent to maintain it as a trade secret. There are no simple rules for demonstrating the intent to maintain information in secret. The owner of the trade secret should do as much as possible to retain the information in secrecy. In one case, the owner of a trade secret was building a chemical plant, but before the roof was put on the plant the trade secret information was visible from the air. A defendant flew over and took pictures before the roof was put on. The court said that this still was a protectable trade secret and taking the pictures was a wrongful act. Of course, if the information is generally available in the trade, then no amount of security effort will turn it into a trade secret.

A trade secret has no time limit. That is, it does not expire from the passage of time alone. It may be maintained forever, so long as it is successfully maintained in secrecy with sufficient security or other acts demonstrating an intent to maintain it in secrecy.

Furthermore, there is no requirement that a trade secret have some degree or quantity of innovation or novelty. Even a very minor improvement can be a trade secret, so long as it is not generally known and attempts are made to retain it as a trade secret.

WRONGFUL ACTS

The use by someone of trade secret information is not alone sufficient to convince a court to stop that use or require payment of damages for that use. If a trade secret can be shown to exist and another uses it, there still must be some wrong committed by a wrongdoer. One such wrongdoing is committed by a person who uses wrongful means to learn of the trade secret. This would include industrial spying or espionage or bribing employees who know of the trade secret to disclose it. Another wrongful act would be fraud. For example, posing as a bona fide customer or disguising yourself as a laborer to get a job and learn of the secret would be wrongful acts. Attempting to negotiate a dealership arrangement with the owner of a trade secret for the sole purpose of learning the trade secret, with no actual intent to be a distributor, would also be fraud.

Another kind of wrongful activity involves people who learned of the trade secret in a lawful manner with the understanding it would be kept in secrecy, but who later violate that understanding. An employee who agrees in an employment contract to maintain a secret in confidence and then discloses it, for example, commits a wrongful act. Some courts have also said that if you learn of a trade secret by mistake or from someone who themselves obtained the secret by wrongdoing, the law imposes a duty to protect that trade secret, even though you yourself are guilty of no wrongdoing.

The courts will protect specific information, but will not protect general knowledge acquired by an employee based upon his or her experience in the business. An employee must be able to practice his or her trade and have job mobility, and consequently can even go to work for a competitor. While an employee cannot disclose specific trade secrets, he or she can utilize the general knowledge acquired on the job. Whether the information is general or specific will depend in part upon whether the secret can be described in a concise, specific description. For example, the drawings, the customer list, or a particular paint formulation would be regarded as a trade secret. Probably, how to design a house would not.

Trade secret law permits anyone learning of a trade secret by fair and honest means to use it. For example, anyone who independently thinks of or obtains the same information as someone else's trade secret may use it, so long as it was not learned from the owner. It is lawful to inspect a product and utilize any trade secret information that is apparent from the product itself. You can use what you see by walking in public areas of a place of business. Of course, even though trade secret law permits use, a patent or copyright may still prevent use.

Reverse engineering is also recognized as lawful activity. For example, a product can be taken apart to see how it operates. Lawfully obtained software can be examined to see and learn about its underlying ideas. While the software can't be copied, the underlying ideas can be used. Products may be chemically analyzed to determine their constituent parts. Of course, others may learn the information in the literature. Anyone reading an obscure, expired patent containing the information and who learned of the information from that patent, rather than from a trade secret owner, is free to use that information.

REMEDIES TO RIGHT THE WRONG

Some states provide criminal penalties for stealing trade secrets. The criminal activity is specifically described in a statute and can result in misdemeanor or felony penalties. The statute of each state needs to be consulted to determine what activity is criminal. However, criminal penalties do not provide much help to the owner of the trade secret. Non-criminal activities can still be wrongful and allow a trade secret owner to get a remedy from a court.

The usual remedies available to trade secret owners include injunctions against disclosure or use of a trade secret, the award of damages or profits for use of the trade secret, and delivery or destruction of things that contain or use the trade secret.

In deciding whether activities of a wrongdoer should be prevented in the future, the judge must decide whether an injunction should simply undo the wrong and put the trade secret owner in the position he or she would have been in had the wrongdoing not occurred. Alternatively, the judge may decide to prevent the wrongdoer from getting any benefit or use from the trade secret, even a benefit to which the wrongdoer would have been entitled if the wrongdoer had not committed the wrongful act. If the court decides solely to undo the wrong, the court may apply what is called the "head start rule." For example, if someone wrongfully obtains trade secret information about a product that a competitor will introduce in the future and uses that information to introduce its own product, then what should the court do? If the trade secret would be apparent from the product when introduced by the competitor, then the wrongdoer has received a time lead benefit by not being required to wait until the product was introduced to see it. The court, under the head start rule, may enjoin the wrongdoer from introducing the product for a period of time, such as six months, and thereby deprive the wrongdoer of the head start, but allow the wrongdoer to utilize the information that is available from the product. However, if the wrongdoing was sufficiently evil, the court may deny all use of that trade secret, even though others in the trade may use it after the product is introduced. An Ohio court summed it up well by saying that an injunction should generally terminate when the trade secret becomes known, but in some cases the misappropriation may be so egregious as to justify the ultimate sanction of a permanent injunction.

The wrongdoer may also be required to pay the trade secret owner profits that the trade secret owner lost as a result of the wrongdoing. The court may, in some cases, require that the wrongdoer pay all ill-gotten profits to the trade secret owner. Courts do not try to find a fair market or replacement value for a trade secret, because that is essentially impossible to do.

Finally, some courts have ordered products that embody a trade secret, or plans, patterns, or photographs showing the trade secret, to be destroyed or given back to the trade secret owner.

RELATIONSHIP TO PATENTS AND COPYRIGHTS

Trade secret law is so different from patent and copyright law that there is very little overlap. A patent or copyright may be infringed even in the absence of any violation of trade secret law. For example, learning information in a fair manner, such as by reading it or by inspecting a product, will entirely eliminate any trade secret law violation, but patent or copyright infringement could still occur.

There is, however, some interrelationship between patent and copyright law and trade secret law. The filing of a U.S. patent application does not destroy a trade secret, because patent applications are maintained in secrecy in the U.S. Patent and Trademark Office. However, foreign patent applications may destroy a trade secret because they are published after filing, regardless of whether a patent is issued. In any event, the issuance of a patent will destroy trade secret information that is disclosed in an issued patent. Consequently, an applicant for a patent must recognize that a choice is being made and that the issuance of a patent will result in the loss of any trade secret rights to the information disclosed in the patent.

Furthermore, patent law requires the disclosure of the best mode of practicing the invention. Consequently, the filing of a patent application requires the information be disclosed that is necessary for a person to practice the invention. Disclosing in a patent application only the main concepts of the invention, but concealing important, practical information, which may be needed to operate the invention in the best way, may destroy the patent and make it invalid. Consequently, careful choices must be made when determining whether to file a patent application or depend upon trade secret law.

CONCLUSION

Trade secret law, more than most areas of the law, is pretty much the application of seat-of-the-pants justice. Courts have significant latitude and must weigh the competing interests to determine what is fair conduct and what should be done to remedy unfair conduct. In that sense, trade secret law is common law at its best. To be protectable under trade secret law, the information can be almost anything that has value in the trade and for which steps were taken to intentionally keep it secret. There must be some wrongdoing, either wrongful conduct in obtaining the trade secret or a failure to meet a duty to retain it in secrecy and not use it. If a trade secret is found to exist and a wrongdoing is found in connection with it, a court will then construct a remedy based on balancing the interest of protecting the property in order to provide incentive and protecting the need of the public to utilize prior knowledge.

MYTHS, TRIVIA, AND MOST FREQUENTLY ASKED QUESTIONS ABOUT PATENTS, COPYRIGHTS, AND TRADEMARKS

VII

MYTHS

17

There are many existing myths and fallacies about patents, copyrights, and trademarks. After reading this book, hopefully, you now understand enough about the subject that certain of your misconceptions no longer exist. The following comments about some of these common myths may provide you with some additional insight about patents, copyrights, and trademarks.

Myth   *It is becoming increasingly more difficult to receive a patent on an invention since so many good ideas have already been patented.*

Fact   Though it may appear that most of the good ideas have already been taken, we can assure you this is not true. In fact, as a result of technological advances, there are more opportunities for new patents today than ever before. Consider, for instance, the incredible advances that are presently being made in such fields as medicine, computers, space, et cetera. During John Quincy Adams' administration (1825–1829), Congress came within three votes of discontinuing the U.S. Patent Office. They believed that all of the good ideas had been conceived and wanted to save the taxpayers' money. Since then, inventions such as the automobile, airplane, telephone, television, and thousands of other things have been patented. If the future is anything like the past, the vast majority of new things have yet to be invented.

Myth *Once a patent is granted, financial success is guaranteed.*

Fact There are no guarantees that a patented invention promises monetary gain. In fact, the vast majority of patented products do not produce significant wealth for their inventors.

Myth *With a patent, an inventor will have little difficulty lining up a big company to be his "partner" in developing, manufacturing, and marketing the patented product.*

Fact Contrary to what many people believe, for most patented inventions, it is extremely difficult to find somebody else to handle the business end of product development, manufacturing, advertising, distribution, promotion, et cetera. If the patent owner is not himself skilled in these areas, his chances of success are greatly diminished. *It is up to you, the patent owner, to make things happen.* You cannot rely on somebody doing it for you.

Myth *If you build a better mousetrap, the world will beat a path to your door.*

Fact In truth, after you have built your better mousetrap, you must beat a path to the door of the rest of the world. Once your mousetrap is patented, you must go out and sell it.

Myth *An inventor must make up a working model of his or her invention in order to get it patented.*

Fact A working model isn't necessary to file a patent application.

Myth *An individual could copy an invention that she sees in a foreign country and get it patented in the United States.*

Fact A patent applicant must sign an oath stating that she believes herself to be the first inventor, which means inventions cannot be copied from an inventor in another country.

Myth *Big companies sometimes buy up patents that are an improvement of their existing products to keep the improved product out of the marketplace.*

Fact Although many people believe this, there is no evidence that we have ever seen to substantiate this practice. For instance, many people erroneously think that the major oil companies have attempted to keep fuel-efficient automobiles from entering the marketplace. In a highly competitive worldwide marketplace that exists in the automobile industry, curtailing competition is an absurd notion. The oil industry has never attempted this practice.

Myth	*When an individual takes his invention to a big company, the company is likely to steal it rather than give the inventor a fair deal.*
Fact	This is a greatly overexaggerated concern that has little merit. The vast majority of major companies are reputable and do not steal. The roots of this myth probably stem from the fact that an idea may be presented to a company that was already in the process of doing the same thing when the inventor approached it. So, while the company independently thought of the idea, it appeared as if the idea was stolen from the inventor. For this reason, many companies are skeptical about even talking to an outsider who approaches them with an idea.
Myth	*If a person writes a description of her invention on a piece of paper and mails it to herself via registered mail, it will serve as proof of when she thought of her idea.*
Fact	Doing this is a very unreliable way to protect your invention and does not prove too much. It is simply too easy for an unscrupulous person to unseal an envelope and place a false document into it.
Myth	*Another way to prove the original date of an invention is to describe it on paper and then have the document notarized.*
Fact	A notary is just one witness and his or her act of notarization has no special effect or value.
Myth	*A patent is always the best way to prevent the competition from copying your product. At least, for a 17-year period.*
Fact	Though a patent provides a monopoly that lasts for 17 years, a good secret can last forever. Had Coca-Cola's formula been patented, for example, it would have expired years ago. By keeping it a secret, Coca-Cola has been able to enjoy its exclusivity for many more years. Bear in mind, however, that keeping a secret can be very difficult. You must make a choice based on the nature of your product.
Myth	*To avoid infringement, a person only needs to make a slight improvement of a patented invention.*
Fact	An inventor could patent the improvement itself but that does not excuse copying the underlying invention. This means he would still be infringing on the basic patented product. The patented improvement probably would not do him much good unless he was able to sell or license it to the

patent owner of the basic product or get a license from the owner.

Myth   *A major service of a vanity publisher is that it will register the copyright of the author's works.*

Fact   Registering an author's works with the copyright office is not so difficult that it should be a significant factor in determining who publishes a book. When a vanity publisher uses this service as a major selling point, it is likely that the company has little else to sell.

Myth   *As long as an employer does not sell the copies, it is permissible for it to photocopy a copyrighted work and distribute it to its employees, customers, et cetera.*

Fact   This is deemed copyright infringement, although many people frequently do make copies of such copyrighted works. It is a difficult task, however, for a copyright owner to police and, as we stated previously, it is up to her, not the copyright office, to police infringement activities concerning her work.

Myth   *It is not necessary for a nonprofit organization to obtain permission from a copyright owner to produce a play.*

Fact   Lack of profit motive does not excuse copyright infringement. However, by special exemption a nonprofit school may perform a play for classroom use and libraries may make one copy under some conditions without infringing.

Myth   *If a famous person gives an exclusive right to a writer to do her autobiography, no other writer is permitted to write a biography without being authorized to do so.*

Fact   The exclusive right given to an author only means that an agreement has been made whereby the individual will not work with another writer on her autobiography. This would not prevent anyone else from writing a biography.

Myth   *If a manuscript is sent via the U.S. Mail, it is automatically protected under copyright law.*

Fact   Mailing a manuscript has no effect on the copyright status of a published or unpublished work.

Myth   *Unlike other books that contain a copyright notice (©), it is never permissible to copy any portion from a work when the notice reads, "All rights reserved. No part of this book may be reproduced or utilized in any form or by any means, electronic or mechanical, including photocopying, recording, or by any information storage and retrieval system, without permission in writing from the author."*

Fact   The above statement is no more protective than any other copyright notice. Keep in mind that under the "fair use" section of the Copyright Act, it is permissible to copy some portion of a copyrighted work in some circumstances. The question of how much is fair is sometimes debatable.

Myth   *When an author's work is published, the publisher automatically owns the copyright rights.*

Fact   Unless otherwise agreed on, the copyright rights always belong to the author, not the publisher.

Myth   *It is permissible to use one paragraph or so from a literary work, two measures or eight notes from a musical composition, four frames from a motion picture, and so on, without constituting copyright infringement.*

Fact   While this may be true in some instances, there is no general rule in this regard.

Myth   *If credit is given to a literary work, it is permissible to copy it; or if not the entire work, significant portions of it.*

Fact   When it comes to determining fair use of a copyrighted work, it does not matter that the copyright owner is given credit or the work itself is acknowledged as a source. The citation may be an element considered by a court in determining whether fair use has been made—but don't count on it.

Myth   *Once you own a trademark that has been well accepted by the public, it is valuable because you can then license it to others, sit back, and enjoy the royalties.*

Fact   You must remember that when a trademark is licensed to others, you must maintain control of the quality of the licensee's goods. If you fail to do so, you can lose your trademark rights. For this reason, you would be making a foolish mistake by failing to be selective on whom you choose as your licensee(s).

Myth   *A person always has the right to use his surname as his trademark.*

Fact   Generally, this is true, but if a surname is already used as a trademark by a company and the public associates it with the products of that company, then a later user would be an infringer because his use would be deceptive to the public. For instance, if two brothers with the surname of Brooks decided to open a men's clothing store, they would be denied the right to use the name Brooks Brothers. Likewise, if your surname is Bloomingdale, you might have to choose another name for your newly formed department store.

Myth *It is permissible to use a famous person's name as your trademark because public figures are considered as public domain.*

Fact You must obtain the written consent of a living person in order to use or register his or her name, portrait, or signature as your trademark.

Myth *It is essential to register your trademark at the earliest possible date in order to obtain it as your mark.*

Fact Trademark ownership is determined principally by use, not by registration. However, legal rights are substantially enhanced by registration.

Myth *A trademark that is registered with the U.S. Patent and Trademark Office is similarly protected under existing treaties in foreign countries.*

Fact You must register your trademark country by country. Your registration in the United States does not extend your trademark rights to other countries.

TRIVIA

18

On June 4, 1963, perhaps the youngest person ever to receive a patent was Robert W. Patch. At age six, his toy truck received patent number 3,091,888.

◆◆◆

The patent with the record number of 21 inventors was issued to Patrick B. Close and 20 co-inventors. Their invention was a computer.

◆◆◆

The average patent search is estimated to take about 15 hours.

◆◆◆

In 1785, Benjamin Franklin invented bifocals because he hated carrying two pairs of glasses.

◆◆◆

On May 5, 1809, Mary Kies of Killingly, Connecticut, became the first American woman to receive a patent. Her invention was a device that weaved straw with silk or thread.

◆◆◆

On October 14, 1834, Henry Blair received a patent for a corn planter, thus becoming the first black patentee.

Patent leather got its name because the process by which the polished black finish is applied to leather used in shoes and handbags was once protected by a patent.

General Electric owns by far the most patents of any company in the world, more than 50,000 of them. Interestingly, the company was founded in 1878 by Thomas Edison and originally called the Edison Electric Light Company.

The individual granted the most number of patents by the U.S. Patent and Trademark Office is Thomas Edison, owner of 1,093. In 1868, at age 21, he received his first patent for the electrical vote recorder.

Persistence for invention is paramount. Thomas Edison recorded 25,000 failures in his attempt to invent a storage battery. When once interviewed about his work on the storage battery, Edison replied, "Those were not failures. I just learned 25,000 ways not to make a storage battery."

It is estimated that there are 2.5 million Americans who are presently working on their own inventions.

Our favorite quote about patents is Mark Twain's "A country without a patent office is just a crab that can't travel any way but sideways and backways."

Our favorite remark about inventions was made by Ben Franklin in response to the question, "What possible good could spring from the first balloon ascension?" Franklin answered, "Of what use is a newborn baby?"

Samuel Hopkins of Pittford, Vermont received the first U.S. patent in 1790 on an improved process to make potash. The patent was signed by George Washington.

There are 385 classifications and 100,000 subclassifications of things that are patentable at the U.S. Patent and Trademark Office.

There are 25 million documents, over 5 million U.S. patents, and 90,000 bound periodical volumes in the search room of the patent office.

Thomas Jefferson, the first secretary of state, was the first person to head the U.S. Patent Office.

The first design patent was granted to George Bruce in 1842 for a type face.

Auguste Bartholdi received a design patent for the Statue of Liberty in 1879.

In 1904, George L. Gillespie received a design patent for the Congressional Medal of Honor.

In 1980, the Supreme Court ruled that living organisms were patentable.

More patent applications for inventions on perpetual motion have been rejected by the U.S. Patent Office than any single other thing.

Abraham Lincoln received a patent for a set of bellows that could be attached to the hull of a ship below the waterline and be inflated as the craft approached a shallow area.

In 1859, James E. B. Stuart, a well-known Confederate general, received a patent for his method of attaching sabers to belts.

Samuel L. Clemens, known as Mark Twain, had a patent for a self-pasting scrapbook that was actually a collection of blank pages coated with gum or veneer. He also received a patent for an improvement for suspenders that had an adjustable and detachable strap.

Actress Lillian Russell patented a dresser-trunk in 1912. Instead of her stage name, the operatic soprano's real name, Helen Louise Leonard, appeared on the patent.

Albert Einstein, with co-inventor Leo Szilard, received a patent for a refrigeration apparatus in 1930.

In 1942, actress Hedy Lamarr, along with a co-inventor, George Antheil, a composer, patented a complex communications system designed to direct torpedoes at moving ship targets. The patent was put in her real name, Hedy Kiesler Markey.

Mrs. Richard Rodgers, wife of the composer, received a patent for inventing the "Johnny Mop," a device for cleaning toilet bowls.

Harry Houdini, the great magician, received a patent in 1921 for a diver's suit designed to enable the wearer to escape from it underwater. His patent is in his real name, Ehrick Weiss.

Entertainer Danny Kaye, with his co-inventor, Edward Dukoff, got a design patent for a blowout toy in 1952. Three snakes unrolled when the toy was inflated, and it had feathers extended at the end for tickling noses. The toy also delivered a mild Bronx cheer.

Winifred Guglielmi, otherwise known as Mrs. Rudolf Valentino, co-invented a doll that could serve as a wrap and received a patent for it in 1912.

In 1960, comedian Herb Schriner was a copatentee of the Harmonigun, a combination harmonica and water pistol.

In 1950 and 1951, entertainer Lawrence Welk was listed as the patent designer of two different lunch boxes.

Actress Edie Adams received a 1965 patent for her ring-shaped cigarette and cigar holders.

Herbert Zeppo Marx in 1969 was the co-inventor of two patents for a heart alarm to be worn on the wrist.

Henry F. Bosenberg was granted the first plant patent for his climbing or trailing rose in 1931.

In the late 1970s, Dan Bricklin invented VisiCalc, the first computer spreadsheet for personal computers, but did not patent its technology. He received no royalties from many top-selling programs that subsequently used the spreadsheets. "I may go down in history as the inventor of VisiCalc," Bricklin claims, "but with a patent, there'd be a difference, however. Some several hundred million dollars worth."

In 1867, when George Westinghouse invented the air brake, a device that revolutionized railroading, he attempted to sell it to Cornelius Vanderbilt, the business tycoon whose vast holdings included the New York Central Railroad. Vanderbilt told Westinghouse that he did not have time to waste on dreamers with "fool ideas that won't work," and threw the young inventor out of his office.

There were 77,251 patents issued in the United States during 1985. Of that total, 43,370 were granted to Americans and 33,881 went to foreigners.

♦♦♦

The first antibiotic, penicillin, was the discovery of Alexander Fleming in 1929. Under British law, chemical substances could not be patented. Its use was delayed for more than 10 years due to the absence of adequate equipment to purify the crude drug. This represents a good example of the value of a patent system. The patent system serves as a strong impetus for the research and development of a product.

In 1925, about 20 years after he and his brother, Wilbur, invented the airplane, Orville Wright received a patent for a flying doll. With the use of a spring, the doll could fly through the air, somersault, and land on a swinging frame to which it clung with wire arms.

The first American to be granted a patent for an automobile was George B. Selden, who applied for it on May 8, 1879, but did not build his machine until 16 years later. Interestingly, although there were more than 50 companies producing automobiles by 1898, the first commercially successful American-made vehicle was a three-horsepower Oldsmobile. In 1901, the company sold 425 of them; in 1904, it sold 5,000.

In 1884, when Joshua Lionel Cowen was only seven years old, he attached a small steam engine to a wooden locomotive that he had carved. The incident marked the beginning of Lionel Trains.

In 1986, there were more than 600,000 active trademarks that were registered with the U.S. Patent and Trademark Office.

The famous Brooks Brothers clothing store, founded in 1817, is America's oldest clothier. Abraham Lincoln was wearing Brooks Brothers clothing the night he was assassinated. So were Teddy Roosevelt and Woodrow Wilson during their inaugurations. Brooks Brothers' golden fleece is a valuable trademark that has been well recognized for many years.

First introduced in 1898, the familiar red-and-white Campbell Soup cans were the idea of John Dorrance, a nephew of founder Joseph Campbell's partner, Arthur Dorrance. The young Dorrance's choice of colors was inspired by Cornell University football team uniforms.

The famous Aunt Jemima trademark is named from an old vaudeville song, "Aunt Jemima."

The Shell Oil Company got its name and famous trademark because its founder originally owned a small shop in which he sold shell-covered boxes made by his children.

The Miltown tranquilizers were named after Milltown, New Jersey, a nearby town to the laboratory where the tranquilizers were developed. One *l* was dropped from the spelling to avoid having the trademark being classified as a geographical term.

Although Owens-Corning was able to use the color pink as its trademark for home insulation, Deere & Company, the tractor manufacturer, was not permitted to use a particular shade of green for its trademark. The court ruled that green, the color of grass, has a "natural" association with farming and therefore would unduly restrict competition.

Just as companies change their line of products, so are trademarks and trade names subject to change. Founded in 1914, the Computing-Tabulating-Recording Company manufactured butcher scales and time clocks. It was not until 1924 that the company changed its name to International Business Machines.

Reverend Sylvester Graham believed that the way to a man's soul was through his stomach. During the 1830s, he traveled the East preaching the evils of meat, alcohol, and processed flour. His disciples, "Grahamites," followed a strict vegetarian diet, drank only water, and throughout the year slept with their windows open. In 1837, Graham published a treatise urging his followers to bake their own bread and avoid highly processed baked goods. Thus, the Graham Cracker was born.

Albert W. Edgerly was a famous health foods advocate, nutrition expert, and author who was known by the general public as Dr. Ralston in the late 1800s. Later Dr. Ralston endorsed the Purina whole wheat cereal manufactured in St. Louis by Miller William Danforth. The doctor's name was so strongly associated with good nutrition that Danforth renamed his company the Ralston Purina Company in 1902.

Daniel Haynes founded the Haynes Mattress Company in Sealy, Texas in 1884. Since people mostly referred to his product as "the mattress from Sealy," when he sold out to a group of investors in 1906, the firm's name was officially changed to the Sealy Mattress Company.

Lunsford Richardson originally called his product Richardson's Croup and Pneumonia Cure. However, the North Carolina pharmacist, in search of a more catchy name, borrowed the surname of his brother-in-law, Joshua Vick, who, in fact, had nothing to do with the product's development. In 1905, Richardson's salve was renamed Vick's Vaporub.

Back in the 1930s, Samuel Ruben wanted to give his newly formed cosmetics firm an image of continental elegance, so he used the surname of Peter Carl Fabergé, the world renowned goldsmith who, during the late nineteenth century, designed the ornate jeweled Easter eggs and other elegant baubles for the czar's court. Today Fabergé Cosmetics is one of the most well-known firms of its kind in the world.

Chicago confectioner Otto Schnering created a five cent, nut-roll candy bar that he initially called "Kandy Kake." In 1921, one of his employees, in response to a company contest, suggested that the name be changed to Baby Ruth after ex-President Grover Cleveland's daughter, Ruth. As you can see, contrary to public belief, the famous trademark did not come about due to the popularity of baseball's immortal home-run slugger, Babe Ruth.

The copyright office has employees who carefully supervise people that inspect deposited works, and it does not permit deposit copies to be photocopied. Records of people who inspect deposit copies are also kept. For this reason, the risk of "stealing" is minimal.

The Writer's Guild of America (West) has a registration service to assist writers in establishing the completion date and the identity of their scripts written for theatrical motion pictures, television and radio. Though there is no statutory protection provided by the guild's service, it does provide evidence of the writer's prior claim to authorship of his work and the completion date. The guild, like copyright law, does not protect the registration of titles.

In 1965, two movies titled *Harlow* were produced. The first *Harlow* was an expensive big-screen version produced by Joseph E. Levine starring Carroll Baker. While it was being made, promoter Bill Sargent completed an inexpensive *Harlow* in black and white (starring Carol Lynley) in eight days and rushed it to the theaters to get the jump on the Levine movie. As angry as Levine was, no copyright infringement occurred. In an effort to promote his movie, he placed full-page ads in various publications stating, "Let there be no confusion! The *only* 'Harlow' produced by Joseph E. Levine and Paramount Pictures will open on August 11. It's the *only* 'Harlow' starring Carroll Baker, the *only* 'Harlow' filmed in breathtaking Technicolor, the *only* 'Harlow' produced at the world-famous studios of Paramount Pictures." The *Harlow* movies illustrate two important facts about copyright law. First, a title cannot be copyrighted, and second, it is not considered infringement for two or more biographers and historians to produce works on the same subject.

United Artists purchased the rights to *Alive*, a best-selling book about an Andes plane crash that occurred in 1972. Around the same time, a Mexican film called *Survive*, based on another book about the same plane crash, was made. Paramount subsequently released (in 1976) another movie about the event—prior to the *Alive* movie's release. Consequently, the United Artist's version of *Alive* movie project was canned, and the people who planned to make it had no legal recourse. Then, in early 1993, Touchstone Pictures released its version of *Alive*.

One of the most famous cases on the subject of literary property rights in conversations concerns Ernest Hemingway, who, before his death, had many lengthy conversations with A. E. Hotchner, his writer companion. Hotchner then wrote *Papa Hemingway*, based on the conversations, and it became a bestseller. Hemingway's estate later sued Hotchner and claimed proprietary rights in the book. In 1968, the New York courts rejected the suit, and determined that Hemingway's estate could not enforce any literary property rights in the conversations that were chronicled in the book. Although it is an overstatement to say *no* proprietary rights can exist in conversations, it is usually a good idea to write down or record your conversations if you wish to guard the expression of your ideas.

Titles are not copyrightable since a title does not possess sufficient expressive content. If you were the first person to write a book titled *Family*, copyright law could not be used to prevent others from using this title. However, you could not write a book titled *Gone With the Wind*, even one totally unlike the Mitchell civil war story, with total impunity. The *Gone With the Wind* copyright owners might have legal recourse, perhaps under unfair competition law rather than copyright law.

In an effort to change its somewhat staid and aloof image, IBM obtained reproduction rights from Bubbles, the Chaplin family company that licenses the use of Charlie Chaplin's image of the Tramp. IBM's advertising campaign was brilliant in projecting a user-friendly image. The Tramp is said to have given IBM a human face.

The United States has entered into treaties with many countries that give reciprocal protection to the copyrighted works in each country. This does not mean, however, when claims are made such as "International Copyright Secured" that there is an actual "international copyright" or a unitary "international copyright law."

During the years 1913, 1914, and 1915, playwright Eugene O'Neill copyrighted several of his plays by registering them with the copyright office. He was not fond of these works and did not want them published. When he later failed to renew his copyrights on these works for additional 28-year terms after his original copyright terms expired, the plays went into the public domain, making the works available to anyone who wished to copy, perform, or publish them. New Fathoms Press, Limited published these "O'Neill rejects" as *Lost Plays of Eugene O'Neill* and promoted them as a collection of "lost" work, a historic event. In addition to O'Neill being upset about his work being published against his wishes, he never received any compensation from the publication.

The list of ingredients on a food container cannot be copyrighted; however, if creativity is added, such as in a recipe, the work is copyrightable.

An example of a work that was initially denied registration at the copyright office occurred when a book with pages consisting entirely of a series of numbers arranged in particular patterns was rejected. Later, however, it was explained that these patterns of numbers were a teaching tool designed to communicate mathematical principles, and the copyright office reversed its original decision and registered the copyright.

For an additional fee, a copyright owner can request the copyright office to retain the deposit of the work for the life of the copyright.

It is advisable for a copyright owner to keep an exact copy of the work he or she deposits with the copyright office. You should not rely on your registered copyright at the copyright office as a permanent record of your work. Works can be lost. For instance, Charles Darrow's first set of rules for his game "Monopoly" was destroyed.

MOST FREQUENTLY ASKED QUESTIONS | 19

This final chapter includes many of the most frequently asked questions about patents, copyrights, and trademarks. Some of this information has already appeared in this book; other questions will provide answers that also need to be addressed.

PATENTS

Q *I have an idea for an invention that I would like to patent. What is the first step I should take?*

A You should first secure records that provide evidence of the date when you first thought of your invention. In fact, from the time your invention is simply an idea, you should begin to write a description of it, including how it works, and, if possible, make up some sketches. Explain your invention and notes to two associates and have them sign and date your records. As your work progresses, keep a log including experiments, successes, and failures, and also have it witnessed on a regular basis as things begin to happen. Be sure to keep your papers in a safe place.

Q *What if I only have an idea for a needed product that I document and have witnessed, but do not know how to make the product? For example, a liquid ink that can be erased.*

A An idea by itself cannot be patented, so you have nothing. Unless, of course, you do something about it. You must find the chemicals that will work.

Q *What is the purpose of a patent search if a patent office examiner will conduct a search when he or she reviews my application?*

A By conducting a search, you can find out if your invention has a chance of being patented. It is considerably less expensive to do a search before filing your application than it is to file the application and be denied a patent; additionally, what you learn from the search may be helpful in defining your invention in the application.

Q *Is there any reason for me to visit the patent office if an attorney is representing me?*

A No. However, the patent office is an interesting and educational place to visit.

Q *Once my patent attorney does a search, how do I determine whether to pursue applying for a patent?*

A Both of you must carefully analyze what the search reveals. The patent attorney will render an opinion on whether you are likely to get a patent based on experience in the field of patents. You must weigh the cost, the likelihood of getting the patent, and the potential commercial value of the patent to decide whether to proceed.

Q *How much detail is necessary in patent drawings in order to have an effective application?*

A The drawings should show every basic part of the invention in sufficient detail so that, when combined with the written description, the invention could be made, without undue experimentation, by a person of ordinary skill in the art.

Q *Can I obtain a copy of the patent for any invention that has been patented with the U.S. Patent and Trademark Office? If so, how?*

A Yes, by sending a check in the amount of $3.00 for each patent to the U.S. Patent and Trademark Office. You should indicate the patent number. If you do not know the patent number, some kind of search based on what you do know will be needed to find the number.

Q *What purpose is served by marking my invention "Patent Pending" or "Patent Applied For" while my application is being evaluated by the patent office?*

A These terms have no legal meaning. There is only a legal significance when you have the word "patent" followed by its issued number. However, the former does notify the public that an application is pending at the patent office and thereby serves as a notice to discourage competitors from investing in an infringement.

Q *If I file a patent application, can other people get a copy or read it?*
A Only after a patent is issued can the public see what you wrote. Before that, applications, including ones that are abandoned, are kept in secrecy and only patent office employees and persons authorized by the inventor or owner can see the application.

Q *Once my application is filed with the patent office, what legal recourse do I have if somebody infringes while my patent is pending? In other words, can I stop the person before having my patent granted?*
A You have no legal recourse for events before the patent issues. The patent office will, however, expedite the processing of an application where there is an infringer.

Q *What does "Reg U.S. Pat. Office" have to do with a patent?*
A It has nothing to do with a patent. It signifies the registration of a trademark.

Q *Can I enter a licensing agreement with somebody before a patent is granted on my invention? What are the consequences if my patent is not granted and I have licensed certain rights to another party?*
A Yes, licenses are often granted for an application. Such a license is really the guarantee of a license after the patent issues. If the patent is not granted, the consequences will be those stated in the agreement, which could be none. However, if the patent does not issue, you may have nothing left to license and therefore the license could simply cease to be operable.

Q *Why does it take so long for a patent application to be processed if the examiner only averages about 15 hours per invention?*
A There is an 18- to 24-month backlog because there simply are not enough examiners to handle the number of patents filed at the patent office. Besides, many applicants want some time delay while they try to test and commercialize the invention.

Q *What are the odds of my patent being granted on the first submission of my application?*

A Very low. Almost always further communication to the patent examiner is necessary. Often extensive effort is required.

Q *What is recommended if a patent is not granted initially?*

A First, you and your patent attorney should review why the examiner rejected it. On doing so, you may want to amend it (see following question) and/or explain to the examiner why it should be allowed. You may choose to appeal the examiner's decision, and, if so, you are advised to employ a patent attorney since it can be quite complicated. Of course, your patent might be denied because your invention is public domain. If so, you can still take your product into the marketplace with the same rights that everyone else has. After all, many people in our free enterprise system succeed without the advantage of a 17-year monopoly.

Q *If my patent application is turned down, can I amend it and try to change the patent examiner's mind?*

A Yes, you can address a letter to the patent office and request such things as having some of the original claims canceled or perhaps restate the language of a claim(s). Your letter should point out why you believe a patent should be granted. In submitting an amendment, you should avoid adding limitations that will restrict your patent unreasonably, but at the same time, you must remember that the broader your claims are, the more difficult it is to get your invention patented.

Q *Is it likely that an examiner will reconsider my application after it has been rejected?*

A Yes, on receiving your amendment, he or she will again study the application and a second office action will be taken. You may receive a notice of allowance that informs you that your patent will be granted, a rejection of all your claims, or a rejection of some claims while allowing others. There may be several office actions and responses before the examiner states that the rejection is final or a patent is granted. You always have a right to a second office action.

Q *Am I permitted to make some changes and improvements in my invention after my patent application has been filed and then add a description or illustration of these new features?*

A No new matter can be introduced into the disclosure of a patent application. However, a new application can be filed in which the new matter is added. If done properly, the benefit of your original filing date can be retained with respect to the originally disclosed subject matter.

Q *Can I get advice from the patent office about my patent?*

A The patent office can only consider the patentability of an invention when this question comes regularly before it in the form of a patent application. They cannot give you legal advice, but they can give some help on procedures.

Q *Will the patent office answer my correspondence pertaining to my application once I have filed it?*

A Yes, but in the event that you use an attorney or agent, the patent office will correspond only with him or her unless otherwise instructed. The patent office will not respond to both of you. For this reason, you must forward your inquiries through your representative.

Q *Is it possible to extend the six-month period that is allowed by the patent office in order to respond to an office action in a pending application?*

A No, this is the maximum time allowed by patent law. If you fail to respond within this period, your patent application will be abandoned. There are some conditions under which it can still be revived, however.

Q *I published an article on my invention 15 months ago, and now I want to have it patented. Am I still able to do so?*

A No, you cannot sell it or publish anything about it more than one year prior to filing your patent application. If you do, you lose your right to a patent on it.

Q *What happens if the inventor dies before a patent application is filed or is granted?*

A An application may be filed by the executor or administrator.

Q *In the event that the rights to a patent or patent application are sold or transferred, who then files the application?*

A While all or part of the inventor's interest may be assigned to another party, the application must be filed only in the name of the actual inventor, not the person who owns the rights. After that, the owner can file and record the assignment and then have complete control of the application.

Q *Once my patent is granted, are there fees to keep it in force?*
A Maintenance fees have been enacted and should be paid 6 to 12 months in advance to continue the patent after 4, 8, and 12 years.

Q *A patent is granted for 17 years beginning from what date?*
A Your 17-year monopoly begins on the actual date that your patent is granted—not the date when you filed your application. (This is important because of the length of time it takes for a patent application to be processed.)

Q *What happens to my patent after it has been in force for 17 years?*
A It becomes public domain—you no longer have a monopoly! A recent exception permits drug patents to be extended where lack of FDA approval prevented marketing a drug after the patent issued.

Q *What if somebody infringes on my patent, but I do not want to spend the money to stop him? How can I avoid the high cost of bringing an infringement suit against somebody, but at the same time, protect my rights?*
A Unfortunately, you cannot, unless the infringer and you are willing to enter into a settlement agreement.

Q *I realize that the consequences for infringement can be severe. What can I do to avoid unknowingly infringing on an existing patent?*
A Start by looking for patents on similar products. Get a copy and have your patent attorney tell you whether you infringe. You can search in the patent office for patents that you might infringe.

Q *Once my patent application is filed in the United States, can it be copied in another country?*
A Yes, copying is prohibited only after a patent actually issues in the country where the copying occurs.

Q *How can I determine whether it is worth the effort and cost to apply for a patent in a foreign country?*
A You must discuss the issue with your attorney and then, as with any other business decision, evaluate the facts and act accordingly. It is simply a question of whether the potential market in the country and the probability of getting the patent justify the cost and whether you can afford it.

Q *Once my invention has been granted in the United States, and I wish to have it patented abroad, what are the chances of it not being granted in foreign countries?*

A A foreign patent application must be filed *before* your U.S. patent issues or within one year of filing the U.S. application or you cannot get a foreign patent.

Q *Is my patent automatically granted in Canada or any other countries when it is granted by the U.S. Patent and Trademark Office?*

A No. Each country or each group of countries under a treaty makes its own decision.

Q *What happens if my copatentee and I have a disagreement and want to go our separate ways?*

A In the absence of an agreement, each of you is on your own. Each of you has the right to market, distribute, license, et cetera, and compete head-on against one another. It is generally better to have an agreement and avoid such a situation.

Q *Under what circumstances can I lose my patent after it has been issued?*

A If you fail to pay the maintenance fee (or annual tax in foreign countries) or if a court declares your patent invalid.

Q *Can an invention be patented if it changes the chemical proportion of the ingredients of a chemical mixture, resulting in a different kind of material?*

A Yes. For instance, you can obtain a soft rubber in one proportion of rubber ingredients and develop a hard rubber with a different proportion of ingredients that exhibits different properties. Ordinarily, changing proportions will not be patentable.

Q *Is an invention patentable that substitutes a superior and stronger material in a machine that has weaker materials?*

A Not unless the superior materials change the machine's actual function and/or result in unexpected, increased efficiency such as increased saving in the cost of operation.

Q *Can an invention that applies an old invention to a new use be patentable?*

A It is possible, but very difficult. The new use must not be an "obvious" use.

Q *Can a newly discovered theory or law of nature be patented?*
A No, because it is simply an idea. Of course, a patent could be granted on a device that puts a theory into operational form.

Q *Can a method of doing business be patented?*
A No.

Q *Is every patent good for a period of 17 years?*
A A patent is good for a 17-year period from the date it is issued, except for patents on ornamental designs, which are granted for 14 years, and except for drug patents where sales of the drug were delayed significantly beyond the patent issue date by the FDA. Only by a special act of Congress, which can occur in the most rare of instances, could the term of a patent be extended.

Q *Will the patent office give me any information on whether or not my patent attorney is good at her trade?*
A All patent attorneys and agents who are registered to practice before the patent office are expected to be reliable and trustworthy. The patent office will only inform you that a particular person is, or is not, in good standing on the register. The patent office will not help you select a patent attorney.

Q *Is it more difficult to obtain a design patent than a copyright?*
A Yes, since copyright law requires only minor originality, but a design patent requires invention. Also, as with any other patentable invention, a design must be nonobvious to those skilled in a particular field.

Q *What is an example of an article that falls under the design patent laws rather than the copyright laws?*
A A new and inventive bottle design with ornamental features, such as its shape, that are novel and nonobvious would be protected under design patent law rather than copyright law. It would not qualify for a copyright because it is a useful article and does not contain pictorial, graphic, or sculptural work that could be separately recognized from the bottle.

Q *What would make a useful article, such as a bottle, also copyrightable?*
A It might have a design such as a bird or a house embossed into the side that could be recognized apart from the bottle

itself. However, the embossed design, and not the bottle, is copyrightable.

Q *How much more effort and cost is a design patent versus registering a copyright?*

A Like other patents, the cost is considerably greater than the relatively low cost of obtaining a copyright, but is considerably less than utility patents. Sometimes, however, you are wise to spend the extra money, because with some products, such as jewelry or a vase with utilitarian purposes, it would be relatively easy for somebody to make a similar product that would not be a copyright infringement but would infringe on a patent.

Q *What is the major difference between design patent protection versus copyright protection?*

A A patent infringer can recreate the design without ever having seen the patent or patented article and still be an infringer. By contrast, copyright infringement requires access to the copyright owner's work and use or copying of the work. For this reason, independent creation of a product still constitutes design patent infringement, but it is not considered copyright infringement.

COPYRIGHTS

Q *When do I have a copyright—at the time of creation, publication, or registration?*

A Under the new law, on the creation of your work, it is copyrighted. Your work is considered created when it is fixed in a tangible medium. Keep in mind that you do not have to publish your work or have your copyright registered—your copyright protection begins from the time you put your work into a tangible form. Under the old law, the date of publication determined when statutory copyright protection was effective. Note that you do not obtain a copyright by filing your work with the copyright office—you get your certificate of registration from the copyright office, which is a public record of the existence of your claim to copyright.

Q *When do you recommend putting a copyright notice on my work?*

A It takes so little effort to place a copyright notice on your work that you should give yourself this protection as soon as it is in a tangible form. That is, of course, if you consider it something worthy of protecting.

Q *Can somebody other than the author be granted a copyright on my work?*

A No, since the rights automatically are the property of the author on the creation of the work. As the author, you may transfer ownership of the copyright before or after registration. In the case of being employed to create a work made "for hire," your employer is the actual legal author, and possesses all of the exclusive rights, regardless of your being the creator.

Q *If I create a painting and sell it, do I still own the copyright?*

A An original work such as a painting is considered to be a "copy" and protected under copyright law. The purchaser does not have the right to make copies of your work, even though he owns the original painting (no more than a person who buys a book has the right to reproduce it). The owner of the painting is infringing on your copyright if he makes copies of *his* possession.

Q *If I hang my painting in an art gallery, does it constitute publication?*

A No, a public display of your work is not considered publication.

Q *Can I transfer a part of my copyright, or do I have to transfer the entire work?*

A Not only can you divide the copyright in the work itself (you can sell the audio rights, the video rights, the paperback rights, and so on of a book to one or more parties), but when the work permits, you can divide the copyright in portions of the work. For example, you can excerpt and license use of a chapter of your book.

Q *Are there certain conditions I should want when I give consent or permission to use my work?*

A Depending on the amount of your work that is used, you may or may not receive monetary compensation. However, as a condition for your consent to use your work, you may require being given credit for your contribution, such as a proper copyright notice. If you want to play it safe, you might reserve the right to review how your work will be used before granting permission—by doing this, you can avoid being misquoted.

Q *How do I get permission from somebody else to use a portion of his or her work?*

A Depending on what is "fair use," you might or might not need permission. If you think you do, simply contact the copyright owner and ask for his or her written permission. You might want to do a search at the copyright office to determine who the current owner of the work actually is.

Q *What is the importance of recording an assignment or other transfer of copyright ownership with the copyright office?*

A It serves as notice to everyone, regardless of whether he or she actually saw it, that you are the copyright owner. You can look in the records of the copyright office to make sure that the person granting rights to you is actually authorized to do so. If you record the assignment to you and the person who sold it to you attempts to sell the rights a second time, you will avoid a potential conflict with the second buyer.

Q *Should the copyright office be informed of a transfer on the death of the copyright owner?*

A Yes. With a registered work, you should record a certified copy of the decree of distribution of the estate, showing the new owner or owners, the registration number, the title of the work, the author, and the registration date. With an unregistered work, the executor should register the work before the assets of the estate are distributed. After the registration, the decree of distribution identifying the work, and the heir or legatee receiving the same, can be recorded. By doing this, the heirs will be able to bring a suit for copyright infringement without both registration of the work and a record of the transfer to them.

Q *What can you tell me about cowriting a book, screenplay, et cetera?*

A When you do a "joint work" with another person, both of you co-own the entire work. Typically, as collaborators, you should register the copyright in the names of both, and you will share equally with all rights of the work. It is recommended to enter a formal collaborator agreement that spells out the terms of such matters as artistic rights, division of income, how nonexclusive licenses will be handled, and so on. Of course, one collaborator can have a higher interest than another—they can agree to whatever they choose in a separate agreement.

Q *What is the difference between joint work and ghostwriting?*
A When a person ghostwrites a work, he or she is generally an employee for hire and is not considered to be the author of the work. This is dependent on the extent of the supervision and control exercised by his or her employer. Under a separate agreement, the author and ghostwriter should specify what rights belong to each party.

Q *Is there a statute of limitations for copyright infringement?*
A Yes, you have three years from the infringement date to bring suit. There may be claims other than copyright infringement, such as unfair competition that does not fall under copyright law, and other claims might have shorter statutes of limitations. In general, you should attempt to avoid delaying your action against an infringer. As soon as you are aware of unauthorized use of your work, you should consult an attorney immediately.

Q *How does a publisher protect herself from infringement claims?*
A First, she may want to do a copyright title search before entering an agreement with a writer. Additionally, the publisher will typically require the writer to make a written warranty that the property is original to the author and that the property does not violate the copyright of any third party. The publisher will require the writer to indemnify her for claims that are inconsistent with the warranties. For this reason, a writer takes a risk of being sued for infringement and also paying the legal fees while the publisher's risk is reduced (although she will likely be named in the suit too).

Q *How much of a work can I use and have it be deemed "fair use"?*
A While many works use parts of copyrighted works, the test includes whether the amount used is substantial. The extent of damage to the copyright owner is also a factor. There is not an exact standard measure of what amount constitutes infringement. (See the discussion of "Fair Use" in Chapter 8.)

TRADEMARKS

Q *Who may own a trademark?*
A A trademark can be owned by any individual, partnership, firm, corporation, or an association or other collective group.

Q *What is a trade name and how is one registered?*

A A trade name is a name of a business used by manufacturers, merchants and others to identify their business or occupations. Unlike a trademark that identifies a source of a product, a trade name identifies an enterprise. Under the federal Trademark Act, there is no provision to register a trade name that simply identifies a business entity. They can be registered in most states.

Q *Is there a time limitation to file a trademark application?*

A No. You can register your trademark any time after your mark has been used on a product or service that is offered for sale. For a federal application it must be offered in interstate, foreign, or territorial commerce. You cannot federally register your trademark if your product is only being sold or shipped in intrastate commerce. However, the courts have expanded the definition of "interstate commerce" to include most of what you might ordinarily consider to be intrastate.

Q *If I have a great idea for a trademark, can I register my concept and save it to be used for a future date?*

A No, not in the United States, but you can in most foreign countries. A trademark is eligible for federal registration based on using it in commerce that may lawfully be regulated by Congress, such as interstate commerce at the time the application is filed. However, you can file an application to register the trademark federally if you have a good faith intent to use it. Actual registration must await your use within a limited time.

Q *If my trademark is registered in the United States, does this give me protection in other countries?*

A No. You must obtain a registration in each country where you want protection. Your U.S. registration, however, can be helpful for obtaining registration in several other countries. In some countries, it is essential to first register your trademark here in the United States.

Q *Do foreign countries require the use of a trademark prior to its registration?*

A No, many countries do not have this requirement that we have in the United States. In fact, a resident may obtain a registration that he or she never intends to use in order to prevent somebody else from using it! To avoid this, many multinational

American companies that have secured a domestic registration of their trademark frequently register it in foreign countries before actually using the mark there.

Q *What are the requirements for drawings to register my trademark?*

A First, you can use a pen or a process that gives the drawing satisfactory reproduction characteristics. A photolithographic reproduction, printer's proof, or quality xerographic copy may be used. Every line and letter must be in black, no matter how fine, including shading. All lines must be clean, sharp, and solid, and they must not be too fine or crowded. Surface shading, when used, must be created by solid black lines or dots. The rules also limit drawing size.

Q *What kind of paper and ink should I use for my drawings?*

A You must use smooth, white, durable paper, the surface of which is smooth and not shiny, such as a good grade of bond paper. India ink alone must be used for pen drawings to secure perfectly solid lines. The use of white pigment to cover lines is not acceptable. The size of the sheet on which the drawing is made must be 8 to $8\frac{1}{2}$ inches wide and 11 inches long. The margin should be at least 1 inch on the sides and bottom of the paper, and there must be at least 1 inch between the the margin and the heading. Xerographic copies can be used if they produce solid black lines.

Q *Since India ink alone must be used for pen drawings, how do I indicate the color of my trademark when registering it?*

A When color is a feature of a mark, you use symbolic linings in your drawing. These are shown in the rules of the U.S. Patent and Trademark Office, which can be purchased from the Government Printing Office or found in a library in Volume 37 of the Code of Federal Regulations.

Q *Can I submit an informal drawing?*

A Yes, for the purpose of examination. But, before the application can be allowed, you must make the necessary corrections.

Q *Are many trademark infringements litigated in the United States?*

A The latest figures indicate that 4337 trademark infringement cases were litigated in the United States in 1984. These are only a handful of the more than 600,000 active trademarks on the register of the U.S. Patent and Trademark Office in that year, as well as the thousands of others registered in individual states, plus the untold number of trademarks in use but not registered.

Q *What is the difference between Principal and Supplemental Register Marks?*

A There are two registers at the trademark office—designated as the Principal Register, and the other as the Supplemental Register. Coined, arbitrary, fanciful, or suggestive marks and marks that customers recognize as distinctive may, if otherwise qualified, be registered on the Principal Register. Marks that are not qualified for the Principal Register, but are capable of distinguishing the applicant's goods and have been in lawful use in commerce for at least one year, may be registered on the Supplemental Register.

Q *What are some examples of kinds of marks that would be registered on the Supplemental Register?*

A These marks may include any trademark, symbol, label, package, descriptive language, configuration of goods, name, word, slogan, phrase, surname, geographical name, numeral, or device, or any combination of any of the foregoing.

Q *Is a signature and verification required on a trademark registration application?*

A Yes, the application must be signed and verified (sworn to) or include a declaration by the applicant or by a member of the firm or an officer of the corporation or association applying.

Q *Do I submit a specimen of my trademark when I register it?*

A Three specimens are to be submitted and shall be duplicates of the actually used labels, tags, containers, or displays, or portions thereof, when made of suitable material and capable of being arranged flat and on a size not larger than $8\frac{1}{2}$ by 13 inches. Specimens of three-dimensional or bulky material will not be accepted, but photographs can be used.

Q *Can I submit a facsimile of my trademark when I register it?*

A Yes, when it is not feasible to submit a specimen. In this case, you should furnish the trademark office with three copies of a suitable photograph or other acceptable reproduction, not larger than $8\frac{1}{2}$ by 11 inches and clearly and legibly showing the mark and all matters used in connection therewith.

Q *What should I use to register my trademark when, due to its nature, it is not possible to furnish a specimen or facsimile?*

A With certain marks, such as sounds (like the NBC chimes), it is permissible to submit some other form of representation of your trademark. In the case of service marks not used in printed or written form, for example, three recordings will be accepted.

Q *What is a service mark?*

A This term is used in reference to the sale or advertising of services. A service mark is used to identify the services of one person and distinguish his or hers from the services from others. Titles, character names, and other distinctive features of radio or television programs are examples that can be registered as service marks notwithstanding that they, or the programs, may advertise the goods of the sponsor.

Q *What is a certification mark?*

A This term is used in reference to a mark used on or in connection with the products or services of one or more persons other than the owner of the mark to certify regional or other origin, material, mode of manufacture, quality, accuracy, or other characteristics of such goods or services or that the work or labor of the goods or services was performed by members of a union or other organization.

Q *What is a collective mark?*

A This term means a trademark or service mark used by the members of a cooperative, an association, or other collective group or organization. Marks used to indicate membership in a union, an association, or other organization may be registered as Collective Membership Marks.

Q *Can I use a notice of registration prior to registering my trademark?*

A No, you cannot use a notice of "Registered in U.S. Patent and Trademark Office," or "Reg. U.S. Pat and Tm Off.," or the letter R enclosed with a circle (®) before the actual issuance of a certificate of registration of your mark. To do so may be the basis for refusal of registration—but use is ordinarily excused if there is suitable explanation.

Q *What are the fees and charges in connection with various trademark matters?*

A The fees are increased often. As of the date of this writing they are:

Trademark Processing Fees

2.6(a)(1)	Application for registration, per class	210.00
2.6(a)(2)	Filing an Amendment to Allege Use under § 1(c), per class	100.00
2.6(a)(3)	Filing a Statement of Use under § 1(d)(1), per class	100.00
2.6(a)(4)	Filing a Request for a Six-month Extension of Time for Filing a Statement of Use under § 1(d)(1), per class	100.00
2.6(a)(5)	Application for renewal, per class	300.00
2.6(a)(6)	Additional fee for late renewal, per class	100.00
2.6(a)(7)	Publication of mark under § 12(c), per class	100.00
2.6(a)(8)	Issuing new certificate of registration	100.00
2.6(a)(9)	Certificate of Correction, registrant's error	100.00
2.6(a)(10)	Filing disclaimer to registration	100.00
2.6(a)(11)	Filing amendment to registration	100.00
2.6(a)(12)	Filing § 8 affidavit, per class	100.00
2.6(a)(13)	Filing § 15 affidavit, per class	100.00
2.6(a)(14)	Filing combined §§ 8 & 15 affidavit, per class	200.00
2.6(a)(15)	Petition to the Commissioner	100.00
2.6(a)(16)	Petition for cancellation, per class	200.00
2.6(a)(17)	Notice of opposition, per class	200.00
2.6(a)(18)	Ex parte appeal, per class	100.00
2.6(a)(19)	Dividing an application, per new application (file wrapper) created	100.00

Trademark Service Fees

2.6(b)(1)(i)	Printed copy of each registered mark, regular service	3.00
2.6(b)(1)(ii)	Printed copy of each registered mark, expedited service	6.00
2.6(b)(1)(iii)	Printed copy of each registered mark ordered via EOS, expedited service	25.00
2.6(b)(4)(i)	Certified copy of registered mark with title and/or status, regular service	10.00
2.6(b)(4)(ii)	Certified copy of registered mark, with title and/or status, expedited local service	20.00
2.6(b)(2)(i)	Certified or uncertified copy of trademark application as filed, regular service	12.00
2.6(b)(2)(ii)	Certified or uncertified copy of trademark application as filed, expedited local service	24.00
2.6(b)(3)	Certified or uncertified copy of trademark-related file wrapper and contents	50.00
2.6(b)(5)	Certified or uncertified copy of trademark document, unless otherwise provided	25.00
2.6(b)(7)	For assignment records, abstracts of title and certification per registration	25.00

1.19(g)	Comparing and certifying copies, per document, per copy	25.00
2.6(b)(9)	Self-service copy charge, per page	0.25
2.6(b)(6)	Recording trademark assignment, agreement or other paper, first mark per document	40.00
	For second and subsequent marks in the same document	25.00
2.6(b)(10)	Labor charges for services, per hour or fraction thereof	30.00
2.6(b)(11)	Unspecified other services	AT COST
2.6(b)(8)	Each hour of T-SEARCH terminal session time	40.00
1.24	Trademark coupons	3.00

Q *Is there a digest of registered marks available at the trademark office?*

A Yes, in the search room of Trademark Examining Operations, which is open to the public. This digest comprises a set of the registered word marks, arranged alphabetically, and a set of registrations comprised of symbols such as birds and animals, arranged according to the classification of the goods or services with which they are used. We recommend using this digest or doing some alternative searching before you select your trademark.

Q *What is The Official Gazette of the Patent and Trademark Office, and how may I get a copy of it?*

A This weekly publication contains information relating to patents and trademarks, including marks published for opposition, marks registered, amended, canceled and renewed, and marks published under section 12 (c) of the 1946 Act. Single copies and subscriptions are sold by the Superintendent of Documents, U.S. Government Printing Office, Washington, D.C., 20402. The trademark material and the patent material are printed separately as the Trademark Section and the Patent Section and each may be purchased or subscribed to separately.

INDEX